Advance praise for *Books, Crooks and Counselors*

A mystery writer's bible. Clear, concise and infinitely useful … a smart, easy-to-understand legal guide for mystery writers that will keep your mystery accurate and your story moving. The ultimate mystery writer's handbook!
— Laura Childs, *New York Times* bestselling author of
Fiber & Brimstone, *Scones & Bones*, and *The Teaberry Strangler*

Need to know what laws your antagonist is trampling? Need a handle on how the legal system responds to his criminal activities? Need to grasp the rhythm of the courtroom? In *Books, Crooks and Counselors*, Leslie Budewitz takes you into the legal world with the sure hand and knowledge of an insider. If you write crime fiction, you need this book.
— D. P. Lyle, MD, Edgar-nominated and Macavity-winning author of
Forensics for Dummies, *Murder and Mayhem*, and *Forensics and Fiction*

Books, Crooks and Counselors is terrific. It answers all kinds of questions that I had, and, more important, all kinds of questions that I didn't even know I had. It's one of those books that is going to make me look smarter. I'd want it even if it weren't well-written, which it is. I've had the same fourteen reference books that stay right on my desk all the time, regardless of what particular book I'm working on. From now on there will be fifteen.
— Aaron Elkins, Edgar-winning and Agatha-nominated creator of forensic anthropologist Gideon Oliver, the Skeleton Detective, and other mysteries and thrillers

Concise, user-friendly, and geared toward writers, *Books, Crooks and Counselors* puts everything the crime writer needs to know about using the law in fiction right at hand—no more hours wasted tracking down experts or sifting through research material. If you write fiction, keep this book close by.
— Leann Sweeney, author of the Yellow Rose Mysteries and the
Cats in Trouble series

Books, Crooks and Counselors is a must-have resource for writers of any genre that relies on a clear understanding of the judicial system. From common terms and phrases to legal issues in criminal investigations and punishment, it's all there in a clear and concise format and easily accessible language. This book sits right next to the dictionary on my bookshelves.
— Brenda Novak, *New York Times* and *USA Today* bestselling author
of *White Heat*, *Body Heat*, and *Killer Heat*

Imagine having a private lawyer available 24/7 to answer your every question without hourly fees. Imagine you can slip that lawyer in your pocket to access at your convenience. In *Books, Crooks and Counselors*, Leslie Budewitz has created a comprehensive, clear resource that's destined to be an essential part of every writer's library. With succinct information delivered in a warm, clear manner, Budewitz unravels our legal system and many of its complexities. *Books, Crooks and Counselors* is a must-have reference for every fiction writer.
— Pari Noskin Taichert, two-time Agatha Award nominee and author
of the Sasha Solomon mystery series

Leslie Budewitz's new book *Books, Crooks and Counselors* is destined to become the Bible of legal research for writers. A copy of it on your desk would be like having your very own legal Dream Team at your beck and call.

— Lee Lofland, The Graveyard Shift blog, founder of The Writers' Police Academy, and author of *Police Procedure and Investigation*

A lawyer who can explain our confusing legal system so even another lawyer can understand it? And who knows what writers need to know before they even ask? Priceless. I have a law degree and 25 years' experience teaching law, and I'm in awe of Leslie's ability to explain the law without losing the reader in the tangled morass. This book gives plenty of information but not too much. You'll want this close at hand as you write.

— Cathy Pickens, President, Sisters in Crime, and author of the Southern Fried Mysteries series

Leslie Budewitz's meticulous research and plain-English explanations of legal and procedural matters make this a welcome reference for any fiction author whose stories involve the law. Mystery writers will find it indispensable, not only as a source of accurate information but also as inspiration for new and different plot developments.

— Sandra Parshall, award-winning author of the Rachel Goddard mysteries

Attorney and author Leslie Budewitz has compiled the perfect deskside reference for all genre writers who want to get the details just right. *Books, Crooks and Counselors* is a guide to the legal world that defines terms, explains procedures and gets into the specifics of culprits, crime and courtrooms. From A to Z—arrest through the appeal process with zealous advocacy in between—this thorough, yet engagingly written legal manual for writers is an excellent addition to a reference shelf. Topnotch tips for the criminally creative.

— Nancy Martin, author of the Blackbird Sisters and Roxy Abruzo mysteries

The perfect resource for any writer's desk! Leslie Budewitz has a keen sense of just what a writer needs to know about all things legal. *Books, Crooks and Counselors* is superb!

— Carla Neggers, *New York Times* bestselling romantic suspense author

If you're not a lawyer and you're writing crime fiction, you need Leslie Budewitz's *Books, Crooks and Counselors*. It's got everything a writer needs to write about the law—and do it accurately. I'll be consulting it with every new book I write.

— Lorna Barrett, *New York Times* bestselling author of *Sentenced to Death* and the rest of the Booktown Mysteries

What Leslie Budewitz has created in *Books, Crooks and Counselors* is an essential tool box for the crime and mystery writer, a veritable hand book of legal procedure, precedent and resource from an insider's perspective within the criminal justice system. Simply put, no serious crime or mystery writer should be without it.

—Jeff Boxer, forensic specialist and expert witness

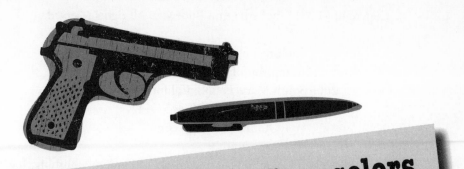

Books, Crooks and Counselors

How to Write Accurately About Criminal Law and Courtroom Procedure

Leslie Budewitz
Mystery Writer and
Attorney at Law

Quill
Driver
Books

Fresno, California

Published by Quill Driver Books
an imprint of Linden Publishing
2006 South Mary, Fresno, California 93721
559-233-6633 / 800-345-4447
QuillDriverBooks.com

Quill Driver Books and Colophon are trademarks of Linden Publishing, Inc.

ISBN 978-1-610350-19-8
135798642

Printed in the United States of America on acid-free paper.

The information in this book is presented for educational purposes only, and is not intended as legal advice.

Library of Congress Cataloging-in-Publication Data

Budewitz, Leslie.
  Books, crooks and counselors : how to write accurately about criminal law and court-room procedure / Leslie Budewitz.
     p. cm.
  Summary: "Addressing the misunderstood and misrepresented aspects of the law in today's writing, this reliable guidebook demonstrates how to use legal concepts, ter-minology, and procedure to create fiction that is true to life and crackling with real-world tension. Examples from actual cases are provided along with excerpts of authentic courtroom dialogue. Topics covered include criminal and civil law; differences between federal, state, and Native American jurisdiction; police and private investigation; wills and inheritances; and the written and unwritten codes that govern the public and private conduct of lawyers and judges. Providing a quick and simple legal reference, this hand-book is the key to creating innovative plots, strong conflicts, authentic characters, and gritty realism"-- Provided by publisher.
  Includes bibliographical references and index.
  ISBN 978-1-61035-019-8 (pbk.)
  1. Criminal law--United States. 2. Procedure (Law)--United States. 3. Legal stories--Authorship. 4. Crime writing. 5. Law and literature. 6. Procedure (Law)--United States. 7. Authors--Handbooks, manuals, etc. I. Title.
  KF9219.85B83 2011
  808'.06634--dc23
                                      2011026983

Table of Contents

C. Evidence

D. Witnesses

E. Burden of Proof

4. ...And Punishment 79

8. Legal Miscellany **137**

9. Thinking Like a Lawyer **151**

10. Thinking Like a Judge **165**

Introduction

A legal thread runs through the fictional world. Writers of novels, short stories, plays, screenplays, and television scripts often find themselves telling stories that involve legal issues—whether those issues are central to the plot, fill in the backstory, or illustrate an aspect of a character's personal history. Mysteries and thrillers in particular involve the "real world" of the law, courts, and crimes. Writers want to use the law realistically and accurately, while telling a good story.

But the law can be complicated and confusing. Even writers who enjoy research can be daunted by the volume of resources available or overwhelmed by misinformation. Writers can easily feel like Alice after she's fallen down the rabbit hole, unable to sort truth from illusion. With a better understanding of the legal world, writers can use the legal aspects of their story to full advantage and avoid the mistakes that annoy readers.

Books, Crooks and Counselors teaches you, the writer:

- **The Facts**. With fifty states plus the federal and tribal systems, the American legal system is enormous and varied. Figuring out the terminology and procedure takes time away from your focus on plot and character, language and setting. Is the prosecutor known as the district attorney or DA (New York), the county prosecutor (Washington State), or the county attorney (Montana)? Will a grand jury be called? Might a character's conviction be appealed? How long does an appeal take, and will the process affect your story's time line? *Books, Crooks and Counselors* shows you how to identify critical legal issues in your stories and handle them correctly, using the right terms.

- **The Thinking**. Lay people don't think about the law the way lawyers and judges do. Courtroom behavior follows its own code, largely unwritten and largely unknown to the public. This book gives you the insight to create more compelling characters and action.

- **The Dialogue**. Courtroom dialogue is a unique language. This book answers writers' questions about common legal terms and phrases.

- **The Procedure**. Whether the protagonist is a professional or an amateur, crime stories often involve both an official and an unofficial investigation. This book answers questions about legal procedure, such as when a suspect is arraigned, how bond is set, and other inside details that will add veracity to your story.

- **The Setting**. This book helps writers visualize how a law firm works, how a courthouse runs, and how a lawyer navigates his or her way through the system.

Books, Crooks and Counselors answers questions on more than 160 legal topics in twelve chapters. Because state law varies, answers focus on legal concepts and principles, and on common variations. Some questions relate to civil law, such as adoption, probate, and malpractice. Where civil and criminal procedures differ significantly, I've explained the differences. I've also included a short guide to research, with resources for finding local laws and procedure.

Readers expect writers to get the facts behind their stories right—or, at the very least, to create a plausible scenario that seems logical and true. Yet it's not enough to know what the law is; writers need to possess the knowledge of how best to use a legal problem, procedure, or scenario to advance their story. I've practiced law for more than twenty-five years, in two states, in the federal system, and in tribal courts. This book gives writers the benefit of my experience, tempered by my perspective as a published fiction writer.

A Few Notes

Of course, nothing in this book is intended as legal advice, and nothing included here should be relied on in handling specific "real world" legal problems. These pages are intended solely for use by writers devising fictional plights.

Keep in mind that because laws and procedures vary widely and sometimes change, you should check the status of any law that affects key elements of your story. I've been as accurate as I could be, but the law is always in flux. I hope by the end of this book you'll know how to research key issues yourself.

Many resources and references mentioned here are websites. Whenever you see "Check Book Links" in the text, you'll find a link on the "Book Links" page on my website, LawAndFiction.com.

Most of the questions in this book came from writers; however, I created others to address topics writers often ask about at mystery conferences or on Internet discussion lists. A few involve problems I've seen in books and manuscripts. I give my thanks to the writers who've asked the questions. I hope my answers give writers of all variety of stories concrete, reliable information so you can portray legal predicaments credibly and accurately, and keep on thrilling us all with the stories you tell.

1

Trial and Error

THE TRIAL IS THE DRIVING FORCE IN CIVIL and criminal litigation, and the focal point of most legal plots and subplots. In this section, we'll examine the role of the trial in the legal process, then turn to a few key topics where writers can add realism and avoid pitfalls. First, we'll look at the pretrial process—the stage that starts when charges are filed and ends when the jury is called. We'll talk about some common issues related to evidence and witnesses, and look at the "burden of proof"—who's got it, and what it means. Last, we'll look at what really happens on appeal.

A. JUDICIAL SYSTEM BASICS

Getting the facts right—even in fiction—helps writers eliminate the risk that an astute reader or viewer will lose interest and put a book aside or change the channel because the world the writer has created no longer seems realistic. Like most citizens, writers know the basics of the American judicial system, but with fifty states and the federal system often structured differently and using varied terminology, the details can be confusing. So, to avoid what lawyers call "reversible error," the place to start is with a primer on the system and terminology.

What's the difference between a criminal action and a civil action?

A criminal action charges the suspect with a crime—a violation of the rules of society as agreed on and adopted by the state or federal legislature, codified in the criminal statutes. A crime is an offense against the peace and order of society. In theory, the wrong or offense is against society, not just the individual victim. That's why crimes are prosecuted in the name of the government: the United States of America against Jeffrey K. Skilling, the State of Florida against Theodore Robert Bundy, the People of New York against Bernhard Goetz.

In contrast, civil law involves private rights. Examples of civil cases:

- suits for money damages, such as personal injury claims, contract disputes, and claims for property damage;

- suits by the government for violations of statutes that aren't criminal, e.g., tax or professional licensing issues;

- domestic relations cases, such as custody, paternity, support, dissolutions of marriage, or adoption; and

- guardianship and probate.

Of course, civil cases aren't always civil—the parties can be just as nasty and contentious as in a criminal case.

> Of course, civil cases aren't always civil—the parties can be just as nasty and contentious as in a criminal case.

(The phrase "civil law" also refers to a legal system derived from the French system—a modified version is used in Louisiana—in contrast to the common law system, descended from English courts, used in American federal courts and most states.)

My story involves a courtroom scene. Should I set it in federal or state court?

It depends on the case. Two court systems—federal and state—exist side by side, with different, sometimes overlapping, jurisdiction. Jurisdiction means a court's authority, and it may be defined by geography, subject matter, or the amount of money at stake. (Specialized courts, like tax and bankruptcy courts and state workers' compensation courts, are rarely the setting for thrilling drama, either in real life or on the page.)

Simply put, federal courts handle federal issues. On the criminal side, examples abound:

- Violations of federal statutes making specific acts criminal. Most are easily recognized as crimes: drug possession or sales, kidnaping across state lines, firearms offenses, and hundreds more. Some regulatory offenses, such as pollution violations, may also be crimes.

- Virtually any offense related to securities (stocks and bonds) or banking. Martha Stewart was charged with obstruction of justice for lying about a stock sale—a federal offense. Federal criminal charges filed against Enron executives Ken Lay and Jeff Skilling asserted conspiracy, insider trading, wire fraud, and bank fraud. The infamous Montana Freemen violated federal banking laws by circulating false bank notes.

- Immigration offenses.

- War crimes and acts of terrorism, which may also involve military courts.

- Crimes involving interstate communication systems, such as postal fraud, wire fraud, and cybercrime.

- Crimes committed on federal property, such as a prison, or an American embassy in a foreign country.

- Most crime committed in Indian country (reservations and other specified areas), including violent crime, corruption, and gaming violations. Under a federal law known as PL-280, some states exercise full or limited criminal jurisdiction over Indians in Indian country. For example, on the Flathead Reservation in western Montana, the state investigates and prosecutes all felonies and some misdemeanors, while the tribes handle other misdemeanors and all juvenile matters. But on other reservations, most crimes are federal matters, as portrayed in Tony Hillerman's Leaphorn and Chee series.

State court systems handle the majority of criminal and civil litigation—estimates are as much as 95 percent. State courts handle criminal cases of all variety. If a crime is a violation of state law, the state prosecutes.

Civil suits involving personal injuries, property damage, or contracts may be federal or state cases. Suits between individuals or companies land in federal court if they involve "a federal issue," such as pension rights or violations of federal discrimination laws, or if they are between citizens of different states (called "diversity jurisdiction") and involve more than $75,000. However, some areas of civil law are handled only by state courts. These include domestic relations cases, probate, adoption, and guardianship.

My story involves a drug deal violating both state and federal law. Who prosecutes?

Both state and federal authorities may file charges, then decide who will pursue the case and who will wait. Or they may agree in advance that only one will file charges. The decision may be made in an informal conversation between the prosecutors, in person or otherwise, or during a more formal meeting, particularly if multiple jurisdictions are involved. Most such discussions are collegial. If no agreement is reached and both state and federal prosecutors file charges, federal law requires state prosecutions to be suspended while a federal case arising from the same incident is pending, even if the charges differ. Factors in the decision include the nature of the crime, which entity has better resources to pursue the case, and the penalties in each jurisdiction. If an incident violates one federal statute and four state statutes, the state will probably take the lead, unless the federal crime is major and the state crimes are minor.

My bad guy kidnaps a banker in one state, holds him hostage in another, then kills him. Where should he be prosecuted?

A string of crimes crossing state lines is distressingly common. The state where the suspect is arrested has the right to prosecute first. But states generally respect the rights and interests of other states, and the arresting state may send the suspect to the first state and wait in line if the crimes committed there occurred first or were more serious. If the crimes committed in the second state were relatively minor, it may choose not to prosecute.

> The state where the suspect is arrested has the right to prosecute first.

In May 2005, Joseph Duncan murdered a woman, her boyfriend, and her teenage son in northern Idaho and kidnaped her younger children, a boy and a girl. The three camped in Montana for several weeks, where Duncan molested both children and killed the boy. He returned to Idaho with the girl and was arrested when a sharp-eyed waitress recognized her from published photos.

Idaho had the right to prosecute the first three murders and the kidnaping. When Duncan crossed state lines with the children, the kidnaping became a federal crime, giving the United States jurisdiction to prosecute. Federal authorities could prosecute the boy's homicide in the state where the kidnaping occurred—Idaho—or where the homicide occurred—Montana. Montana could also prosecute the kidnaping (because Duncan held the children there), as well as the molestation and homicide.

The prosecutors discussed charges and priorities. Idaho, where Duncan was arrested, filed charges first. Federal charges followed. Ultimately, he was convicted in Idaho and pled guilty in federal court, resolving all charges without the necessity of further prosecution.

In January 2007, Duncan confessed to killing two girls in Washington State and a boy in California; other states are still investigating him for child rape or murder.

Sometimes the waiting line is long.

On the news and in TV shows, I hear some judges referred to as "justices." What's the difference?

The difference in title is a mark of respect for the office. "Justice" is reserved for the members of the U.S. Supreme Court or a state's highest court (also usually referred to as "Supreme Court"). Members of other courts are called "judge." A notable exception: In New York, the general trial courts are called Supreme Court and County Court, served by both justices and judges, the intermediate appellate court is the Appellate Division (judges), and the highest court is the Court of Appeals (judges). So check before you write.

Despite the formal title, a "justice of the peace" is a judge, often called "the JP."

A judge may also be referred to as "the court."

In person, the correct term of address is Judge, Justice, Chief Justice, or "your honor." Out of their hearing, of course, judges and justices may be called many other things.

I'd like the criminal charges in my story to be filed in federal court. What's the structure and terminology for the federal system?

There are three levels of federal courts:

1. **The District Court**, also called the trial court. Jurisdiction is defined in the Constitution, Art. III, Sect. 2. Most action occurs at the trial court level, so most stories will be set here.

2. **The Court of Appeals**, which is divided into twelve regional courts, also called circuit courts, plus the Federal Circuit, which hears specialized appeals such as patent claims and international trade cases. These are sometimes called the Circuit Court or by number, e.g., the Ninth Circuit. Judges are appointed from throughout the circuit. While the circuit's official headquarters are in one city, e.g., San Francisco for the Ninth Circuit and Denver for the Tenth, individual judges may have their offices or "chambers" in a federal courthouse or office building anywhere in the circuit.

3. **The Supreme Court**, the court of last resort.

Each state has at least one federal district, with a Chief Judge who handles administrative matters in addition to hearing cases. A district may cover part of a state—the Eastern District of New York, for example, covers several counties and includes Queens and Brooklyn. Or, it may cover an entire state, e.g., Delaware, Minnesota, Wyoming. A district may be split into geographical divisions, each with its own courthouse. In sparsely populated states, federal judges travel regularly. Some courts use video-conferencing to conduct procedural hearings.

Federal judges employ secretaries and law clerks (lawyers, often recent graduates, who research the law). Judges and their staffs work closely with the Clerk of Court, an appointed position. Senior or retired judges may work part-time, which helps the courts manage their case loads. Retired Supreme Court Justice David Souter regularly hears cases on the First Circuit, covering New England.

Federal cases are appealed from District Court to the Court of Appeals. Most decisions are made by a three-judge panel, but larger panels occasionally convene. Some cases are decided based on written briefs without oral argument.

Cases may then be appealed to the United States Supreme Court by petitions called writs of certiorari, or cert. Roughly 7,000 such petitions are filed each year, and about 100 are accepted. The Supreme Court has discretion to decide which appeals it will consider, and it may also consider state court cases that raise federal constitutional issues. If the Supreme Court decides not to take an appeal, the most recent court decision stands.

Remember that the Court reviews the constitutionality of statutes and government actions, and interprets statutes—it does not determine their wisdom or effectiveness. The Supreme Court is also the trial court for actions between states or by foreign governments, and the Chief Justice presides over presidential impeachments.

> Remember that the Court reviews the constitutionality of statutes and government actions, and interprets statutes—it does not determine their wisdom or effectiveness.

Woodward and Armstrong's juicy classic, *The Brethren: Inside the Supreme Court* (1979), illuminates the Court's daily workings, and Jeffrey Toobin gives an updated perspective in *The Nine: Inside the Secret World of the Supreme Court* (2007).

Who gets to be a federal judge?

Federal judges are appointed by the president with the "advice and consent" of the Senate. In practice, this means the president nominates candidates—after consulting with the state's senior senator—and the Senate holds confirmation hearings. Although the Constitution sets no requirements, such as age or education, the Department of Justice evaluates potential candidates. The American Bar Association (ABA)—a voluntary national organization of lawyers—assists in the process by rating prospective nominees' qualifications for integrity, professional competence, and judicial temperament. The Bush administration chose not to submit names to the ABA before their official nomination, although the ABA evaluated the nominees at the request of the Senate Judiciary committee. The Obama administration has resumed the practice of allowing potential nominees for lower court positions to be evaluated before nomination. While most judicial nominations fly under the radar, some develop a higher profile because of the nominee's prior decisions, outside activities, or even his or her spouse's work. Or, a nomination may be held up by unrelated partisan politicking. Imagine the fictional possibilities.

Federal judges are appointed for life—a critical factor in preserving the independence of the judiciary and assuring that decisions are impartial and made without fear of recrimination. Federal judges may be impeached for misconduct, including criminal convictions, and tried by a streamlined version of the process used against the president; if convicted, they are removed. The process is rarely used—Congress has impeached only fifteen federal judges, convicting and removing from office only eight. However, the cases often involve fascinating personal trainwrecks that could make great plots or subplots.

> Federal judges are appointed for life—a critical factor in preserving the independence of the judiciary.

Nominees to the federal bench usually share the president's political philosophy, or at least his political affiliation. But surprises do occur. In 1970, Richard Nixon nominated Harry Blackmun, a Court of Appeals judge, to the Supreme Court and expected a conservative. But Justice Blackmun wrote the majority opinion in *Roe v. Wade* (1973), the case that recognizes a right to privacy in the federal constitution and guarantees a woman's right to choose, and many observers claim his judicial philosophy became more liberal over time. The justice, though, maintained that the rest of the court simply became more conservative. *New York Times* Supreme Court reporter Linda Greenlaw's *Becoming Justice Blackmun: Harry Blackmun's Supreme Court Journey* (2005) draws on his extensive personal papers to examine a long and fascinating career.

And, while Earl Warren ranks as one of the greatest chief justices—for his leadership as much as his opinions—the Republican California governor and former prosecutor departed so much from Dwight Eisenhower's expectations that the president called the appointment one of his biggest mistakes.

If I set my story in state court, what structure and what terminology should I use?

State court systems vary widely. The basic structure looks like this:

Courts of Limited Jurisdiction: Common names for these include county court, district court, justice court, city or municipal court, traffic court, and small claims court. These courts handle only the types of cases specified by statute, such as misdemeanor criminal cases, initial appearances in felony cases, traffic claims, or civil cases involving less than a specified amount (ranging from $500 to $10,000 and up), and, in some states, domestic relations cases. Some states do not require judges in these courts to be lawyers.

In Margaret Maron's long-running Deborah Knott mystery series, Judge Knott, a lawyer, serves at this level in the North Carolina courts.

Courts of General Jurisdiction: Most action occurs here. These courts, the general trial courts, handle most criminal and civil cases. Their names vary: Superior Court (California, Washington State), District Court (Montana, Wyoming), Circuit Court (Illinois, Oregon), and even Supreme Court (New York).

A few states—most notably Texas—separate civil and criminal cases. Some states maintain specific courts at the limited or general level for probate, youth, or family matters. This specialized focus improves efficiency, but may accelerate burnout for judges and staff.

Intermediate Courts of Appeal: Many states have an intermediate Court of Appeals, a stop between the general trial court and the state's Supreme Court. New York calls this court the Appellate Division. Texas and a few others separate civil and criminal appeals, and some less-populated states do not have an intermediate appellate court.

These are workhorse courts, hearing thousands of appeals each year. Jurisdiction is mandatory, meaning the court must accept any case appealed.

Highest Court of Appeal: A state's Supreme Court is its court of last resort. New York and Maryland call their highest court the Court of Appeals, rather than Supreme Court. Jurisdiction is largely discretionary, meaning that one party must petition the Supreme Court to accept an appeal in a case already decided by the intermediate appeals court, or to accept an appeal directly from the trial court. Jurisdiction is mandatory in some cases, e.g., capital cases (those punishable by death), and in states without an intermediate court of appeal.

NOTE: Writers of historicals, be aware that court names and organization may have changed over time.

TIP: Expect readers familiar with your setting to know what local courts are called. For greater credibility, use the right names. The National Center for State Courts maintains a directory of state court websites, including a state-by-state court structure chart. (See the Book Links section at the back of this book.)

A lawyer in my crime novel aspires to become a judge. How are state court judges chosen?

Methods of choosing state court judges vary widely. In some states, judges are elected; mid-term vacancies are filled by appointment and the appointee must run for election at either the next general election or the end of the term. Unopposed judges may face a "retention ballot," meaning voters are asked whether to retain the judge. If "Mr. No" wins, to quote a Montana judge, the resulting vacancy is filled by appointment.

In other states, judges are appointed, typically by the governor with advice from a judicial nominations commission. A third variation is a combination, with positions in some types of courts elected and others appointed. The National Center for State Courts website gives state-by-state particulars. (See Book Links.)

I've heard about drug courts and would like to use one in my novel. Can you tell me how they work?

Drug courts are special programs operated within a state's existing court system. Their purpose is to give defendants with addiction problems the opportunity to avoid jail, treat their addictions, and turn their lives around. If they complete the program, drug or alcohol-related convictions are taken off their record.

Drug courts typically handle only adult defendants charged with nonviolent misdemeanor drug or alcohol offenses. Not all applicants are accepted. Some defendants choose not to participate—jail time is easier. If your character doesn't follow the program, he can be sanctioned or dropped, which usually means going to jail.

These programs involve intensive oversight by a team of judges, prosecutors and defense counsel, social workers, chemical dependency and mental health counselors, and other professionals. Obviously, such close supervision is expensive, but the programs aim to save money by reducing time in custody, preventing recidivism, and cutting the costs to courts, law enforcement, and victims for re-arrests. Success rates and cost benefit figures vary, but the National Association of Drug Court Professionals says 75 percent of graduates remain arrest-free for at least two years and that cost savings range from $4,000 to $12,000 per participant. (See Book Links.) Other studies show that graduates tend to stay in treatment programs, including AA, far longer than other defendants. Your character may return in a sequel clean and sober, or back in trouble, whichever suits your story.

Other intensive supervision courts focus on DUI, mental health, families, and fathers. By 2010, more than two dozen courts nationwide focused on veterans who had committed crimes, addressing the special needs of vets with post-traumatic stress disorder (PTSD), traumatic brain injury, and other combat-related issues.

In 2006, the Billings, Montana, drug court graduated its first defendant. In twelve months, the twenty-one-year-old drug user and dealer:

- appeared in court thirty-four times;
- visited his probation officer fifty-two times;
- underwent urinalysis to check for drugs 200 times;
- attended 151 treatment sessions;
- performed forty hours of voluntary community service;
- attended at least 114 AA meetings, the minimum required; and
- worked full-time; unemployed participants must find work or attend a job-training program.

Can you give me an overview of a trial?

First, we'll discuss jury selection, called *voir dire*, from the French "to see and speak," or as I think of it, "show and tell." Six, eight, or twelve jurors may be seated, depending on the court and the nature of the case. Alternates are chosen in lengthy felony cases and complex civil trials. Each side gets a specified number of peremptory challenges used to bump a potential juror without explanation. The parties may challenge for cause any obviously biased persons. In complicated or high-dollar cases, outside jury consultants may advise counsel, as in John Grisham's *The Runaway Juror* and Perri O'Shaughnessy's *Breach of Promise*.

Once jurors are chosen, the judge gives opening instructions describing the order of trial (the basic structure of the trial), the jurors' role, and how to behave.

Next come opening statements or arguments. Criminal defense counsel may defer opening until after the prosecution presents its case-in-chief, that is, its witnesses and exhibits. Doing so creates a risk that jurors will have already made up their minds. But a deferred opening allows the defense to put off making some strategic decisions, such as whether the defendant will testify.

Next, the prosecution in a criminal case, or the plaintiff in a civil case, presents its case-in-chief. A civil example: The plaintiff calls witnesses and introduces physical things and documents to prove the elements of the case, e.g., that a car wreck occurred, the defendant caused it, and, as a result, the plaintiff was injured and incurred specific financial losses. After the case-in-chief, the defense may ask the judge to dismiss the case, asserting that a key element has not been proven. If the request is denied—and most are—it's the defendant's turn. The defense may argue that the wreck was really the plaintiff's fault or that her injuries were pre-existing or not as severe as claimed. After the defense rests, the plaintiff may call rebuttal witnesses to respond to assertions made by the defense.

Closing statements—also called arguments or summations—follow. The prosecution or plaintiff goes first and gets a chance to give two closings—before and after the defense—because they have the burden of proof.

The judge instructs the jury before closings in some courts, and afterward in others. The jury deliberates in the closed jury room; jury members take with them written copies of the instructions, along with the documents and physical evidence, and their own notes. They may send written questions to the judge or ask to hear testimony again, read from the court reporter's transcript.

Jurors deliberate until they reach a verdict. Unanimous verdicts are required in criminal cases and in federal civil cases. Requirements in civil cases in state court vary; if unanimity is not required, typically eight of twelve jurors must agree. If jurors can't agree, they're "hung," and the judge declares a mistrial. Later, the prosecutor—or the plaintiff's lawyer in a civil case—must decide whether to retry the case. The verdict is read in court by the judge, bailiff, or jury foreman, sometimes called the presiding juror or chief juror. If the point of view you choose allows you to tell part of the story from a juror's perspective, you can present a wide-ranging debate filled with human tension.

> If the point of view you choose allows you to tell part of the story from a juror's perspective, you can present a wide-ranging debate filled with human tension.

If the jury convicts a capital defendant, a second phase immediately follows, with the same jury, to decide whether to impose a death sentence. The purpose of separating the two phases is to prevent the jury from considering factors such as a criminal defendant's record or abusive childhood in deciding guilt.

Similarly, if a plaintiff in a civil suit seeks punitive damages, liability and compensatory damages are determined in the first phase and punitive damages are determined in a second phase. Compensatory damages are those intended to compensate the injured person for his losses, such as medical expenses, lost wages, and pain and suffering, while punitive or exemplary damages are intended to punish the defendant. The separation prevents a jury from considering the defendant's finances or previous adverse judgments when it decides liability and compensatory damages.

After the verdict, either side may file post-trial motions asking the judge to set aside the verdict, order a new trial, or raise or lower monetary awards.

> The prosecution may not appeal a "not guilty" verdict in a criminal case, although it can appeal procedural or evidentiary rulings.

Appeals may follow. The prosecution may not appeal a "not guilty" verdict in a criminal case, although it can appeal procedural or evidentiary rulings. A criminal defendant is usually sentenced before appeal.

At long last, a final judgment is entered and the case is over. Its impact on the parties, witness, and sometimes on counsel may continue a long time.

B. Before the Trial

Before my character is charged with a crime, does she have to go through a grand jury investigation?

That depends on the state and court where you set your story. Federal criminal charges are filed only after a grand jury hearing, as required by the Fifth Amendment. State prosecutions may begin in two ways: The prosecutor may call a grand jury, or use his or her discretion to file charges based on a law enforcement investigation. In some states, especially in the West, prosecutorial discretion is the norm and grand juries rare.

A grand jury does not actively investigate, although jurors may ask witnesses questions. Instead, the prosecutor presents evidence—live testimony and documents—and asks jurors to decide whether there is probable cause to file an indictment charging the target with a crime. The prosecutor may compel witnesses to testify by issuing subpoenas and may grant witnesses immunity for any crimes they reveal.

Grand jurors come from the same pool as trial jurors, but they are not questioned in advance for bias. Hearings are held without a judge, although a judge may be called on to decide disputes, such as whether certain evidence is admissible. If the grand jury votes to indict, an indictment is filed with the clerk of court and a judge may issue an arrest warrant or summons.

The target is not present, cannot participate by asking questions or calling witnesses, and might not even know about the investigation unless called to testify. In the federal system, a target who is called to testify may not bring a lawyer into the courtroom, though he or she can leave to consult a lawyer; some states allow lawyers to be present during their clients' testimony. The prosecutor may present conflicting evidence, including testimony favoring the defendant, but isn't required to do so. The target has no right to confront the witnesses at this stage—only at trial.

Grand jury proceedings are closed to the public. Jurors, prosecutors, and staff may not speak about the proceedings except by court order. This secrecy protects jurors from outside pressure or tampering, allows witnesses to testify freely, and prevents targets from fleeing before arrest. It also protects those who are being investigated, but not charged, from public knowledge of the investigation and resulting rumor. All proceedings occurring after the indictment is filed are public.

In my story, a vengeful prosecutor threatens my protagonist with indictment. What is an indictment?

An indictment is a formal written accusation issued by a grand jury, at the request of a prosecutor, charging a person with a crime. In the federal system and some state courts, an indictment is the procedural means of bringing a person to trial. In states that don't use the grand jury system, or where it's optional, the defendant is brought to trial through a written charge called a Complaint or an Information.

Some indictments are more specific than others, but generally they identify the crimes charged, sometimes listing the criminal code section allegedly violated. They may state the date and place the crime occurred, give a short description of the crime, and identify the victim. When your character learns she's been indicted, she should immediately hire a defense lawyer, who will ask for more details about the crimes alleged in discovery (the formal process of exchanging information about a case).

A Complaint or Information contains the same details as an indictment. It is filed by the prosecutor in his or her discretion, typically as the result of law enforcement investigation.

How does a prosecutor decide whether to prosecute a specific case?

The prosecutor represents the people. His or her job is to prosecute all crimes committed within the jurisdiction while upholding the rights and privileges of all citizens. That means the prosecutor has a duty to seek the truth, no matter what it is.

And, the truth is, some suspects are innocent, and some crimes are never solved.

A prosecutor can't bring charges just because a crime occurs—he or she needs probable cause to believe that the person charged committed the crime. The prosecutor needs to weigh all the evidence and decide whether he honestly believes a jury will convict the person after weighing all the evidence. But in the early stages, evidence may be incomplete. If you want to delay the process or complicate the prosecutor's job, there are many options: Witnesses may disappear, or new ones may emerge. They may reveal new facts on the brink of trial. Lab results may be delayed or surprising. New appellate decisions may change the law. As a result, your prosecutor may be forced to lower, increase, or drop charges.

> A prosecutor can't bring charges just because a crime occurs—he or she needs probable cause to believe that the person charged committed the crime.

TIP: Watch your terms. Readers are TV-educated and may think every prosecutor is a DA, but that usage is limited to jurisdictions with district attorneys. Others use county attorneys, county prosecutors, or a combination. In some states, for example, the DA handles criminal matters while the county attorney is responsible for civil cases.

Evidence is often hard to evaluate. In close calls, the prosecutor considers the nature of the crime, the effect of trial on victims and witnesses, and the need to send a message to the community that certain conduct is unacceptable and justice will be sought. Expense may be a factor, particularly if the suspect has been tried once already or if expert witnesses will be needed, e.g., forensic accountants or psychiatrists with specialized knowledge.

But prosecutors can be misguided or mistaken. Prosecutors may rely on erroneous or deliberately false information—numerous convictions in several states, including Washington, Montana, and Texas, have been overturned because unethical employees of state crime labs provided false information or lied on the witness stand. Prosecutors may be disciplined by the court for misconduct if they violate

> A defendant wrongfully convicted as a result of deliberate prosecutorial misconduct may be able to sue for money damages.

court rules or orders, or by the state bar for violating the rules of professional conduct. A defendant wrongfully convicted as a result of deliberate prosecutorial misconduct may be able to sue for money damages.

It's a tough job, in the flesh and on the page.

The victim is afraid her assailant will hurt her if she pursues her complaint. Can she stop the prosecutor from filing charges? What are the consequences if she refuses to cooperate?

Once a victim or witness reports a possible crime to police, the state becomes responsible for investigating and prosecuting. Remember, crimes are seen as offenses against society, not just the individual victims. So, the prosecutor, not the victim, decides whether to prosecute.

But some cases can't be proven without the victim's cooperation. This is a frequent problem in domestic assault cases, where one spouse refuses to testify against the other. Unless other evidence is sufficient to prove the case—e.g., witness testimony, photographs of injuries, or medical reports—charges may be dropped. In a bizarre Montana case, homicide charges against a man accused of kidnaping and eating a ten-year-old boy were dropped days before trial because the boy's mother, convinced by a photograph of an American boy living in Italy who could have been her son's twin, planned to testify that her son was still alive. (The defendant was sentenced to 130 years for kidnaping and sexual assault, including torture, in another case, and later died in prison of natural causes.)

A victim who wants to drop charges or refuses to testify may fear retaliation. In some counties, victims' advocates work with victims to obtain restraining orders, counseling, and other services.

The greatest consequence of your character's refusal to cooperate with an investigation may be her vulnerability to future crimes, especially in domestic assault cases.

A character wants to create trouble for her ex-boyfriend by telling police that he assaulted her. What are the potential consequences if she makes a false complaint?

She may be charged with making a false report or obstructing police, both misdemeanors. A Wisconsin college student who was reported missing and found several days later in a marsh claimed to have been abducted at knife point, bound, and drugged. Surveillance tapes from a store near her apartment just before her disappearance showed her buying a knife, duct tape, rope, and cold medication. Witnesses reported seeing her alone and unharmed near the marsh after her disappearance. She was sentenced to probation and ordered to reimburse the police department $250 a month.

The infamous Runaway Bride, who in 2005 fled Georgia to avoid her wedding, then called police to claim she'd been kidnapped and assaulted and taken to New Mexico, was charged with giving police false information and filing a false report; she pled guilty and was sentenced to probation, community service, and restitution.

The father of the six-year-old "Balloon Boy," falsely reported missing in a homemade helium balloon, pled guilty to a felony charge of attempting to influence a public servant; the mother pled guilty to a misdemeanor charge of making a false report. Both received short jail sentences, fines, and probation.

Your character can expect similar charges and sentencing.

My protagonist has been arrested. What happens next?

Arraignment is the defendant's first appearance in court after arrest. Sometimes called a probable cause hearing, arraignment must be held within the time set by statute, usually 48 to 72 hours, unless circumstances necessitate a delay (e.g., the suspect is wounded and hospitalized). The judge formally reads the charges and gives the defendant a written copy. The defendant makes or "enters" an initial plea, which is "entered" into the written record of the case. Witnesses may be called, usually law enforcement officers. Most defendants plead not guilty at this stage, even if they expect to plead guilty later after more information is exchanged and sentencing options are discussed.

This initial appearance may be waived under limited circumstances. In the federal system and some states, court rules permit arraignment by video conference. Bail may be set at arraignment, or at a later hearing. The more serious the charges, the more likely it is that a separate hearing will be scheduled.

I want to have my protagonist released on bail, so she can find the person who actually sent the victim threatening letters. How is bail or pretrial release decided?

The right to bail is grounded in the Eighth Amendment to the Constitution, prohibiting excessive bail. Although state statutes governing specifics vary, the premise is that a defendant is released from official custody before trial on the least restrictive combination of conditions intended to ensure that:

- she appears for trial and other hearings;
- she commit no further crimes; and
- the victim and the public remain safe.

Factors in deciding whether to release a defendant and on what conditions include:

- the severity of the crime charged;
- the weight of evidence against the defendant, although the full extent of the evidence may not yet be known;

- risk of flight;

- personal characteristics such as physical and mental condition, family ties, employment, financial resources, length of time in the community, past conduct, a history of alcohol or drug abuse, criminal history, and past record of appearing in court when required;

- the danger to the community that the release might present; and

- whether the defendant is able to post property as bond or collateral to ensure her appearance. Bond may be posted by the defendant, a friend or relative, or a professional bail bondsman, but not by defense counsel. Bail is forfeited if the defendant does not appear in court when scheduled. Mystery readers know that bondsmen sometimes use bounty hunters to track down clients who skip out—Janet Evanovich's Stephanie Plum is the best-known fictional bounty hunter, though not the only one.

> **Bail is forfeited if the defendant does not appear in court when scheduled.**

Alternatively, a person may be "released on personal recognizance," meaning she alone is responsible for assuring that she appears in court when required and complies with all conditions.

In many states and the federal system, a person charged with a capital offense is not eligible for bail. Notorious cases often lead to calls for stricter rules, including higher bail or its elimination. The 2010 murders of four police officers in Lakewood, Washington, by a man released on bail on child rape charges reopened debate over what offenses should not be bailable.

Your character's release will be subject to conditions which depend on the crime and circumstances. They commonly include orders to:

- stay within the county or state, unless the court gives permission for travel;

- have no contact with witnesses or victims, or with potential victims, for example, an accused child molester ordered to stay away from children under a certain age, schools, parks, and other places where children are likely to be;

- stay away from co-defendants or others involved in the alleged crime;

- undergo treatment or counseling;

- obey any restraining orders—especially important in domestic assault or stalking cases;

- avoid drugs and alcohol, particularly for substance-related offenses;

- commit no other criminal offenses—crimes committed on release can result in much stiffer sentences for the earlier crimes;

- maintain or seek employment;

- possess no weapons, particularly in cases involving violence or hunting violations; and

- report regularly to the supervising agency.

A defendant may be released into a supervised living center, government-run or privately owned, leaving only for work, school, or other approved purposes.

The bond amount or terms of release may be changed for good cause. In one case, a defendant released before trial had been ordered not to drink. After a witness reported seeing him buy beer, the defendant claimed the beer was for a visiting friend and that he didn't partake. The court did not revoke bail, but revised the conditions of release to also ban buying or possessing alcohol.

A defendant may also be released on bail, with conditions, after she is convicted, pending sentencing. Release during appeal is possible, but unusual.

Pretrial release sometimes angers victims and their friends and relatives, especially when the victim is seriously injured or dies. Survivors often feel that the defendant has more rights than the victim. Keeping this in mind may lead you to more story conflicts.

How will the amount of her bail bond be set?

Some states set a schedule of amounts for specific offenses, mainly traffic violations. For more serious crimes, the amount is set based on the facts of the case, although criminal lawyers get a feel for the range a particular judge is likely to use.

The Eighth Amendment prohibits excessive bail. What's excessive or appropriate depends on the facts. The amount should be enough to ensure that your character appears in court and complies with conditions set, but should also be commensurate with the crime charged—what's reasonable for manslaughter or arson is probably excessive for minor assault or possession of drugs for personal use. Your character's finances will be considered, along with all the other factors for determining conditions of release discussed above.

But how does all that translate into dollars and cents? Some examples:

- A suspected Brooklyn mobster, charged with operating a multimillion dollar gambling ring and failing to report gambling income, a felony punishable by up to twenty-five years in prison, was granted bail of $250,000. Bail for co-defendants charged with felonies punishable by up to four years in prison ranged from $5,000 to $20,000.

- A Montana man charged with negligent homicide and felony criminal endangerment for one death and one serious injury in an alcohol-related car crash was released on $100,000 property bond.

- Another Montana man, charged with double negligent homicide, faced an initial six-figure bond, which was later reduced to $25,000. While out, he was arrested for DUI, and bail was revoked and increased.

- A New Jersey couple charged with four counts of aggravated assault and fourteen counts of child endangerment for failure to feed several foster children were released on $200,000 bail.

- In Seattle, a man charged with forcing his way into the offices of a Jewish charity, killing one and wounding five, was held on $50 million bail.

- Another Seattle man, charged with beating and stabbing a woman out walking with her young daughter, was held on bail of $1 million dollars.

Bail is deposited with the clerk of court, by the defendant, bail bondsman, or friends or relatives posting it for the defendant. Defense counsel can't pay the bail from their own funds or advance the funds, but can physically make the deposit. Some courts take credit cards or provide financing. Bail is returned if the defendant makes all required court appearances, less a private bond seller's fee and, sometimes, a court administrative charge.

Daniel Woodrell's *Winter's Bone*—also a 2010 film—is the grim but gripping story of a teenager in the Missouri Ozarks who must find her missing father before his bail is forfeited, in order to save the family homestead.

What is the right to a jury trial?

The Sixth Amendment to the Constitution, and every state constitution, guarantees a criminal trial by jury. That right is limited to serious cases, meaning those punishable by more than six months imprisonment. Adult defendants may waive the right and be tried by the judge, called a bench trial. Juvenile cases in youth court are handled without a jury; the constitutional right does not apply, because juveniles are not subject to the same punishment as adults.

> Juvenile cases in youth court are handled without a jury; the constitutional right does not apply, because juveniles are not subject to the same punishment as adults.

The Seventh Amendment and state constitutions and statutes also guarantee trial by jury in civil cases, although that right is limited to the types of claims recognized at the time the Bill of Rights was adopted. Generally, if money damages are involved, there's a right to trial by jury.

Bench trials are shorter, and they can usually be scheduled sooner.

Should my criminal defendant choose a trial by a judge instead of a jury?

An adult defendant may waive the right to a jury trial and be tried by a judge, called a bench trial or a judge trial. The decision is complex. A case might turn on technical legal arguments easier to explain to a judge than to a jury, or a particular judge might be considered sympathetic to the defense. The defendant might fear that the jury would be improperly influenced by harmful testimony, confused by complicated evidence, or overly sympathetic to the victim. But because most criminal prosecutions require unanimity, a defendant only has to persuade one juror of reasonable doubt—easier to do with a jury of twelve than a jury of one. In addition, the defense can participate in jury selection, but doesn't get to choose the judge. (Either side can challenge a judge by showing bias. In some jurisdictions, a party can "bump" one judge without showing bias, but must accept the replacement.)

In most civil cases, either party has the right to request a jury trial. Bench trials are typically shorter and easier to schedule, making them less expensive and quicker to go to trial, an additional factor in the judge-or-jury decision.

A scapegoat is arrested for murder, and the protagonist needs time to investigate the crime and identify the real killer. Will the right to a speedy trial cut that short?

The Sixth Amendment to the U.S. Constitution states:

> *In all criminal prosecutions, the accused shall enjoy the right to a speedy and public trial, by an impartial jury ...*

State constitutions provide the same guarantee.

The Supreme Court established guidelines for analyzing speedy trial violations in *Barker v. Wingo* (1972). The Court recognized that delay skews the fairness of the entire judicial system. The government must diligently pursue charges and cannot leave them hanging, unresolved, over a defendant's head. The remedy is dismissal.

Four factors must be balanced, based on the facts of the case. Judges and lawyers love multi-part tests. They make complex decisions seem easier. They also promote consistency and provide grounds for appeal when not applied properly.

- *Length of delay*. The trigger period varies by state, running roughly seventy to 200 days from arrest, indictment, or custody to trial. Length alone does not decide the issue; shorter delays may violate the right, while longer delays may be permitted.

- *Reasons for delay.* Delays are charged to the party responsible. A defendant cannot complain about a delay attributable to him or his conduct or condition: e.g., a postponement he requested, time to brief a motion he filed, a rescinded plea, or his unavailability for trial because he fled the jurisdiction or was mentally ill. Once the defendant demonstrates sufficient delay attributable to the prosecution, the burden shifts to the state to prove the lack of prejudice. The defendant then has a final chance to establish prejudice. Intentional delay by the prosecution may eliminate the need to show prejudice.

- *Assertion or waiver.* The judge must next consider whether the right was timely asserted, or whether it was expressly waived. A defendant may only object that his right to a speedy trial was violated if he asserted the right before trial—in other words, he can't accept a delay but later complain about it.

    If the prosecution anticipates delays, e.g., to allow a mental exam or when new evidence is discovered, it may request that the defendant sign a waiver of the right. Waivers are usually time-limited. In the Beltway Sniper case, the trial judge ordered the right waived because of trial complications, logistics, and expected length of trial.

> In the Beltway Sniper case, the trial judge ordered the right waived because of trial complications, logistics, and expected length of trial.

- *Prejudice.* Courts recognize that prejudice, or harm to the defendant's case, can be difficult to prove. The three traditional bases—the problems a speedy trial is intended to prevent—all relate to prejudice. They are pretrial incarceration, anxiety and concern, and impairment of the defense, particularly by fading memories or the death of witnesses.

Federal prosecutions are governed by the Speedy Trial Act of 1974. Criminal trials in federal court must start within seventy days of the indictment or initial appearance, unless "the ends of justice" warrant an extension. The Speedy Trial Act of 1974 specifies what delays will be counted in federal prosecutions.

Some practical effects of the speedy trial rule are:

- limited time can affect both sides' preparation;

- as the trial date approaches, prosecutors and defense lawyers work longer days;

- a short time to trial gives skittish witnesses less time to change their stories—or disappear altogether;

- police officers and crime lab witnesses may be called to testify on short notice, taking them off the streets or away from their microscopes;

- slow lab results may force trial delays, or an approaching trial date may force lab techs to put other work on hold; and

- the criminal trial calendar may bump civil trials at the last minute.

If your suspect is cooperating with the protagonist's investigation, she may request that trial be delayed and sign a waiver. If not, or if the judge denies the request because of concerns that witnesses may die or disappear, use a rapidly approaching trial date to pressure your protagonist and raise the stakes.

C. EVIDENCE

What is evidence?

Evidence is anything that tends to prove a fact important to the case. Evidence may be witness testimony. Or it may be documentary, such as records of a stock sale, medical reports, building plans, or photographs. Evidence may also be physical things: drugs, blood-stained clothing, a broken bolt, or a knife or gun. Except when the justice system breaks down—due to human failure or corruption—your characters will be convicted or acquitted based on the evidence presented.

> Except when the justice system breaks down— due to human failure or corruption—your characters will be convicted or acquitted based on the evidence.

The rules for excluding or admitting evidence may seem unduly technical at times. They have evolved to ensure that jurors hear and consider only reliable evidence that's been properly disclosed— "subjected to scrutiny and challenge from both sides," as one law professor put it.

And, as a judge I knew on the Washington State Court of Appeals liked to say, the law *is* technical.

How is physical evidence protected for trial?

To insure the accuracy and integrity of physical evidence, and to prevent tampering, the party introducing physical evidence at trial must be able to show where it has been at all times by establishing the chain of custody. This applies equally to a gun, a tire iron, a blood sample, or a baggie of green leafy vegetable matter. From the moment an item is seized, it's accompanied by a form describing the item, and the date and time and name of each person in possession.

For example, a detective finds a pipe in a car after an accident. The detective bags it and labels the bag with the date and time, the case number, his initials, a brief description, and where the pipe was found. At the crime lab, he fills out a chain of custody form. The lab clerk initials receipt of the evidence and locks the bag away. The tech who tests the pipe for drug residue initials the form, noting date, time, and purpose; when the test is complete, the pipe goes back to the clerk who again initials the form. And so on. When the item is introduced into evidence at trial, the chain of custody form goes with it and is part of the authentication process.

Though chain of custody may seem like a formality, it's crucial insurance against false testimony or shoddy evidence handling. Imagine a fatal accident where a hash pipe came from the car of the person killed but was mistakenly thought to have come from the defendant's car. That simple mistake could destroy yet more lives. (See a sample form in the Book Links section.)

The crime in my story involves a gun and several letters. How will this physical evidence be handled at trial and stored afterwards?

The clerk of court takes charge of all physical objects admitted into evidence. At the end of the trial day, the gun and original letters will be stored in a locked room or cabinet in the clerk's office. After trial, physical evidence is kept at the trial court until the time for appeal expires. After any appeals and retrials are complete, all evidence is returned to the clerk. Very large evidence, such as a truck or a tractor, may be kept in an impound yard.

In civil cases, the lawyer who introduced the evidence—photographs, blueprints, machine parts, and the like—may reclaim them; anything not reclaimed is destroyed. In criminal cases, about half the states have statutes requiring preservation of evidence in felony cases where there's been a conviction—DNA and biological evidence, at a minimum, and all evidence in some states. This allows for future retesting, if the conviction or sentence is later challenged. How long? It depends; in some states, for as long as the defendant is incarcerated; in others, preservation is limited to certain crimes. The Innocence Project maintains a directory of state laws. (See Book Links.) In states without statutes, or in cases not covered, local practice may vary, and will depend on whether there's a conviction, the crime charged, and the nature of the evidence. Check with your local prosecutor or clerk of court.

Why do lawyers make objections? How do judges respond? What terms are commonly used?

Most objections at trial are to admission of specific testimony or exhibits, or to a portion of an argument. Rulings are based on the Rules of Evidence and "precedent"—previously decided cases interpreting the rules. Objections to testimony may be to a question ("Objection: irrelevant," "argumentative," "asked and answered," "calls for speculation"), a line of questioning ("Objection: relevance"), or an answer ("Objection: non-responsive," or "hearsay"). An objection may be "sustained," meaning the objection is accepted and the question or answer is disallowed. If the question's already been answered, the judge may instruct the jury to disregard it. Or, an objection may be "overruled," meaning it's rejected and the testimony or argument is admitted. If the judge allows a line of questioning despite an objection, counsel may request "a continuing objection," so he doesn't have to stand and object to every related or follow-up question. This is important because evidentiary rulings can only be appealed if the evidence was objected to "below," meaning at the trial court.

TV lawyers frequently object to "hearsay," but sometimes the evidence they object to is allowed and sometimes it isn't. How do I know whether hearsay evidence will be admitted or not?

Hearsay is second-hand testimony, based not on personal knowledge but on something the witness heard from someone else. Of course, ordinary people rely on hearsay every day—we make decisions, form opinions, and discipline our children based on what other people tell us. However, with so much at stake in a trial, especially in a criminal case, hearsay is not considered sufficiently reliable.

> Hearsay is second-hand testimony, based not on personal knowledge but on something the witness heard from someone else.

The hearsay exclusion is riddled with exceptions, most both practical and obvious. For example:

- "Excited utterance." A witness may testify to what someone else said while an event was occurring or immediately after. A pedestrian hit by a car can testify that the first thing the driver said was, "I was texting and I never saw you."

- "Statements made for medical diagnosis or treatment." A doctor charts a patient's description of an accident. If the patient describes it differently at trial, the doctor's chart may be used for impeachment—that is, to challenge the witness's credibility.

- "Recorded recollections." Memos or notes made at a time when the witness had a better memory of events than now, usually used to refresh his memory, or by the opponent to impeach his testimony.
- "Public records and reports." A notable exception: reports of law enforcement investigations are inadmissible because they routinely contain not only the investigating officer's personal observations, but also conclusions based on statements of others and his own inferences.
- "Records of religious organizations," such as births, marriages, divorces, deaths, or ancestry.
- "Family records," such as Bibles, genealogies, even engravings on rings, portraits, or tombstones.
- Statements made "under belief of impending death," also called "dying declarations." Courts presume that the dying are generally truthful, even if they later recover.
- "Statements against interest." Because most of us don't blame ourselves unnecessarily, the driver who admitted not seeing the pedestrian is presumed to have been telling the truth.

> Courts presume that the dying are generally truthful, even if they later recover.

- "Prior inconsistent statements." A witness's testimony on the same point in another case may be used against him in a later trial.

Hearsay is also the name of lawyer Mitch McDeere's dog in John Grisham's *The Firm*.

Can I use ancient documents such as letters or the family Bible to prove my character is descended from a particular person?

Yes. Your character will need to establish that the letters or Bible are genuine, e.g., that she inherited the Bible from her grandmother, who kept it on a lace-covered bedroom table and often recounted receiving it from her own mother. If your character also remembers seeing her grandmother receive the letters or record births, deaths, and marriages inside the Bible, admissibility is almost certain.

What's the difference between direct and circumstantial evidence?

Direct evidence is testimony or physical evidence of a fact. Circumstantial evidence is evidence of one fact that leads to an inference or presumption. For example, Clete Purcel testifies that he saw the mobster take a shot at Dave Robicheaux. That's direct evidence. But if Clete testifies that he watched Dave enter the mobster's office and a few minutes later heard a shot, went in, and found the mobster standing over Dave with a gun in his hand, that's circumstantial evidence. The witness did not see what happened, but because of the circumstances, we infer or presume that the mobster shot at Dave.

If, instead, a witness saw Dave and Clete enter the office together, heard a shot, saw Clete run out of the room and leave the building, then found Dave checking the prostrate mobster for a pulse, the witness's testimony is direct evidence that Clete fled the scene. However, it's only circumstantial evidence that Clete shot the mobster. And, you know Dave didn't see a thing.

Circumstantial evidence may be enough to prove a defendant's guilt. But because circumstantial evidence is not conclusive proof, the judge must decide if it's relevant before admitting it at trial, considering what facts the evidence is intended to prove, and whether it makes those facts more probable. The judge looks through the lens of experience, judgment, and knowledge of human behavior, and asks what inferences a juror is likely to make fairly, reasonably, and consistently in light of all the other evidence.

All evidence rises and falls on the credibility of the witness. If you're counting on Clete Purcel to make your case, expect problems.

D. WITNESSES

Are witnesses in a murder trial held somewhere in the courthouse until called so they don't taint each other's testimony?

Not usually. In both criminal and civil cases, either side may invoke the "witness exclusion rule"—sometimes just called "the rule"—excluding witnesses from the courtroom until after they testify. Exceptions are typically made for parents of minor children. Exceptions may also be made for spouses, depending on the nature of their testimony, its importance to the case, and whether the opposing lawyer believes the spouse is likely to lie or be influenced by other testimony.

Some courthouses have public conference rooms where witnesses can wait, but many courthouses are crowded and don't have that extra space.

The rule does not apply to parties—that is, plaintiffs and defendants—including representatives of corporate parties.

Witnesses excluded from the courtroom are free to roam as long as they can be reached on short notice to testify. Witnesses for the state may be allowed to wait in the prosecutor's office, usually in or near the courthouse. A defense lawyer whose office is close to the courthouse might park a witness there. Some courthouses have public conference rooms where witnesses can wait, but many courthouses are crowded and don't have that extra space.

The courtroom bailiff, who is responsible for security, makes sure excluded witnesses don't enter the courtroom. Judges may order lawyers to instruct their witnesses not to talk to or come into contact with witnesses who have not yet testified. Judges may sanction lawyers whose witnesses intentionally or repeatedly violate any part of an exclusion or no contact order.

In either criminal or civil cases, a junior lawyer ("second chair") or a legal assistant might babysit a nervous witness or sit in the hallway with a witness who fears being confronted.

Witnesses can't be sequestered (confined to a specific location against their will), which would be an unconstitutional restriction on a person's liberty. But there are two exceptions:

> In either criminal or civil cases, a junior lawyer ("second chair") or a legal assistant might babysit a nervous witness or sit in the hallway with a witness who fears being confronted.

- a witness whom police have probable cause to believe would go into hiding or flee the jurisdiction could be held as a material witness; and

- a witness, such as an informant, who might be physically harmed by others could be held in protective custody.

In my story, the sole witness against the defendant is his wife. May she testify against him?

That depends on the case. No one may refuse to testify unless a privilege is provided by constitution (e.g., the right to avoid self-incrimination), statute, or the rules of evidence. The spousal privilege combines two elements: the right not to be compelled to testify against one's spouse and the protection of marital confidences.

Let's look at the Montana statute as an example. Most states' laws are similar.

> ***Spousal privilege.*** *A husband cannot be examined for or against his wife without her consent or a wife for or against her husband without his consent; nor can either, during the marriage or afterward, be, without the consent of the other, examined as to any communication made by one to the other during the marriage; but this exception does not apply to a civil*

action or proceeding by one against the other or to a criminal action or proceeding for a crime committed by one against the other.

The privilege applies equally to husbands and wives. Neither spouse may testify about communications between them during the marriage; the protection continues even after the marriage ends. However, the privilege does not apply in a civil suit between spouses, such as a divorce or custody proceeding, or when one spouse is charged with a crime against the other.

A few specifics:

- Like all privileges, the spousal privilege is waived if the statement is made in the presence of another person. It's also waived if the spouse who holds the privilege (the one who made the statement—usually the one being testified against) discusses the privileged communication with someone besides the spouse. The reason for this is those circumstances imply that the speaker did not consider the statement confidential. (Keep in mind, though, that disclosures may be subject to another privilege, such as attorney-client or physician-patient.)

- Some states limit spousal privilege to criminal cases. Even then, it does not apply in criminal cases charging spousal assault or child abuse, neglect, or molestation. If a husband is charged with assault against his wife or a child of either of them, the spousal privilege does not apply, and the wife can testify to any statements he made about the alleged crime.

- No witness or attorney can comment on the claim of privilege. A prosecutor cannot suggest, for example, that if the defendant's wife had been allowed to testify, the jury would have a fuller picture of his cruelty and abuse.

- The privilege is intended to protect communications, not acts or observations.

- A privileged communication must have been made in reliance on the marital relationship. A statement made as a threat or to assert control through fear is not privileged.

- The privilege applies in pretrial proceedings, including depositions, and at trial.

- The privilege assumes a legal marriage. Some states extend the privilege to long-established relationships that have many characteristics of marriage, such as property ownership, shared assets, and children.

Writers of historical fiction should note that the privilege was fairly well-established in both England and the United States by about 1850.

In TV crime shows, judges sometimes question witnesses. Is that realistic? Can jurors question witnesses?

Unlike British judges, American judges don't often question witnesses at trial or sentencing. A judge may ask a question to clarify some point, but a judge is unlikely to delve into subjects that the attorneys have not raised.

Some states allow grand jurors to ask questions. All states allow jurors to ask questions in civil cases, and most allow questions in criminal cases, but in practice, it's not common. A 2006 survey by the National Center for State Courts found that judges permitted juror questions in only 15 percent of criminal trials. The process goes like this: After a witness testifies, jurors submit written questions to the judge, who screens them with counsel and decides which questions to pose. Jurors are cautioned that some questions may not be asked for legal reasons. The lawyers may then ask follow-up questions.

Advantages: Jurors occasionally catch something the lawyers overlooked. More often, their questions highlight misunderstandings—lawyers and judges may know a case too well to understand how the testimony and arguments sound to someone hearing them for the first time. Jurors may feel more comfortable deciding another person's fate when they've actively participated in the trial. The more clearly they understand the case, the sounder their verdicts, and the greater their satisfaction with the judicial system.

Disadvantages: Juror questioning takes time. Jurors may become advocates rather than impartial decision-makers.

During deliberations, the jury may send written questions to the judge about the law, or request that the court reporter read the jury a portion of testimony.

> During deliberations, the jury may send written questions to the judge about the law, or request that the court reporter read the jury a portion of testimony.

A curious juror researches the case during trial. Is that allowed?

No. But whether it results in a mistrial depends on the circumstances. Judges have long given jurors standard instructions against doing any research, visiting the scene, or discussing the case with anyone. Increasingly often, those instructions now include a caution against online research or mentioning the case in Facebook updates or other social media.

What's the risk? The rules of civil procedure and evidence have evolved to ensure that jurors hear and consider only evidence that's been properly disclosed and subjected to "scrutiny and challenge" from both sides. Jurors who research a case on their own may see news accounts of evidence the judge excluded from trial, or they may consult a biased or unreliable website. If jury deliberations and decisions are influenced by outside sources, that's juror misconduct, and the judge should declare a mistrial if there's a risk that it interfered with the right to a fair trial.

In a federal drug trial in Florida, a juror admitted researching the case online. When the judge questioned the rest of the jury, he discovered that eight others had done the same thing. He declared a mistrial, and all the work and expense of the eight-week case was wasted. A Montana juror looked up the word "preponderance" in an Internet dictionary; the definition matched the judge's instructions, and she didn't share her research until after the jury voted. Some jurors later changed their minds for other reasons and the losing side requested a mistrial. The jurors testified that they based their decision on the evidence at trial, not the Internet research. The judge found no prejudice and denied the request. In other cases, a defendant sought to overturn a multi-million dollar judgment after learning that a juror sent Twitter updates during the trial, and a juror in a federal corruption trial posted updates on Twitter and Facebook.

State Supreme Courts and rules committees are now working on recommendations and rules changes to limit jurors' misuse of new technology. However, it isn't just jurors—the judge in former Illinois governor Rod Blagojevich's corruption trial ordered him not to continue his Twitter campaign to clear his name.

E. BURDEN OF PROOF

Can you explain the presumption of innocence?

A fundamental principle of American criminal law, the presumption of innocence, means that the prosecution—the government, representing the people—has the burden of proving a defendant's guilt beyond a reasonable doubt. A defendant is not legally considered guilty until convicted.

Defendants are not required to prove or disprove anything, or even to present evidence. Most defendants cross-examine witnesses and present their own evidence to rebut arguments against them and attempt to show doubt about their guilt. Some testify, but they don't have to.

> The presumption of innocence emphasizes to the jury and the public the importance of judging a person's guilt on the evidence presented in court, and not on suspicions arising from arrest, indictment, or pre-trial publicity.

The presumption of innocence emphasizes to the jury and the public the importance of judging a person's guilt on the evidence presented in court and not on suspicions arising from arrest, indictment, or pre-trial publicity.

In the United Kingdom, a third verdict option is "not proven." In some authoritarian systems, an accused is presumed guilty and required to prove his innocence—often a dicey proposition.

I know the prosecution must prove a criminal defendant's guilt beyond a reasonable doubt, but what is reasonable doubt?

Reasonable doubt is easier to recognize than describe. Here's a typical definition, from the West Virginia model jury instructions:

> *It is not required that the state prove guilt beyond all possible doubt. The test is one of reasonable doubt. A reasonable doubt is a doubt based upon reason and common sense—the kind of doubt that would make a reasonable person hesitate to act. Proof beyond a reasonable doubt, therefore, must be proof of such a convincing character that a reasonable person would not hesitate to rely and act upon it. The jury will remember that a defendant is never to be convicted on mere suspicion or conjecture.*

New Jersey phrases it differently, but the underlying principle is the same:

> *A reasonable doubt is an honest and reasonable uncertainty in your minds about the guilt of the defendant after you have given full and impartial consideration to all of the evidence. A reasonable doubt may arise from the evidence itself or from a lack of evidence. It is a doubt that a reasonable person hearing the same evidence would have.*
>
> *Proof beyond a reasonable doubt is proof, for example, that leaves you firmly convinced of the defendant's guilt. In this world, we know very few things with absolute certainty. In criminal cases the law does not require proof that overcomes every possible doubt. If, based on your consideration of the evidence, you are firmly convinced that the defendant is guilty of the crime charged, you must find [him/her] guilty. If, on the other hand, you are not firmly convinced of defendant's guilt, you must give defendant the benefit of the doubt and find [him/her] not guilty.*

Reasonable doubt is sometimes described as proof "to a moral certainty" or "an abiding conviction" in the accused's guilt. The test is subjective—not every juror will view the evidence the same way. Although the government's burden is heavy, as it should be, the government isn't required to prove the charges beyond all doubt. But doubts or mistakes favor the defendant because of what's at stake: liberty and, sometimes, life.

Every element of the crime must be proven beyond a reasonable doubt. For example, your character is charged with arson for setting a fire that destroyed an office building. Your story state's code defines the crime as know-ingly or purposely damaging or destroy-ing a structure by fire or explosion. (Arson can apply to other situations, but we'll limit the definition for now.) The ele-ments of the charge are:

> Every element of the crime must be proven beyond a reasonable doubt.

- your character did the deed;
- he acted with the knowledge or purpose of damaging or destroying the building;
- the building was in fact damaged or destroyed; and
- the damage or destruction occurred by fire or explosion, and not by some other cause.

If the prosecution fails to prove any element of the crime charged beyond a reasonable doubt (e.g., that your character knew or intended that the building would be destroyed), the character must be acquitted.

Show me a more wrenching debate over reasonable doubt than in the movie *Twelve Angry Men* and I'll refund the price of this book.

In my story, a character is sued for causing a five-car chain collision on a mountain highway that injures several people. What standard will the judge and jury use to decide liability and damages?

In most civil cases, the plaintiff must prove the elements of the claim by "a preponderance of the evidence." The burden of proof is lower than in criminal cases because civil cases involve money judgments, not life or liberty.

A preponderance means that the claim is more probably true than not true, considering all the evidence, no matter which side introduced it. That is, the evidence supporting the claim outweighs the evidence against it. What matters is not the amount of evidence, but which evidence is more convincing. It's a common sense standard, calling on jurors to use their own experience in judging both the credibility and the weight of the evidence.

The O. J. Simpson case illustrates the differences between the criminal and civil standards. California could not convince a criminal jury of each element of the crimes charged beyond a reasonable doubt. However, civil claims that Simpson wrongfully caused Ron Goldman's death carried a lower burden of proof, one the Goldman family successfully met.

So how do you recognize a preponderance of the evidence when you meet one? A plaintiff in a personal injury case arising from a car accident testifies that she had a green light, and that the defendant was speeding and ran a red light. She calls two witnesses who testify that she had a green light. One admits she only vaguely recalls the incident, saw it out of the corner of her eye, and was paying more attention to her two-year-old in the backseat than to the accident. The other witness is firmly convinced of what she saw, but also insists that the defendant was a thin white man in a green Chevy—when in fact, he's Asian, on the round side, and he drove a blue Honda. The defendant testifies that he had just turned on to the street half a block before the light, and thus he could not have been speeding, although he was accelerating. He testifies that he had a green light and that the plaintiff ran a red light and T-boned him. He does not produce any witnesses to the collision. The jury may choose to accept the defendant's explanation, believing a single witness and disbelieving the other three testimonies if, say, the defendant's memory is clear and that of the others appear hazy, their descriptions are vague or inconsistent, they were not in a good a position to see what happened, they do not seem as credible, or it appears to the jurors from the overall circumstances that the accident simply could not have happened the way the plaintiff contends. The jurors are the judges of the facts, including the credibility of the witnesses.

F. Appeals

The judge in my story admitted evidence that drugs were found in the defendant's car, without evidence that he'd taken the drugs or that they caused the accident. He was convicted. Is this an error that can be reversed on appeal?

Yes. Your criminal defendant may appeal the verdict and challenge evidentiary rulings made during trial, like the decision to admit the drug evidence. Your character will need to show reversible error—that is, an error that might have affected the outcome of the case. If a toxicologist or other expert testified that the drugs played no role in causing the accident—because they weren't found in the defendant's system or were found at levels that don't impair driving—then evidence that the drugs were found in his car could have prejudiced the jury and affected the verdict. The conviction should be reversed and the case remanded (that is, sent back for a new trial).

The flip side of reversible error is harmless error, a trivial or technical mistake not likely to have affected the verdict. Errors that don't affect the substantial rights of the parties or the outcome of the case are not grounds for reversal.

Convicted defendants may also appeal their sentences, although many states have set up sentence review boards to ease the burden on the trial courts.

The prosecution cannot appeal a not guilty verdict. But it can appeal specific rulings, such as orders dismissing a case, quashing an arrest or search warrant, suppressing evidence or a confession, or imposing a sentence contrary to law. Each side may raise different issues on appeal, called cross-appeal.

Once an appeal is filed, deadlines for briefing begin. The time to resolve an appeal varies widely, but it will generally take six months to two years. Remember that no new evidence is submitted on appeal. The appellate court is limited to reviewing the actions of the trial judge for reversible error.

Critics sometimes complain that a conviction was reversed "on a technicality." The phrase trivializes a legitimate decision

> Constitutional rights are never technicalities.

that the critic disagrees with. The standards for reversible and harmless error prevent groundless reversals. Constitutional rights are never technicalities.

After my character was convicted and sent to prison, someone else confessed to the crime. How do I free my character?

First, your character and his attorney must convince the prosecutor who convicted him that the confession is genuine and proves your character's innocence. If the prosecutor is persuaded, then your character's lawyer should file a *habeas corpus* petition asking the court to review the new evidence, along with a copy of the written or taped confession. If charges have been filed against the confessor, get that evidence before the new judge, too, along with any law enforcement investigation that shows how the new confession came about and why it's credible.

In some cases, the new confession is so obviously true that the previously convicted person is promptly released, but it's rarely that simple. Some mentally ill people compulsively confess at any suggestion that they committed a crime or are easily coerced into a false confession. If the prosecutor isn't persuaded that the new evidence exonerates your defendant, the problem is tougher. In that situation, your character is likely to remain in prison until a full hearing is held to examine the circumstances of his conviction, the new confession, and any other new evidence.

If your character has been charged with a crime but not yet tried, the prosecutor may agree to dismiss the charges. If not, your character's lawyer must file a motion asking the trial judge to consider the matter.

Once your character is released, he can ask the court to strike or expunge the conviction from his criminal record. If the government prosecuted him with false evidence, he may be able to sue for damages for wrongful or malicious prosecution. Defendants have successfully sued states for money damages when a witness employed by the government testified that physical evidence put them at the scene of the crime, but DNA evidence obtained after conviction proved their innocence. Scott Turow's *Ultimate Punishment: A Lawyer's Reflections on Dealing with the Death Penalty* (2003) tells the horrifying true stories of men wrongfully convicted of homicide despite clear evidence that others' confessions were accurate and credible, or that prosecutors and law enforcement knew material evidence was false.

Injustices will occur as long as the judicial system is run by humans. Use them to tell a killer story.

2

Legal Issues in Criminal Investigation

LAWYERS, JUDGES, COURT STAFF, LAW PROFESSORS, EVEN THE companies that publish court decisions would have much easier jobs if criminal law didn't create so many issues. So would fiction writers—but we would miss so many opportunities to make our stories more interesting. We'll look first at probable cause, the foundation for search and arrest. Next, we'll discuss a few issues related to searches, and we'll clear up some common misunderstandings about *Miranda* warnings. We'll also talk about missing witnesses, confidential informants, public defenders, extradition, and recording.

What is probable cause to search or arrest?

Probable cause is a reasonable belief, based on facts, that evidence of a particular crime will be found in a particular place, or that a particular person is responsible for a particular crime. "Mere suspicion" is not enough.

The Fourth Amendment to the Constitution of the United States provides:

> *The right of the people to be secure in their persons, houses, papers, and effects, against unreasonable searches and seizures, shall not be violated, and no warrants shall issue, but upon probable cause, supported by oath or affirmation, and particularly describing the place to be searched, and the persons or things to be seized.*

State constitutions include a similar provision.

In a nutshell:

- no unreasonable search and seizure;

- no warrants without probable cause, supported by oath and particularity.

Keep in mind that these limitations apply only to government action, e.g., actions of law enforcement officers or others acting with government authority, not to private acts.

Consider a case of suspected homicide: A woman is missing. Her husband's alibi for the time she disappeared can't be confirmed. He admits having a girlfriend. A neighbor calls police to report recent digging in the backyard. When police arrive, the husband is packed and ready to go. Do police have probable cause to arrest him or to obtain a warrant to search the home?

That his alibi is uncertain and he is involved with another woman does not establish reasonable factual grounds to believe that a crime has been committed, or to link him to it. Nor does his imminent departure. All that is merely suspicious. But the third factor—the backyard digging—is sufficient grounds for a warrant to search the yard. When the yard is dug up and the missing woman's body or clothing is found, that is evidence of a crime, linked to the husband, and establishes probable cause for his arrest.

If the neighbor had reported that the day the wife disappeared, she saw the husband carry a shovel to the backyard and start digging, visibility was good, and she sees reasonably well, those facts link the digging to a crime, and they link the husband to both. Probable cause to search and to arrest would exist even before the yard was excavated. If the neighbor further saw him struggle with the weight of a large bundle, or her dog dragged home a scarf known to belong to the missing woman, the showing of probable cause would be even stronger.

Another example involves a suspected drug dealer: Police go to Bates' apartment to question him about a suspected drug deal. When the door opens, they see Bates drop a marijuana pipe into a wastebasket. While standing with him in the doorway, officers see other drug paraphernalia in the living room, in plain view. An officer detects a strong odor of smoke. Officers ask if anyone else is in the apartment; Bates says he doesn't think so. Officers then hear a voice in the kitchen. An officer walks into the kitchen, finds it filled with smoke and soot, and sees a man he recognizes as a convicted drug dealer with an outstanding arrest warrant. He also sees a tobacco tin filled with what appears to be marijuana on the living room table.

> If the evidence establishes probable cause to look for a person, officers can only search places where a person might be found in a home, such as in closets, but not in dresser drawers.

Do officers have probable cause for a warrant to search the apartment for drugs? Yes. They saw a pipe and other paraphernalia. They smelled, then saw, evidence of cooking but no food, with a known drug dealer in the kitchen. These facts establish a reasonable belief that evidence of drug dealing will be found in the apartment.

Do officers have probable cause to arrest Bates on the spot? Yes, for possession of marijuana. If possession of drug paraphernalia is illegal in that state, he can be arrested on that charge as well.

In the actual case, a search warrant was obtained and a meth lab was found in a closet off the kitchen. Officers then had probable cause to arrest Bates for illegal manufacture of drugs.

If the evidence establishes probable cause to look for a person, officers can only search places where a person might be found in a home, such as in closets, but not in dresser drawers. If probable cause extends to cash or drugs, the search area includes any place where those items might be found—in other words, almost anywhere.

Not every search or arrest requires a warrant. (Think of an arrest as the seizure of a person.) Police don't need a warrant to seize evidence "in plain view," as in the story of Bates. Another warrantless seizure is the "stop and frisk," also called a *Terry* stop after *Terry v. Ohio* (1968), the Supreme Court case establishing the rule. There, an officer with a lawful reason to stop a suspect can frisk him for guns, knives, or other weapons, in order to protect the officer's safety. Any evidence found in the course of a reasonable patdown to protect the officer's safety may be seized and the person arrested.

Other valid, warrantless searches are those made pursuant to arrest, or to prevent the destruction of evidence. While one officer cuffs a suspect, his partner may follow the suspect's girlfriend into the bathroom to prevent her from flushing the cocaine they were packaging down the toilet or to stop her from feeding papers that establish accounting fraud into the backyard barbecue.

Police don't need a warrant to make an arrest in a public place or in "exigent circumstances," such as when an officer witnesses a crime or is pursuing a person suspected of committing a crime. But officers still need probable cause.

> Police don't need a warrant to make an arrest in a public place.

Remember that the Fourth Amendment comes into play only when there is both a search and a seizure. If an officer unlawfully searches a house but doesn't take anything, the Fourth Amendment is not involved—although other sanctions may apply. And, if he's walking down the street and sees a pot plant in an open window, he can grab it without a warrant—there's a seizure, but no search.

Probable cause matters because it is the legal minimum level of facts that law enforcement must establish before getting a warrant for a search or an arrest. If you want to create both defensible and questionable arrests and warrants in your fiction, keep the elements of probable cause in mind.

How do the police get a search warrant?

The mechanics vary among jurisdictions, but the heart of the process is giving a judge facts that establish probable cause to believe that evidence of a specific crime will be found in the place to be searched. In routine searches, as for drugs, the warrant application may be written by a law enforcement officer, filling in the blanks on a computerized form. In serious felonies or cases with complicated facts, warrant "apps" may be written by a deputy prosecutor, or by a higher-ranking officer working with the prosecutor. Police procedures typically require that supervisors or prosecutors review apps before they go to a judge.

Detectives may receive extra training in drafting warrant requests. The evidence sought must be described "with particularity." The facts showing the link to the crime must be detailed and the link made clear. Property descriptions must be accurate. When an officer applies for a warrant based on knowledge obtained from someone else, he must articulate detailed reasons why the information is reliable. If he can't produce the informant to testify, he must identify the informant—unless he can establish that doing so would put the informant in mortal risk—and state why the informant is reliable. Past reliability is generally sufficient.

Applications are then presented to the judge for review and signature. In some jurisdictions, any judge will do. In others, requests go to a designated judge. On TV and in movies, detectives often shop for a friendly judge—usually seen answering the door at home in a bathrobe—and that is possible on weekends, holidays, or nights, but it's not routine. "Judge-shopping" can be a problem, if a warrant is challenged and the allegations include improper influence or violation of procedures. And, frankly, most judges apply the standards in pretty much the same way. Of course, that doesn't make for interesting fiction, but there's lots of room for legitimate variation.

Some warrant requests can wait to be reviewed; others are more pressing, and the detective and prosecutor may physically walk the request through the process of review and signature. Depending on who is involved, their experience, and the facts of the case, the process could be completed in a couple of hours or less—or it can drag out for days, if that's what your story needs.

Attention to detail is critical because the risks are so high. If a warrant request is denied, evidence may be destroyed or a suspect may flee. If the request is granted but the warrant is later challenged—say for lack of probable cause—the evidence obtained may be thrown out ("suppressed") along with all other evidence discovered as a result. If there isn't enough admissible evidence left, the entire case may be dismissed.

How can my character challenge a warrant?

For a search warrant, the person in control of the premises should ask to see the warrant and question any discrepancies. Does the warrant say "4772 Highline Drive" and the police are on the doorstep of 4272 Highline or 4772 Ridgeline? Does it say "the home of Alfred Moore" and this is the home of "Albert Morris"? Similar questions can be asked before an arrest. Warrant errors could be minor or critical, but they offer good grounds for refusing to allow the police to enter and execute the warrant—that is, to search or arrest.

Most challenges to both search and arrest warrants are made after the fact, once charges have been filed. Motions to suppress evidence obtained in a search are common, and typically assert lack of probable cause. Evidence obtained as a direct result of a constitutional violation—"fruit of the poisonous tree"—must be excluded from trial unless the prosecutor establishes that it would inevitably have been obtained through legitimate means. The exclusionary rule makes law professors grin and detectives work late. Think of all the possibilities it offers you, as a writer.

Can a landlord give police permission to search rented property?

Voluntary consent is a long-recognized exception to search warrant requirements. Only a person with a right of privacy in the premises can give valid consent to search. This includes any adult who lives in the rented house or apartment, not just the adult whose name is on the lease. The key is the right of privacy, not the right of control or ownership. So, a landlord can't consent, because he's given up the right of privacy to rented premises. If the landlord reserved access to a specific portion of the property, say a locked storage room in the basement, he

> Only a person with a right of privacy in the premises can give valid consent to search.

has the right to consent to a search of that room—and no others. However, if the tenant abandons the premises, he has no further expectation of privacy, and the landlord can consent to a search.

Can my character's girlfriend or a visitor consent to a search?

If your character's girlfriend lives on the premises, she too has access and an expectation of privacy, even if she's not the legal tenant. So she can consent to a search, unless like Bluebeard's wife of fairy tale, she's been told not to enter a certain room. Her right to consent would stop at the door of the forbidden room.

Numerous courts have held that overnight visitors have an expectation of privacy in a premises, and they can challenge searches and seizures that incriminate them. Whether they can consent to a search that might incriminate another will depend on the facts, and whether it reasonably appeared to the police that the person had sufficient control over the premises to consent. In *Illinois v. Rodriguez* (1990), the U.S. Supreme Court announced the principle of apparent authority, upholding consent to search where the complainant took a key from her purse and unlocked the apartment for police. They did not know she had moved out two weeks earlier, nor that the defendant did not know she still had a key. Clearly, she no longer had sufficient expectation of privacy rights in the premises to consent to a search. But her exercise of apparent authority led police to reasonably, although mistakenly, believe she had that authority. The Constitution only prohibits *unreasonable* searches and seizures, so the Court upheld the search. Apparent, as opposed to actual, authority may not apply in states with their own constitutional privacy protections. Either way, the concept allows you as the writer to complicate the facts, reward law enforcement officers who use good judgment, and make things difficult for those who don't.

What happens if one occupant consents to a search but the other refuses?

A husband and wife jointly occupy a house. The husband—the suspect— refuses to let the police search the premises, but his wife consents. What then? The Supreme Court held in *Georgia v. Randolph* (2006) that if both occupants are present, both must consent. One's consent can't override the other's refusal. If only one is present and consents, that's sufficient, even if the other occupant later claims he would have refused had he been there. But police can't call a suspect out to the sidewalk and engage him in conversation while other officers ask his wife for consent to search. If he's on the premises, he's got to be given an opportunity to object. Doing otherwise would not be reasonable.

Can a child consent to a search?

Typically, states analyze the validity of a child's consent to a search of the parent's home by looking at age, understanding, and "the totality of the circumstances." (A few states hold that children lack capacity and authority to consent to the search of a parent's home, usually on state constitutional grounds.) There is more room for a challenge because a child is more readily influenced than an adult.

For example, in your story, set in a state allowing a child to consent to a search, a thirteen-year-old is babysitting her younger sisters. It's late and she doesn't know—though your cops do—that Mom is in custody downtown. The girl, visibly sleepy, peeks out the barely-open door at four uniformed officers. A large male officer says they want to come in and search for evidence of illegal drugs. Is her consent voluntary? What if she says "my mother told me not to let anyone in," but the officer says they need to look for something her mother left there? Make her sixteen, set the scene at noon, or put the officers in plain clothes. See how different facts change the situation? Make her seventeen, or limit the request to search her bedroom or backpack, and the situation changes again.

Turn the tables, apply the principles already discussed, and you'll see that a parent has the right to consent to a search of a child's room or personal property in the parent's home. That the child is over eighteen does not change the parent's right to give consent. The result would probably be different, though, in the case of an adult child who returns home and puts a lock on his door, or who lives in an apartment in the basement.

Can school authorities search a student's purse or locker?

Yes. In *New Jersey v. T.L.O.* (1985), the Supreme Court upheld a warrantless search of a student's purse. The Court held that the Fourth Amendment does apply to students, who have a legitimate expectation of privacy, but also acknowledged the interests of schools in maintaining a safe learning place. To balance the interests involved, it established a "reasonable suspicion" standard, less than probable cause. That is, do school administrators have reliable knowledge that shows a "fair probability" or "moderate chance" of discovering evidence of a crime or violation of school rules? Search measures must be "reasonably related to the objectives of the search and not excessively intrusive in light of the age and sex of the student and the nature of the infraction."

A teacher reported that T.L.O. was smoking in the bathroom, in violation of school rules; T.L.O. vehemently denied it. The Court found that the vice principal had reasonable grounds to search her purse for cigarettes. He immediately spotted rolling papers, giving him reasonable suspicion to search more thoroughly. He then found marijuana, a pipe, several empty plastic bags, a substantial number of one-dollar bills, an index card listing students who owed T. L. O. money, and two letters implicating her in marijuana dealing. He called her mother and police. She confessed to dealing. Delinquency charges were brought. She challenged the legality of the search and confession and the admissibility of the evidence as "fruit of the poisonous tree," but lost.

The same principles apply to locker searches. Unlike purses and backpacks, though, lockers are school property, and some argue that students therefore have a reduced expectation of privacy in them. Some school districts require schools to give students written notice that lockers may be searched on reasonable grounds; others have eliminated lockers. While random searches violate the *T.L.O.* principles, searches following a "hit" by a drug-sniffing dog are probably valid. And, a search based on a reliable report that a student brought a gun to school will also be upheld, if it meets the "reasonable grounds" test. Even then, though, the methods and scope must be limited: Administrators can't search for a rifle in a pencil case.

What other situations might be used, successfully or otherwise, to justify a search of a student's locker or backpack? School staff have grounds to suspect a student of drug use or sales and the student is seen making repetitive trips to his or locker, then clustering with small groups of students not known to be his friends. Reports that another student has contraband—alcohol, drugs, knives, guns—at school. Reports that a student possesses stolen items or evidence of other crimes at school. Gang activity or violence between students. A health emergency. An immediate threat to health and safety, such as reports that students plan a shooting or to set off a bomb at school.

Wasn't there a recent decision about searching a student's underwear?

Methods and scope are key to a recent decision that offers considerable story potential. In *Safford Unified School District v. Redding* (2009), the Supreme Court invalidated an underwear search of a middle-schooler suspected of possessing forbidden prescription pain relievers. Administrators had grounds justifying a search of her locker and backpack—to which she consented—but went too far in searching her underwear. Why? No evidence suggested that the pills presented a danger or that they were in her underwear, making the search "excessively intrusive." The search violated the girl's Fourth Amendment right against unreasonable searches.

School search law and policy has changed greatly in recent years, in response to competing concerns about privacy, on the one hand, and over school shootings, bullying, and other violence, on the other. State and local variations abound. Even before *Redding*, some states and school districts specifically prohibited school officials from conducting strip or body cavity searches. Washington State mandates a search where

> School search law and policy has changed a lot in recent years, in response to competing concerns about privacy, on the one hand, and over school shootings, bullying, and other violence, on the other.

there are reasonable grounds to believe a student illegally possesses a gun. You can create local rules or procedures to suit your story, keeping in mind the overriding constitutional principles.

Trial starts in two days and a key witness has gone missing. Now what?

First, pull your hair. Then, get looking. If you find her but she refuses to testify voluntarily, get a subpoena requiring her to appear in court and threaten her with contempt of court if she doesn't appear or if she appears but refuses to testify. Contempt of court covers a lot of ground; the gist is disobedience of a court's order or authority. There are two kinds of contempt: civil and criminal. The terms stem not from the nature of the underlying case or of the contemptuous act, but from the nature of the sanction. If it's intended to ensure compliance with the court order, it's civil. If it's intended to punish and to vindicate the court's authority, it's criminal. Specifics are established by statute.

If your witness has left the area, you may be out of luck. Subpoenas are enforceable only within the issuing state. In some states and the federal system, a witness can't be forced to travel more than 100 miles, even within state.

Think of other ways to get the witness back to the area to serve a subpoena, such as sending a fake party invitation or enlisting a fam-

> If your witness has left the area, you may be out of luck. Subpoenas are enforceable only within the issuing state.

ily member to make an urgent appeal. Deception is okay, to a degree. Seattle police detectives, posing as a non-existent law firm, sent a murder suspect who had moved out of state a letter inviting him to participate in a class action lawsuit, with a return envelope. The lab got his DNA from the envelope (*State of Washington v. Athan* (2007)). In affirming his conviction, the Washington Supreme Court said "police officers are allowed to use some deception, including ruses, for the purpose of investigating criminal activity," as long as the actions do not violate the suspect's due process rights. Let your fictional officers devise a similar ruse to lure a witness back to testify.

Even if your story involves an official search, don't overlook the local telegraph. In a criminal case related to a civil suit my firm filed, the prosecutor lost contact with a witness and feared she would have to drop charges. Every person in our office started calling people we knew in that community to ask for help: a teacher, a business owner, a former client who ranched in the area. Within an hour, the witness called our office saying, "Heard you're looking for me." We called the prosecutor and the case went to trial as scheduled.

That witness was friendly to our case, not suspected of any criminal involvement, and perfectly willing to be found; he'd simply moved, not gotten a phone in his name, and not thought to keep in touch. A witness who doesn't want to be found may present a bigger challenge, but the search will give your story new dimensions.

When can information from confidential informants be used?

Warrant applications frequently include details learned from confidential informants (CIs) who are not named in the application. TV and movies have trained us to think of CIs as shady types, providing information in exchange for getting off the hook for their own crimes. That is sometimes the case, but not always. Those who live on the edge are often the ones who know about suspicious activity, and they may have perfectly good reasons for reporting it other than self-protection—a drug dealer, for example, may draw the line at murder or have no tolerance for child pornography. Other informants are ordinary citizens willing to go to the police, but they don't want their names in the paper or on the public record. They may be neighbors or relatives who fear retaliation from the suspect or his circle. This is especially common in small towns or in insular groups within larger communities, such as the Hasidic community in New York or the Vietnamese in south Seattle.

> TV and movies have trained us to think of CIs as shady types, providing information in exchange for getting off the hook for their own crimes.

Reliable information from a CI may help show probable cause for search or arrest. The application should include an officer's affidavit stating that the CI has provided reliable information in the past. If there are questions, it's smart to get corroboration; whether that's necessary depends on the "totality of the circumstances." If the CI is anonymous, even to police, the application must include corroborating evidence from police investigation, other reliable sources, or a combination. Multiple sources can be used. Here's an example: A CI tells investigators that a suspect has been manufacturing meth, and provides details about locations, sources of materials, and buyers. Police don't know the informant or his reliability. But police have observed the suspect with a known meth dealer five times in the last two months, and a local pharmacist recently reported that the suspect attempted to buy substantial quantities of over-the-counter drugs known to be used in manufacturing meth. When investigators interview the suspect's landlord, she says she's seen people come and go at odd hours and observed the suspect cooking something foul-smelling when she stopped by to collect the rent. No one person corroborates all the informant's statements, but individual details have been corroborated, and taken together, they reinforce the story's reliability. Police can use all the information to support a search warrant application.

Indicators of CI reliability include providing reliable information in the past, making statements against personal interest, personal observation or other first-hand knowledge, and the level of detail provided. Information provided voluntarily by a concerned citizen—the pharmacist in my scenario—is viewed as more inherently reliable than statements by a person known or suspected to be involved in crime.

Defense counsel may file a Motion to Disclose Identity of a Confidential Informant, as part of the hunt for grounds to challenge the showing of probable cause and the CI's credibility. The officer may have accurately testified that the CI provided reliable details in the past, but neglected to point out several instances where the CI's reports were proven false. Was the CI paid for information or given special treatment? Jurors may be given a "cautionary instruction," telling them to consider evidence of motive, bias, or bad character in weighing the informant's testimony or information obtained from a CI.

A CI can't be compelled to testify, which would expose his identity. But if he agreed to testify in exchange for immunity from prosecution and then refuses to testify, he could be held in contempt of court. A confidential informant is a good way to add more CI—character interest—to your stories.

How do public defender systems work?

The Sixth Amendment to the United States Constitution states:

> *In all criminal prosecutions, the accused shall enjoy the right . . . to have the assistance of counsel for his defense.*

Even so, courts and legislatures were slow to grasp that a person cannot get a fair trial without competent defense counsel. Some states recognized the right to counsel in serious cases long ago—Indiana was first, in 1853, grounded in "the principles of a civilized society," although it didn't articulate a constitutional right until 1951. The U.S. Supreme Court recognized the right in federal prosecutions in 1938, but refused to extend it to state prosecutions. Finally, in *Gideon v. Wainwright* (1963), the Court said that the right to counsel is fundamental, and therefore applies to state prosecutions through the Fourteenth Amendment, which extends the Sixth Amendment and other due process protections to state courts. The decision formalized a change in thinking: Twenty-two state attorneys general signed a brief supporting Clarence Gideon's position. Gideon first set out that position in a handwritten petition before the Court appointed appellate counsel for him, future Supreme Court Justice Abe Fortas. On retrial for robbery charges, with appointed counsel, he was acquitted. Journalist Anthony Lewis wrote about the case and its impact in *Gideon's Trumpet* (1966).

In 1972, the Court extended the right to counsel to misdemeanors where liberty is at stake—that is, where sentencing options include incarceration. The right applies to all critical stages of a criminal prosecution, most notably custodial interrogation (we'll talk about *Miranda* shortly), arraignment, plea negotiations, and sentencing, and to "quasi-criminal" proceedings, like mental competency hearings, extradition, and others.

Following *Gideon*, public defender systems were established across the country. (Some local legal services organizations had been providing criminal defense for years; the Los Angeles County Public Defender's office opened in 1914.) State and local systems have evolved over the years. Variations include staff counsel, contract lawyers, and court-appointed counsel drafted from the community. Contract and drafting systems allow flexibility based on need, but experience varies and quality may suffer, although no doubt some lawyers tired of chasing clients for money appreciate the guaranteed pay. Now, some systems are centralized, as in Minnesota, while others are run by individual counties or judicial districts, as in New York and Washington. Oregon manages its system centrally, using a mix of staff and contract lawyers for different services. Florida elects its public defenders, who then hire staff counsel.

Studies by the American Bar Association and American Civil Liberties Union have prompted critical changes, but more change is needed. In Montana, an ACLU lawsuit resulted in a statewide system, replacing the prior patchwork. Similar suits have prompted reform in other states. A class action suit in New York brought the issue to a boil in 2010; at this writing, claims that the state's system is inadequate are still pending. In 2010, the Justice Department launched a new Access to Justice program to expand indigent defense. The National Center for State Courts' (NCSC) Indigent Defense FAQs page gives details on current state systems. (See Book Links.)

Public defenders have the same obligations to their clients as private defense counsel. The only real difference is that defenders don't pick their clients—they take whoever qualifies for services under local guidelines. The NSCS estimates that 80–90 percent of criminal defendants qualify for indigent defense. Clients can be ordered to repay the costs of their defense, if able to do so.

> Public defenders have the same obligations to their clients as private defense counsel.

48

So, can't I have a real lawyer?

Public defenders are real lawyers, of course, but this not-uncommon question reveals some recurring problems with access to the justice system. Despite the changes, issues still exist which affect the quality of service. Underfunding and inconsistent organization create problems in recruiting and retention. High case loads and turnover mean defendants in less serious cases might work with a series of lawyers who often lack time to dive deeply into the case. Limitations on other resources—access to investigators, experts, exhibit preparation, and the like—affect both experiences and outcomes. However, many public defenders are seriously committed to their work and make a career of public defense. The ABA reports that starting salaries for public defenders and prosecutors are now about equal, but this is not true everywhere. By law, federal defenders must be paid the same as their counterparts in the U.S. Attorneys' offices. Some defenders, as in Cook County, Illinois, are unionized.

The systems still face funding problems, as demands continue while resources disappear. The challenge of maintaining quality service requires commitment from the entire community, in recognition of the constitutional importance of public defense.

> The ABA reports that starting salaries for public defender and prosecutors are now about equal, but this is not true everywhere.

An ever-changing, stress-filled system creates great possibilities for fiction. While quite a few mystery series involve criminal defense lawyers—think of John Lescroart's Dismas Hardy, Michael Connolly's Mickey Haller, and of course, Erle Stanley Gardner's Perry Mason—public defenders are rare in fiction. Horace Rumpole was known to accept appointment, and Ayelet Waldman's "Mommy Track" series featured a former public defender turned amateur sleuth. On TV, both Perry Mason (Raymond Burr) and Ben Matlock (Andy Griffith) usually prevailed, often identifying the real culprit right there in the courtroom. The cases the father-and-son lawyers (E. G. Marshall and Robert Reed) handled in *The Defenders* involved many hot legal issues of the early 1960s.

As major or minor characters, public defenders deal with good people in bad situations, and with bad people in worse situations. Their friends and relatives may challenge why they do the work, asking how they can defend people they know are guilty and why they don't get a real job. Some of the most horrific cases present the most interesting intellectual and philosophical issues. How will your defender character respond? What drives him to pursue this work: the experience of someone close, his own troubled youth, the belief that everyone deserves a good defense?

What's the deal about *Miranda* warnings?

"You have the right to remain silent. Anything you say can and will be used against you in a court of law. You have the right to speak to an attorney, and to have an attorney present during any questioning. If you cannot afford an attorney, one will be provided for you at government expense."

In *Miranda v. Arizona* (1966), the U.S. Supreme Court decided several cases from around the country that raised a critical issue: Must a suspect be warned of his rights before being interrogated? Which rights? Under what circumstances? And, what are the consequences if he isn't warned? The Court said the Constitution requires that suspects in custody be informed of their right to silence, which is grounded in the Fifth Amendment right against self-incrimination, that anything they do say could be used against them, and that they have the right to counsel. Only if the suspect understood those rights and voluntarily waived them can statements made during custodial interrogation be used against the suspect in court.

A noteworthy exception to the warning mandate is the "public safety exception" of *New York v. Quarles* (1984), where an officer or public safety is at risk.

The Supreme Court decided two *Miranda* cases in 2010. In *Maryland v. Shatzer*, the suspect requested a lawyer and questioning stopped; fourteen days later, he was taken into custody, waived his right to counsel, and voluntarily confessed. His initial request for counsel did not bar the later interrogation or prevent an effective waiver.

Ernesto Miranda was convicted of rape and kidnaping, based on his confession and the victim's identification. He was not advised of his right to counsel or to silence, although the written confession form included a preprinted statement that he knew his rights and that his statements could be used against him. After the Supreme Court decision, he was retried, without the confession, and again convicted, based on eyewitness testimony and the testimony of his common-law wife (with whom he was in a custody battle over their daughter) that he had admitted the rape to her. (We talked about the spousal privilege in Chapter 1, and we'll look at common-law marriage in Chapter 7.) Miranda was released in 1972 and returned to prison for a time in 1974. While out, he sold signed *Miranda* cards for $1.50 each. He was stabbed to death at age 34 during a bar fight in 1976; no one was charged.

In *Berghuis v. Thompkins*, the Court held 5-4 that once a suspect has been warned, he must specifically invoke his right to silence—an explicit waiver is not required—and that a brief response amounting to a confession will be taken as a waiver and will be admissible. The Michigan detectives asked Thompkins if he prayed to God, and when he said yes, they asked him if he prayed for forgiveness for "shooting that boy down;" yes, he replied again. That, the majority held, was a choice to respond, and thus to waive the right to silence. The result of the decision may be that police will continue to question suspects who remain silent after being warned, hoping to increase the likelihood of an eventual response. Keep in mind, though, that some states may hold otherwise under their constitutions, and individual police departments may require explicit waivers.

Keys for writers to remember about *Miranda* warnings:

- only suspects in custody are entitled to warnings;

- warnings are required only before interrogation—that is, questioning;

- voluntary statements not made under questioning are admissible;

- a suspect who's been warned can waive his rights and agree to be questioned;

- it's the substance of the warning, not the exact language, that matters. But most law enforcement departments require officers to use standard language to prevent later disputes over what was said.

Consider this scenario, looking first at custody: Police ask a man to come to headquarters to talk about the disappearance of a child in his neighborhood. He agrees, drives his own car, and is interviewed in an unlocked office; everyone is cordial and it's clear that he's free to leave any time. He's not in custody. Contrast this with the same man ordered to get into the back of a police car, which then takes off; he hasn't been told he can't leave, but under the circumstances, he's not reasonably likely to believe that he can.

Now let's look at interrogation. In the interview room, two officers tell the man they're waiting for a photograph to be printed. They don't warn him. Meanwhile, they discuss the scene they've just left: the blood, the horror, and wonder out loud what kind of person would do such a thing. What kind of warped mind, what kind of terrible childhood, and so on. Squirming, the man finally blurts out, "You leave my mother out of this. She had nothing to do with me killing that girl." He then breaks down in tears and tells the whole story. There was no interrogation, just a conversation between two officers, maybe with the goal of provoking a response, or maybe not. After analyzing all the facts, the judge may conclude that the suspect was not in custody and never consider whether he was interrogated. If the facts establish custody, the judge will consider whether the statement was a voluntary, spontaneous response to the officers' conversation or whether it amounted to an interrogation. That decision determines whether his statements are admissible or must be suppressed.

What if the suspect was warned first? Analysis will focus on whether his statements were coerced, and therefore inadmissible, or made voluntarily with full knowledge of his rights. The facts make all the difference.

Assume the suspect requests a lawyer, either before or after his confession, but keeps talking. The lawyer will move to suppress, in order to determine whether the additional statements are admissible, under the analysis just described.

TIP: By changing the setting, the age, sex, race, and even the size of the suspect and officers, the time of day, how long the suspect remains in custody, and of course, what's said, you can add more tension and plot complexity. Is the conversation on a street corner at mid-day or in a small gray room in the basement of the police station? Is the suspect sixteen or forty-five? Is the door open or shut? Do the officers come and go, take bathroom breaks, eat and drink, but offer the suspect nothing? Is his agreement to waive his rights threatened or coerced, or has he been treated with basic human decency? If the suspect is likely to talk, nothing will shut him up faster than being warned; suspects watch TV, too, and, of course, many have been through the drill before. Is your story better served by a silent suspect or a talkative one, by wrangling over admissibility of a confession or by going to trial quickly?

The *Miranda* decision, written by Chief Justice Earl Warren, isn't easy reading, but it is fascinating. A former prosecutor himself, Warren rightly believed that prosecutors have a responsibility to protect individual rights and ensure fair trials, as well as to prosecute crime. Your fictional prosecutor and detectives might agree, or they may shade the line.

Writers of historicals, remember that attitudes about the rights of the accused changed significantly in the 1960s. *Miranda* was a controversial 5-4 decision, even though the FBI and some states already used similar warnings.

My character is in custody in another state. How do I get him extradited to my state?

Extradition procedures differ depending on why your character is being held in the other state. If he's held on a warrant from your state, the process is fairly simple. But if he was arrested on charges in the other state, more factors come into play.

The process generally goes like this: Your character, David, is arrested in Wisconsin, and authorities discover, through a computerized information-sharing system such as the National Crime Information Center (NCIC) database, that there's an outstanding Minnesota warrant for his arrest. Wisconsin authorities notify their Minnesota counterparts. The Minnesota prosecutor decides whether to send a written request for extradition; if he declines, he will probably be required by law to dismiss both warrant and underlying charges. If return is requested, David must decide to accept or fight the request. He is entitled to a lawyer at this stage, if he wants one. If David agrees to return, paperwork is completed and arrangements for secure transfer are made. The process is usually completed within a short time; two or three weeks is typical. (For a link to one state's extradition form, see Book Links.)

If David decides to fight, matters slow a bit. The requesting state must file a motion and brief with the court in the custody state showing what charges were filed, the evidence in support, and why the arrest warrant is legitimate. To successfully resist, David has to show "good cause" why he shouldn't be returned for trial. The most common reason is lack of probable cause for the warrant. Successful challenges are rare. Again, requests are usually handled quickly—the custody state does not want the expense of playing host any longer than necessary—although resolution could take a few months while each side briefs the issues for the judge.

But what if Wisconsin arrests David on local charges, then discovers the Minnesota warrant? It can keep him and take first crack, return him and request his later return, or drop the charges. The state with custody must act quickly, before arraignment, to prevent the clock from starting on his right to a speedy trial. Factors in the decision include the comparative seriousness of the charges, the strength of the evidence, and whether the cases are related, e.g., part of a cross-state crime spree. If the Wisconsin arrest is for a felony and the evidence is strong, Wisconsin might hold David and try him; if he's acquitted, he'll be sent to Minnesota for trial there. If he's convicted in Wisconsin, he'll have to serve his sentence before being returned for trial in Minnesota. Conversely, Wisconsin could send him to Minnesota for trial and request his return later. The two states' prosecutors will likely talk it over and work out an agreement.

Adjacent states deal with extradition requests regularly, and they typically have a streamlined process in place. The general process remains the same even for distant states, although transport may become a problem and costs, paid by the requesting state, may be a factor.

Adjust the facts to suit your story. If you want David returned to Minnesota, keep his nose clean in Wisconsin; just have him arrested and returned on the

Minnesota warrant. If he commits a crime in the second state, make it a misdemeanor and up the ante in the original state, e.g., multiple felonies, aggravating factors like violence or a particularly vulnerable victim, or a long criminal history in the requesting state.

How does international extradition work?

That's trickier. Consider an American involved in questionable doings in France who then escapes to China. If she stays in China, your American character won't be returned to France to face charges. A key principle of international law is that a country has legal authority over persons within its borders, regardless of their citizenship. Another country wanting to try a suspect must formally request, through legal and diplomatic channels, that the suspect be turned over to its representatives. That can happen only if the two countries have an extradition treaty. But France, like the United States, has no treaty with China, leaving no legal mechanism to request the suspect's return.

> A key principle of international law is that a country has legal authority over persons within its borders, regardless of their citizenship.

What if the fictional suspect returns to America, which does have an extradition treaty with France? Treaties vary widely, but requests typically trigger an analysis of factors like these:

- Is the crime serious? Murder, bombing, rape, then yes. Minor theft, no.

- Has the country requesting extradition shown a "prima facie" case against the person sought, i.e., facts establishing the elements of the crime charged?

- Do the facts constitute a crime in both countries? Rarely is this a factor interstate, because most states treat crimes similarly, but it is a frequent issue in international extradition.

- Can the suspect reasonably expect a fair trial? Again, this is not typically a factor on requests for transfer within the U.S., but it is a serious issue between nations.

- Is the potential sentence proportionate to the crime? This factor often blocks extradition to countries with extreme punishments for drug offenses. As well, countries without the death penalty, such as Canada, Mexico, and many European countries, regularly refuse to extradite to the U.S. if the suspect would face death; as a result, American prosecutors frequently agree not to request the death penalty in exchange for extradition.

- Is the suspect a citizen of the country making or receiving the request? France, for example, is one of many countries prohibited by law from extraditing its own nationals, so it could not return film director Roman Polanski, a French citizen, to the U.S. for sentencing on child sex charges. When Polanski brought a libel case in British courts, he testified by video hookup from France rather than travel and risk arrest in Britain and extradition to the U.S. He took the risk when he traveled to Switzerland in 2009 to accept an award; after his arrest, he challenged the extradition request, which the Swiss court ultimately rejected. In contrast, the U.S. has no blanket ban on extraditing its nationals.

- Are the motivations, and the crime, political? Were charges brought to damage a government's political opponents or retaliate for good-faith decisions that turned out badly? This factor does not immunize former officials from genuine investigations of wrongdoing, as with former Chilean president Augusto Pinochet and former Panamanian dictator Manuel Noriega.

- Are the motivations and crime military? In 2007, Germany decided not to request extradition of alleged CIA operatives on kidnaping allegations because its treaty with the U.S. prohibits extradition for purely military matters and the U.S. was likely to deny any request.

In the U.S., the Department of State makes the ultimate decision whether to request extradition or to grant another country's request, in consultation with the appropriate U.S attorney or state attorney general. Requests may be reviewed by the courts, as in the American review of France's request for the extradition of Noriega. In contrast, in Mexico, a court must review a proposed request to extradite from another country before the request can be made. The court denied permission to request extradition of Duane "Dog, the Bounty Hunter" Chapman from the United States because the crime charged was relatively minor. If the Mexican court had allowed the prosecutor to request Chapman's extradition, the Mexican government would have made a formal request to the U.S. government, triggering State Department review.

Corporate crime can also involve international extradition. Prosecutors in Kansas City indicted Chinese pet food manufacturers on charges related to deliberate product contamination. Without a treaty, the defendants could not be brought to the U.S. for trial, so why bother? Because the case had potential long-term impact on international trade and relationships. Charges could also pressure co-defendants within the court's reach, such as American importers and Chinese distributors doing business in the U.S. And the charges sent a message to everyone in the manufacturing and distribution chain, and to customers, that pet food contamination would be treated seriously.

Extradition and its complications are fertile soil for international thrillers and suspense novels: plots involving terrorism, drug running and money laundering, art theft, and trafficking in weapons or other stolen or illegal goods. Also, extradition may help you deepen the plot of any story with characters from another country. It offers rich potential for emotion and conflict in cases of child abduction or violence against family, especially if the suspect returns to a country that refuses to extradite its own nationals. See the State Department's International Child Abduction web page for more details. (See Book Links.)

Can a conversation—on the phone or in person—be recorded?

The real questions here are whether recorded conversations can be used as evidence in court and what are the potential sanctions for unauthorized recording. As always, state law varies and changes. Some states permit use of recorded conversations at trial if one party consented to the recording; others allow their use in civil trials but not in criminal trials; still others ban their use in court altogether, unless the recording was made by police officers with a valid search warrant.

The U.S. Supreme Court held in *U.S. v. White* (1971) that warrantless electronic monitoring of face-to-face conversations with the consent of one party to the conversation does not constitute a search and, therefore, does not violate the Fourth Amendment. It held that a suspect does not have a reasonable expectation of privacy in conversations with informants, even though the suspect does not know he's talking to an informant.

But as we've discussed, the federal constitution dictates an individual's minimum guarantees, and states are free, through their constitutions, to give their citizens a greater degree of protection. In a classic example, Montana's constitution also guarantees the freedom from unreasonable searches and seizures, and specifically recognizes the individual right to privacy. In *State v. Goetz* (2008), the Montana Supreme Court reviewed the use of a conversation between a confidential informant and a suspected drug dealer that was recorded, via wire, with only the informant's consent and without a warrant. It

> The federal constitution dictates an individual's minimum guarantees, and states are free, through their constitutions, to give their citizens a greater degree of protection.

held that the state constitution narrows the range of permissible warrantless searches, and that the recording—essentially a search of a conversation, rather than of a place—was an unreasonable search and seizure and could not be used at trial. As a result, Montana law enforcement officers need a warrant to record conversations between informants and suspects, even if the informant consents to the recording.

These cases illustrate the range of options. If your story involves an FBI investigation, your investigators can freely wire a character with a concealed recording device, but if your investigators work for a state or local department, you may need to send them for a warrant, and consequently heat up the tensions when they don't get one.

Most states and the federal government also have laws that apply to recording in other contexts, such as court hearings or city council meetings, which are routinely taped, or when an insurance adjuster interviews a witness to a car accident. Most allow recording if one party consents. States that require consent of both parties typically make exceptions for public officials and employees recording a meeting or conversation as part of their official duties, public meetings, and emergency calls to health-care facilities. They also make exception for persons who have been warned that the conversation may be recorded, as in calls to customer service departments at banks and brokerages, or calls by prison inmates. In some states, simply knowing that a conversation is being recorded and then talking is considered consent. Unauthorized recording is typically a misdemeanor. Though violations are not often prosecuted, these statutes have reshaped some business activities and increased individual protection.

Remember these laws deal only with persons involved in the conversation, or those who hear the recording. They don't help your non-law enforcement character who plants a voice-activated recorder to capture a conversation that doesn't involve him. That's unlawful in almost any circumstance.

But what about that insurance adjuster—or a reporter who wants to record a conversation to get the quotes right? None of the typical exceptions apply. The conversation can be recorded if the witness consents. The adjuster or reporter should tell the witness, on the recording, that the conversation is being recorded and ask if the witness consents. That avoids violating the privacy in communication statute, and allows the conversation to be admitted at trial, if necessary.

For state-by-state information, see The Reporters Committee for Freedom of the Press guide. (See Book Links.)

Why does the Montana constitution require a result exactly opposite that of the federal constitution? Montana entered the Union in 1889 using a bare-bones constitution written quickly. In 1972, a Constitutional Convention, or Con-Con, wrote a dramatically different document, approved by voters in a 1973 referendum. The 1972 constitution takes advantage of nearly two centuries of experience in constitutional law in the state and around the country, and expresses values held by the people of the state. It articulates a right to privacy, a right to a clean and healthful environment, and a right to know relating to government agencies, among other rights not stated in the federal constitution. At least fourteen states, including Maryland, Illinois, Connecticut, and Hawaii, require voters to consider every ten or twenty years whether to establish a Con-Con to update their constitutions. In other states, the question can be placed on the ballot by initiative or referendum.

3

Crime...

IN THE LAST CHAPTER, WE TALKED ABOUT CRIMINAL procedure. Now it's on to substantive criminal law. You'll learn the concept of the elements of a crime, how they vary, and how they're proven—and we'll see more of those all-important differences in terminology. Then it's on to a few recurring topics in fact and fiction: gun laws, hacking, juvenile justice, false allegations of abuse, mental competence, and the insanity defense.

What's the difference between a felony and a misdemeanor?

The difference is largely one of degree, a reflection of the legislature's judgment—on behalf of the people—of the seriousness of a crime. Felonies include intentional killings and certain unintentional killings (like vehicular homicide and manslaughter), sexual intercourse without consent, kidnaping, arson, robbery, burglary, escape, and distribution of dangerous drugs. Misdemeanors include possession of small amounts of drugs or drug paraphernalia, disorderly conduct, trespass, indecent exposure, solicitation (aka prostitution), and some traffic offenses.

Black's Law Dictionary says the root of felony is *felonia*, "the act or offense by which a vassal forfeited his fee." Who knew? Misdemeanor, meaning "misdeed," dates back to fifteenth-century England; it initially meant crimes not subject to forfeiture, but evolved to refer generally to less serious crimes. Merriam-Webster traces hoosegow to the Spanish *juzcado*, or courtroom; how it came to mean jail is a mystery.

Some crimes—notably assault—may be either felonies or misdemeanors. Some states classify assaults into aggravated or simple, while others define them separately, e.g., partner assault, assault with a deadly weapon, assault on a sports official, with each classified as a felony or misdemeanor. The degree of intent and possible harm makes the difference.

Some states establish classes of felonies and misdemeanors, e.g., A, B, C, with punishment differing for each class. Felonies typically carry prison terms, while misdemeanors are punished by fines and up to a year in the local hoosegow.

Murder, homicide, manslaughter—what's the difference?

Each state defines crimes by statute, and both names and definitions vary widely. So while it's impossible to summarize those variations here, writers should have an idea of the elements of the most common crime in fiction. As always, check the law in your story state for specifics.

Let's look at examples from three states to give you an idea how the most common terms—and a few less common ones—are used.

Montana: Montana separately defines four types of homicide: deliberate homicide, mitigated deliberate homicide, negligent homicide, and vehicular homicide while under the influence.

"Deliberate homicide" can be charged in two scenarios: when the accused "purposely or knowingly" caused the death of another, or when the accused caused a death while committing or attempting to commit one of several serious felonies or fleeing from the crime or crime attempt (sometimes called felony murder, discussed below). Sentencing is complicated, but the statutory ranges give an idea of the relative seriousness of each crime. For deliberate homicide, the penalty for adult offenders is death, life in prison, or a prison term between 10 and 100 years. (Sect. 45-5-102, MCA (Montana Code Annotated).)

"Mitigated deliberate homicide" occurs when a person "purposely or knowingly causes the death of another human being but does so under the influence of extreme mental or emotional stress for which there is reasonable explanation or excuse. The reasonableness of the explanation or excuse must be determined from the viewpoint of a reasonable person in the actor's situation." In other words, some trigger played a role, lowering the defendant's culpability a notch. The lesser severity of the crime is reflected in the potential prison time: two to forty years (Sect. 45–5–103, MCA). In one case, the victim brought a gun and a knife to a fist fight, prompting the defendant to pull his own knife; the court held that it was reasonable for the jury to conclude that the threat posed by the victim's weapons might cause "extreme mental or emotional stress," justifying the conviction for mitigated deliberate homicide. (*Montana v. Lamere* (2003).)

A young, single mother with financial trouble and a difficult child killed the child during one of his not-infrequent temper tantrums; the trial judge noted that while circumstances did not excuse the killing, they did demonstrate the extreme stress necessary for the lesser charge of mitigated deliberate homicide. She was convicted. (*Montana v. Winger* (1997).) In contrast, anger and intoxication are not sufficient mitigation. (*Montana v. Miller* (1998).)

"Negligent homicide" requires proof only that the defendant negligently caused the death of another person. Criminal negligence is acting with "conscious disregard of the risk of death" or disregarding a risk of causing death that he should be aware of—in other words, a serious failure to use reasonable care in the circumstances. Negligent homicide is most often charged in fatal auto accidents. The potential prison time is up to twenty years. (Sect. 45-5-104, MCA.)

In a case that illustrates the difference between negligent and mitigated deliberate homicide, the defendant struck the victim in the head several times, causing a fatal brain injury. He admitted intending to hurt her, but denied intent to kill, and claimed he was only guilty of negligent homicide. The judge disagreed, saying "a person cannot strike lethal blows and then avoid the consequences of his actions by saying he was surprised his victim died or that he did not intend to kill her." His conviction for mitigated deliberate homicide was upheld. (*Montana v. Koepplin* (1984).)

Last, there's "vehicular homicide while under the influence." This is a species of negligent homicide; it requires proof that a person negligently caused the death of another person while driving under the influence of drugs or alcohol. The potential prison time is up to thirty years, with no deferred sentences, reflecting the legislature's judgment of the seriousness of the crime. (Sect. 45-5-106, MCA.)

Mitigated deliberate homicide, negligent homicide, and vehicular homicide while under the influence are all "lesser included offenses" of deliberate homicide, under its first definition, though not under its felony murder definition. This means a person may be charged with the more serious offense, but if circumstances warrant, the judge could dismiss the greater charge and instruct on a lesser charge, or on both, giving the jury a choice.

Mystery and thriller writers, note that the language "cause the death" of another is broad enough to include murder for hire or directing a murder, even if the person charged did not physically kill the victim.

Washington State: In Washington State, the terminology is different, and so are some of the underlying

> Mystery and thriller writers, note that the language "causes the death" of another is broad enough to include murder for hire or directing a murder.

distinctions. Homicide is the killing of a human being by (1) murder, (2) homicide by abuse, (3) manslaughter, (4) excusable homicide, or (5) justifiable homicide. (RCW 9A.32.010 (Revised Code of Washington).)

Murder can be first or second degree. First degree murder is causing death with premeditated intent; premeditation "must involve more than a moment in point of time." The same conduct, without premeditation, may constitute second degree murder. First degree murder may also occur when, "under circumstances manifesting an extreme indifference to human life, he or she engages in conduct which creates a grave risk of death to any person, and thereby causes the death of a person." Felony murder may be first or second degree murder, depending on the underlying felony.

"Homicide by abuse" applies to the deaths of vulnerable persons, and it requires proof of three elements:

1) "circumstances manifesting an extreme indifference to human life;"

2) causing the death of a child under sixteen, a developmentally disabled person, or an adult who is dependent on another for the basic necessities of life, because of age or physical or mental disability; and

3) a pattern or practice of assault or torture of the victim. (RCW 9A.32.055.)

Washington also defines two degrees of manslaughter. First degree manslaughter occurs when a person recklessly causes the death of another; in second degree, the actions are not reckless, but only negligent. It is also first degree manslaughter to "intentionally and unlawfully kill an unborn quick child by inflicting any injury upon the mother of such child." (RCW 9A.32.060 and .070.)

Washington specifically defines as homicide deaths resulting from illegal drug sales. A "controlled substances homicide" is a death that occurs as a result of the use of a controlled substance unlawfully delivered to the decedent by the person charged with the crime. (RCW 69.50.415.)

In Washington, homicide is excusable "when committed by accident or misfortune in doing any lawful act by lawful means, without criminal negligence, or without any unlawful intent." (RCW 9A.16.030.)

> **There are two categories of justifiable homicide, the first involving law enforcement officers, and the second justifying deadly force.**

There are two categories of justifiable homicide, the first involving law enforcement officers and the second justifying deadly force to protect oneself or another person from an imminent threat of serious injury, death, or another felony, or while resisting a felony in a residence. (RCW 9A.16.040.) Other states also recognize the right to use deadly force in defense of persons, and some, but not all, recognize it in defense of property; however, most don't include it in the definitions of homicide, but define it by other statutes or in case law.

California: If you're setting a fictional killing in California, take a look at the definitions and sentences in Penal Code Sects. 187–99, which include some of the quirky phrases we sometimes hear. California law defines murder as "unlawful killing" "with malice aforethought." (Sect. 187(a).) Malice is an odd word in the law, meaning different things in different contexts. Because the phrase "malice aforethought" catches the ear, I've set out the full California definition:

> *Such malice may be express or implied. It is express when there is manifested a deliberate intention unlawfully to take away the life of a fellow creature. It is implied, when no considerable provocation appears, or when the circumstances attending the killing show an abandoned and malignant heart. When it is shown that the killing resulted from the intentional doing of an act with express or implied malice as defined above, no other mental state need be shown to establish the mental state of malice aforethought. Neither an awareness of the obligation to act within the general body of laws regulating society nor acting despite such awareness is included within the definition of malice.*

(Sect. 188.) Sect. 188 states that murder can be first or second degree, depending on a variety of circumstances.

California defines manslaughter as "the unlawful killing of a human being without malice," and California law recognizes three types: voluntary, involuntary, and vehicular. Voluntary means in "a sudden quarrel or heat of passion." Involuntary refers to killings that occur "in the commission of an unlawful act, not amounting to felony; or in the commission of a lawful act which might produce death, in an unlawful manner, or without due caution and circumspection." Vehicular, of course, refers to deaths occurring as the result of driving a vehicle. California further defines the crime of vehicular manslaughter while intoxicated in two degrees, ordinary and gross.

California also defines excusable and justifiable homicide, much as Washington does.

An unusual defense, based on the elements, rejected: In early 2010, a Kansas judge rejected defense arguments that the jury should be allowed to consider voluntary manslaughter in the trial of Scott Roeder for the murder of Dr. George Tiller in a Wichita church, finding that Roeder's claim that it was necessary to kill Tiller to prevent him from performing abortions did not meet the statutory definition. Had the defense been allowed, Roeder would have been required to show that he had "an unreasonable but honest belief that circumstances existed that justified deadly force." The jury convicted Roeder of premeditated first degree murder.

Several of these statutes—the Montana and California statutes on drunk driving deaths and Washington's "homicide by abuse" and "controlled substances homicide"—are examples of a state legislature determining that existing homicide statutes and penalties were not sufficient to address a particular problem and devising a specific solution. Other states have done the same with other crimes. Those statutes offer writers unexpected opportunities for crime and punishment.

> While phrases like "malice aforethought" and "heat of passion" are intriguing, they are also somewhat antiquated, and no longer widely used.

TIP: While phrases like "malice aforethought" and "heat of passion" are intriguing, they are also somewhat antiquated, and are no longer widely used. If your Seattle police detective uses them, local readers might dismiss him as a know-nothing "Californicator"—or toss your book across the room. Meanwhile, referring to manslaughter in Montana or mitigated deliberate homicide in California might get your book the same treatment. And that would be murder.

What is statutory rape?

Writers often ask about using the threat of criminal charges relating to sex between teenagers of different ages to increase the stakes. The idea is that a person under a certain age—typically 16—is incapable of consenting to sex with a person over a certain age, because age gaps create a power differential in which the younger person can't give voluntary consent.

Note that statutes don't typically say "statutory rape." Common terms include underage sex, sexual intercourse without consent, and nonconsensual sex. The word rape implies physical force, not an element of this crime.

Typical statutes distinguish underage teenage sex from child abuse and establish different punishments depending on the victim's age and the age gap. And, yes, the statutes term the younger person the "victim" and the older the "offender," because of the legislative judgment that the younger person's inability to consent makes the older person's actions a crime.

An FBI study shows that underage sex involves girlfriend-boyfriend in about 30 percent of cases and acquaintances or friends in 62 percent. It also shows that forcible sex crimes involving a juvenile victim are three times more common than crimes based solely on age. The problem of criminalizing sex in underage relationships has led some states to enact what are sometimes called "Romeo and Juliet laws," making evidence of a small age difference and a pre-existing relationship a defense to the charges. Other states make the crime a misdemeanor if the age difference is small, or limit sentencing options to probation, fines, or community service.

Be aware that the victim's age alone may not be determinative; some states require a minimum age gap. For example, the law might say if she's 15 and he's 17, no crime occurs. If the statute criminalizes a four-year gap and he's 19—legally an adult—but not a full four years older, again, no crime. But consider a younger victim: If she's 13 and he's 17 and a half—four or more years older—the sex would be a crime. In that case, he'd be subject to a harsher sentence than if she were older, but a lesser sentence than if he were 18. Of course, the offender may be female and the victim male. As written, some statutes apply only to intercourse, and some apply only to persons of the opposite sex. If either of these is an issue in your story, check state law.

Note that there are also other reasons why a person might be legally incapable of consent to sex: mental or physical disability, including intoxication or sleep, physical helplessness making her unable to resist, and incarcerated persons or mental health patients when the perpetrator is an employee of the facility with supervisory authority over the victim.

So when is a prosecutor likely to pursue a case based on an age difference alone? Only if the facts warrant treating the case as a crime. Factors considered include the following:

- What are the circumstances—why was a complaint made? No prosecutor wants to be used for personal vengeance or moral outrage.

- How wide is the age gap? Charges are more likely at 13 and 17 than at 15 and 17.

- What conduct occurred? Digital penetration or actual intercourse? Vaginal or anal?

- Is there an ongoing relationship between victim and offender?

- The maturity of the individuals involved.

- Multiple victims and evidence of deliberate pursuit of younger victims.

- Evidence that the accused reasonably believed the alleged victim was older than her actual age.

- The offender's age. An 18-year-old male should be treated differently than a forty-year-old, even though he is legally an adult, because he can't be expected to have the same judgment as an older man.

And, of course, if force or physical injury is involved, there can be no consent.

In some states, a teenager convicted of statutory rape may be required to register as a sex offender, depending on whether the registry laws include all sex offenses, limit it to specific offenses, or include only offenders judged on release to be at risk to rape again. Statutory rape is what's called a status offense—not the predatory or violent crime the registries were meant to include. (See the discussion and links to state and national registries in Chapter 4.) If you want a character in your story to face this problem, check the story state's registry requirements.

What is felony murder?

The felony murder rule expands liability for murder to a person who did not actually kill the victim, if the killing occurred during the course of a felony. It covers both killings by accomplices and unintended killings. If two people rob a bank and one shoots and kills a teller, the other is guilty of felony murder, even though he did not pull the trigger or intend that his accomplice do so.

Forty-some states recognize felony murder, which originated in English common law but was abolished in Britain in 1956. In 1990, Canada eliminated it for accomplices as violating "the principle that punishment must be proportionate to the moral blameworthiness of the offender."

> Forty-some states recognize felony murder, which originated in English common law but was abolished in Britain in 1956.

Some states separately define the crime of "felony murder." Others include it in the definitions of murder or homicide, as discussed earlier in this chapter. The underlying or "predicate crimes" must be serious felonies—what are sometimes called forcible felonies—such as robbery, sexual intercourse without consent, arson, burglary, kidnaping, aggravated kidnaping, and felonious escape, or attempted crimes. In the federal system, the felony murder rule also applies to crimes defined as terrorism.

The rule may also apply to killings during flight from the crime, say if one bank robber shoots and kills a bystander on the way out the door. A few states apply it to accidental deaths during the felony or flight. If the getaway driver hits and kills a bystander, a case of negligent homicide would be elevated to deliberate homicide (or the local equivalents).

The defense might argue that the person charged was not armed, did not know that his accomplice was armed, or had no reasonable grounds to believe his accomplice might do something likely to result in death or serious physical injury.

The rationale is that the rule both punishes and deters crimes that create the foreseeable risk of murder, or in jurisdictions that include accidental killings, the foreseeable risk of death. People who jointly participate in a crime are each held responsible for all consequences. The FBI reports that about 16 percent of homicides in 2006 occurred during felonies. Opponents question the deterrent effect and say the rule punishes a person who lacked intent to kill as if he'd had the intent, rather than for his own misconduct.

Some states apply the death penalty to persons convicted of felony murder. This raises questions under the Eighth Amendment, prohibiting cruel and unusual punishment. The death penalty is not usually imposed on minor participants in the crime. (See the analysis of mitigating factors in the death penalty discussion in Chapter 4.)

Here's one example of the felony murder rule in action, from Florida. In March 2003, a young man named Ryan lent his car to four friends who talked about going back to a house where all had just attended a party to steal a safe belonging to the homeowner, a known marijuana dealer. There may have been talk about "knocking off" the dealer's teenage daughter. Ryan testified that he thought they were joking, especially about a killing. During the burglary, the girl was beaten to death with a shotgun found in the home. The man who killed her, the two other burglars, and the driver were all sentenced to life without parole. So was Ryan, who wasn't there and had no criminal record. Prosecutors offered him a plea, because of his lesser culpability, but he took his chances at trial and lost. Is Ryan's felony murder conviction justified, because the crime would not have occurred without the car? Or, is it draconian, because he drank too much and carelessly lent his car to a buddy, as he had without incident many times before?

Can my amateur sleuth legally carry a gun?

Maybe. Not only do state laws vary, but some municipalities have enacted gun laws as well. About half the states prohibit openly carrying handguns or long guns (rifles and shotguns), with numerous exceptions. Hunters with valid licenses may carry openly, with some limitations. Some states allow people to openly carry guns while hiking or fishing, for personal safety against wild animals and humans.

Laws and rules for permits to carry a concealed weapon (CCW or CCP) vary widely and change often; check your story state. Illinois and Wisconsin do not issue any permits, while permits are not required in Alaska or Vermont. Utah offers permits to nonresidents who take a one-day class. Some states allow the issuing authority—typically the county sheriff or local police chief—discretion to deny a permit, while others require permits to be issued if the minimum statutory requirements are met.

Typical requirements include in-state residency, a clean criminal record, no recent mental commitment, no dishonorable military discharges, physical ability to handle a gun, and successful completion of a handgun training class. Domestic violence charges may automatically disqualify applicants. Fugitives need not apply; a background check will be run. Writers occasionally ask how a character's fingerprints might have been taken, other than during a previous arrest—a concealed carry application is one option.

> **Writers occasionally ask how a character's fingerprints might have been taken, other than a previous arrest—a concealed carry application is one option.**

Some issuing agencies require proof of a need for self-defense, such as threats or work-related reasons, justifying permits for private investigators, jewelers, and criminal lawyers. Actor Sean Penn reportedly obtained a CCP after being stalked by a former employee and receiving threatening calls and letters.

Most states have reciprocity agreements, but it isn't always a two-way street. Your Seattle-based sleuth who follows a suspect to Montana will have her permit recognized, but her Montana counterpart won't get the same courtesy when he goes to Washington. Permits issued in California and New York, for example, may be recognized elsewhere, but those states don't return the favor—they recognize no other states' permits. In contrast, Oklahoma and Missouri, among others, recognize all permits. That Utah nonresident permit may get your character reciprocity not available with his home-state permit. If your sleuth crosses state lines with a gun, she may face charges for illegal possession, even if she has a permit in her state and doesn't use the gun.

There is much debate over whether concealed carry permits affect violent crime rates. Some maintain that the possibility that a potential victim or witness might be armed prevents crime, while others believe that more guns means more gun-related crimes. Statistics, of course, can be interpreted in many ways to support either position.

My sleuth has a carry permit for the story state. Are there places where she can't take her gun?

Many states prohibit carrying, even with a permit, in bars, churches, schools, parks, courts and government buildings, correctional facilities, police stations, airports, and polling places. Laws on guns in cars vary widely. Many states require them to be kept in a locked area, even separated from ammunition; local permits may allow guns in locked area of cars if holstered or unloaded.

What are some common exceptions to gun permit requirements?

Keep in mind that your character may or may not need a permit to have a gun in his or her home or business, again depending on state and local law. The law may distinguish handguns from long guns, and semi-automatics from automatics.

> Keep in mind that your character may or may not need a permit to have a gun in his or her home or business.

State and federal gun laws do not apply to active-duty military, including military police.

What gun laws apply in national parks?

Your character might be affected by a recent change on guns in national parks. Effective February 2010, state laws where the park is located now determine the matter. Some parks officials opposed the change, concerned that it would create uncertainty over governing laws among visitors and cause enforcement problems, especially in the thirty-some parks that straddle state lines.

What laws apply to law enforcement officers crossing state borders?

For professional sleuths, be aware that the Law Enforcement Officers Safety Act of 2004 allows qualified state, federal, and local law enforcement officers, active and retired, to carry a concealed firearm in any state, regardless of local laws. The stated purpose is to make it easier for officers to be called into action when needed in response to natural disasters, terrorism, or other problems, without violating conflicting laws. Two primary exceptions: local laws allowing private property owners to ban guns, and local laws permitting state and local governments to prohibit guns on government property, must still be followed. Other federal gun laws, such as restrictions on firearms in federal buildings, also still apply. Not all officers qualify—the key is their right to carry and good standing in their law enforcement job. If your fictional officer crosses state lines in pursuit of a suspect, use an arrest for unlawful possession of a weapon to slow him down.

What legal rights does the Second Amendment provide?

The Second Amendment provides: "A well-regulated militia, being necessary to the security of a free State, the right of the people to keep and bear arms, shall be not be infringed." Astute readers will note that the commas are confusing and could lead to conflicting interpretations. In *District of Columbia v. Heller* (2008), the Supreme Court resolved the long-running dispute over whether the right is individual or belongs only to state-run (that is, official) militia or armies, holding that the right is individual, and overturned the city's outright ban on handguns.

The principle was extended to states in *McDonald v. City of Chicago* (2010).

But Second Amendment rights are still a hot-button issue across the country, sometimes serving as a code phrase for specific beliefs about the role of government and the relationship between government and gun ownership. If your plot involves politics, hunters, anti-government conspiracy theorists, or "white rights" activists, light a fuse under the phrases "Second Amendment" or "gun control," and stand back.

Gun laws change regularly, so consult the laws for your story locale, or check the NRA website, with links to federal, state, and local laws. (See Book Links.)

My protagonist asks her 17-year-old nephew to do some computer research. Is she legally responsible if he hacks into a private computer system without her knowledge or approval?

If he gets caught, yes, although she may be off the hook if she told him to stay legal and had no reason to think he wouldn't. That probably won't work with a younger teen, though—while a 17-year-old is old enough to know the legal limits, a younger child may not be, giving your protagonist more responsibility for supervision.

The murder suspect in my story is thirteen. Will he be tried as a juvenile or an adult? In what court? Where will he be held pending trial?

Your young teen will probably go to juvenile or youth court, which handles delinquency cases—those that would be considered criminal if involving an adult. Rather than trials, juvenile courts hold hearings to "adjudicate" whether the child is "a delinquent youth," sometimes called a "youth in need of intervention." The focus is on supervision, treatment, and rehabilitation to help juvenile offenders avoid becoming adult offenders. Cases are tried to a judge, without a jury. Hearings are generally closed to the public. Juveniles do have the right to counsel, to confront witnesses, and so on.

> Rather than trials, juvenile courts hold hearings to "adjudicate" whether the child is "a delinquent youth."

In some states, the same judges handle both juvenile and adult cases; in others, certain judges handle only juvenile cases, at all times or on rotation. A few states mix it up, with larger counties maintaining separate juvenile court systems and smaller communities depending on the same judges for all cases. Los Angeles County, for example, maintains a separate juvenile court system within Superior Court.

Pending adjudication, your teen will be held in a juvenile holding facility. If he must be kept in an adult facility briefly for initial processing or in an emergency, he should be separated by sight and sound from all adult detainees. Children held in adult facilities can easily be victimized or exposed to inappropriate behavior. These miscarriages of justice do occur, whether intentionally or by mistake, and can form powerful plots or subplots.

After adjudication, your youthful offender will be given a "disposition," that is, a sentence. While in custody, at all stages, he must be given education.

The alternative is criminal court. Each state sets an upper age limit, by statute, for juvenile courts—fifteen, sixteen, or seventeen—but most also allow younger children to be transferred to criminal court and tried as adults. Legislatures expanded transfer significantly during the 1980s and 1990s, in response to a rise in juvenile crime and public outcry. According to a U.S. Department of Justice report, transfer requests increased by 80 percent between 1985 and 1994, but declined by nearly 50 percent between 1995 and 2005, as violent juvenile crime dropped. In 2005, juvenile courts nationwide handled 1.7 million delinquency cases. Transfer to criminal court was requested in 56 percent of the cases, and of those, granted in less than 1 percent—roughly 6900 cases. 51 percent of cases transferred involved offenses against persons, 27 percent property offenses, and 12 percent drug offenses. Eighty-five percent involved males 16 or older; of those, 58 percent were white and 30 percent were black, although the statistical likelihood of transfer was about the same for black and white juveniles.

States use three basic types of transfer laws. The first is "concurrent jurisdiction," giving the prosecutor discretion where to file; if charges are initially filed in criminal court, the juvenile may request transfer to juvenile court. Under "statutory exclusion laws," certain classes of cases must be filed in criminal courts, based on age and offense. Under "judicial waiver laws," cases are filed in juvenile court, but the prosecutor may request transfer to criminal court. A judge may have discretion in some cases but be required to transfer in others.

Most states establish specific criteria for consideration. They vary, but include the age of the offender, personal details like cognitive abilities, any learning disabilities, past behavior, the nature and circumstances of the offense, whether a youth court proceeding and disposition will protect the community, treatment recommendations, and treatment options available in each court. If an older juvenile, about to "age out" of the youth court system, would not remain in state custody long enough to complete a treatment program in a youth facility, but sentencing as an adult might keep him in custody long enough to complete an intensive supervision or "boot camp" type program in adult court, the judge might choose transfer, because youth court would not provide the supervision or structure needed for both the juvenile and community protection.

Back to the very young juvenile in your story. According to a University of Texas report, roughly eighty children 13 and under are transferred to adult court every year. Some states say that children as young as 7 may form criminal intent and be tried as adults, although the youngest child in the United States charged with murder as an adult appears to be an eleven-year-old in Michigan. After his conviction, the judge strongly criticized the law and sentenced him to youth detention rather than life imprisonment, where he reportedly turned his life around.

In *Roper v. Simmons* (2005), the U.S. Supreme Court eliminated the death penalty for crimes committed by minors. In *Graham v. Florida* (2010), the Court held that juvenile offenders may not be sentenced to life without parole for cases other than murder, because of the possibility of maturity and rehabilitation over time. Each of the 129 such prisoners across the country may now request sentence review and a "meaningful opportunity" to show that they have become "fit to rejoin society"; release is not mandatory.

One highly-publicized case of a teen tried as an adult is Lee Malvo, the 17-year-old accomplice of John Muhammad, aka the Beltway Sniper. Malvo was convicted in Virginia and sentenced to life without parole.

Juvenile cases present thorny issues of fairness and justice. Laura Lippman's *Every Secret Thing*—in which two eleven-year-old girls in Baltimore are sent away to a youth facility for the murder of a baby girl they found in an abandoned stroller—touches on social and legal issues in the juvenile justice system.

The transfer statistics are taken from a June 2009 U.S. Department of Justice study. For an overview and state-by-state summary of transfer laws, and a look at children under 12, see "From Time Out to Hard Time: Young Children in the Adult Criminal Justice System," a 2009 project report from the University of Texas. The National Center for Juvenile Justice state profiles are another excellent source of state-by-state specifics. (See the Book Links section.)

How can my character protect himself from his unstable, estranged wife who is threatening to accuse him—falsely—of child molestation?

This is a scenario ripe for conflicting perceptions: Is she unstable or is he covering up?

A report will trigger an investigation by police and child protective services. Assuming there is no question that the accusations are false, he has several options. First, he should document her threats by writing down, in detail, what she said, when, where, and who else was present, and update the list with each additional threat. If he later needs to show that she made the threats, the detailed record will boost his credibility.

He could report the threats to police. This is a two-edged sword, a good tool for a fiction writer. In reality, if he made a report, police and prosecutors aren't likely to take action against her at this stage, unless the threats are repeated or escalate significantly. But the report might help him later, by documenting the threats. But people in hostile domestic situations often don't take steps outsiders think reasonable because of fear—here, loss of custody or visitation.

He and his lawyer should identify potential witnesses to testify that she made the threats and that she acknowledged they were false and meant to harm him—if that's the case. He may also need witnesses to disprove the abuse claims, such as the child's doctors, teachers, and family and friends. In both situations, doctors and therapists who treat either spouse or the child, as well as clergy, could be witnesses; privilege issues might arise in the civil case, but they don't typically apply in criminal proceedings involving suspected abuse. In addition, if there's an investigation, the investigators—police and child protective workers—are important witnesses. An alleged child abuse victim is often evaluated by a therapist who has specialized training and experience and whose opinions will be critical.

Your character's lawyer should strongly urge him to be careful with whom he discusses the threats and not to discuss them with his wife or her friends and family. That could cause a lot of trouble, which might be good for you as the storyteller. If they are in divorce or separation proceedings, his lawyer might discuss the threats with her lawyer; that could fan the flames, or her lawyer might persuade her to stop making false threats, which could affect her own custody and visitation rights. And, of course, she could face charges for knowingly making a false report.

If they are not separated, or have physically separated but neither has filed for divorce, the lawyer should discuss those options, including custody issues. Your character's first priority, of course, is to protect his child from the fallout of false allegations and from any other harm inflicted by an unstable mother.

The average person would probably be tempted to use a pocket recorder during conversations when the threat might be repeated. You can use this to cause your characters all kinds of problems. (See the discussion on recording in Chapter 2.)

What is competence to stand trial and when does it become an issue?

The defendant's mental status may be considered in determining whether he is competent to stand trial, whether mental illness affects his responsibility for the crime, and in sentencing.

The U.S. Supreme Court held in *Dusky v. U.S.* (1960) that a defendant's constitutional right to due process and fundamental fairness give him the right to a competency evaluation before trial. The focus is on his current mental capacity. Does he have the ability to understand the proceedings and help counsel prepare his defense? Can he make the necessary decisions, e.g., can he evaluate a plea offer and make a knowing, voluntary waiver of his right to go to trial?

> The U.S. Supreme Court held that a defendant's constitutional right to due process and fundamental fairness give him the right to a competency evaluation before trial.

Defense counsel raises the issue by motion, although the judge may also raise the issue (called *sua sponte*, meaning on his own). A clinical evaluation by a psychiatrist or psychologist will be ordered. The judge reviews the briefs, reports, and other evidence submitted, such as neurological or neuropsychological testing, and holds a hearing. The judge may interview the defendant. According to one study, about 80 percent of all defendants whose competency is considered are found competent to stand trial.

Competence is decided by the judge, typically during the pretrial phase, although the issue can be raised at any point in criminal proceedings. For example, during trial, a defendant's courtroom outbursts, irrational behavior, or apparent inability to understand what's going on may raise questions about competency.

Mental illness alone does not establish incompetence. Ted Kaczynski, the Unabomber, was diagnosed with paranoid schizophrenia but held competent—he was perfectly lucid and able to understand the criminal process and work with his counsel.

If the defendant is found competent, trial proceeds. If not, he'll be sent to an inpatient facility—options vary by state—for treatment intended to restore his competence. If treatment works, the defendant may then be tried. But if treatment is not successful, he should be released. The Supreme Court held in

Jackson v. Indiana (1972) that an incompetent person can only be held for a reasonable time to determine whether it's possible to restore his competency—he cannot be held indefinitely. This standard arises from past abuses, but is still vague and hard to enforce. Of course, if he presents a danger to himself or others, he may be civilly committed, which requires a separate proceeding.

> Mental illness alone does not establish incompetence. Ted Kaczynski, the Unabomber, was diagnosed with paranoid schizophrenia but held competent.

A related issue is the defendant's right to refuse medication, whether because he dislikes the drugs, or because he wants to avoid trial. The Supreme Court held in *Riggins v. Nevada* (1992) that the defendant had the right to refuse anti-psychotic meds; although the state could prove a need to medicate in some circumstances, it hadn't done so there.

The screenwriters of *Miracle on 34th Street* (1947) asked whether Kris Kringle was competent when he claimed to be Santa Claus, ignoring the legal standard of whether he presented a danger to himself or others in favor of the better story.

Tip: The wide range of factual scenarios and potential legal outcomes make this a terrific area for fictional exploration. However, a finding of incompetence ends the trial, or at least delays it, so this aspect may be best used in a subplot or complication.

What is the insanity defense?

The underlying premise is that a person cannot be held responsible for criminal behavior if mental illness prevented him from understanding that his actions were wrong. This inquiry focuses on the defendant's mental status at the time of the crime.

The test has changed significantly since the defense was first recognized in 1843, and courts applied several standards from the 1950s to the early 1980s. The 1982 trial of John Hinckley, who shot President Reagan, highlighted the controversy and prompted legislative changes. In most cases, there is little doubt that the accused committed the crime; the real issue is insanity. In Hinckley's case, the defense arose early, and psychiatric evaluations—which took four months—began shortly after his arrest. The standard applied at trial was whether Hinckley could "appreciate the wrongfulness" of his actions, and the government had the burden of proving that Hinckley was sane. After three days of deliberations, the jury found him "not guilty by reason of insanity" on all counts.

After the trial, Congress and many states changed their laws to shift the burden of proof to the defendant, meaning that a person claiming the defense must prove its essential elements. In essence, the presumption of innocence is now paired with a presumption of sanity. Currently, in federal cases, the defendant must prove that he has a "severe" mental disease that made him "unable to appreciate the nature and quality or the wrongfulness of his acts." The language of state standards varies somewhat, but is similar in most aspects. Note that as with competence, proof of mental illness alone is not enough.

Several states give jurors an additional verdict choice: "guilty but mentally ill." A handful of states (Idaho, Kansas, Montana, and Utah) do not allow the

The insanity defense is still much in debate. The heart of the disagreement is the tension between treatment or protection, and punishment. Advocates say the defense allows mentally ill offenders to obtain needed treatment and keeps them out of the prison system, where they lack treatment and are often victimized. A humane society must recognize that some people cannot be held to the same standards of conduct as the rest us because of mental illness they can't control. Others believe the defense allows the guilty to escape punishment for their crimes, and suspect defendants of faking mental illness to get an acquittal or avoid prison. Justice Department statistics say the defense is raised in only about 1 percent of cases, and succeeds in only 25 percent of those. A large percentage of acquittals result from plea agreements, where the prosecutor agrees that the defendant should be sent to treatment, not prison. Ideally, the evaluation process detects attempts to fake mental illness, which can trigger an enhanced sentence.

> Ideally, the evaluation process detects attempts to fake mental illness.

But the insanity defense was anathema to Ted Kaczynski, who insisted on representing himself, in part because his court-appointed lawyers wanted to raise the defense, while he believed he was sane. By legal measures, he was right. His writings and his arguments to the court demonstrated that his paranoid schizophrenia—a diagnosis he rejected—did not prevent him from understanding that his actions were wrong.

defense at all, but allow the defendant to introduce evidence of mental conditions to show that he did not have the level of knowledge or intent ("*mens rea*") for the crime charged. In other words, he tries to prove that he could not form the intent to purposefully or knowingly kill another. If he meets his burden, the state will be unable to prove all elements of the crime charged, and he will be acquitted by reason of mental disease or defect—essentially the same result as under the insanity defense.

A defendant found not guilty but mentally ill may be confined to a mental institution if commitment standards are met and released if he becomes no longer mentally ill. Hinckley is confined to St. Elizabeth's Hospital in Washington, D.C. In 2003, a judge ruled he no longer presented "a serious danger" to himself or others and approved unsupervised visits with his parents. If he establishes that he is no longer a threat to himself or others, he will be released.

In contrast, a defendant found guilty but mentally ill will be sentenced and kept in government custody for the length of his sentence. Where he is held depends on that state's procedures and facilities, but it's typically a prison mental health unit. If he becomes no longer mentally ill while still serving his sentence, he will be transferred to an ordinary prison unit. Once his sentence is complete, he must be released, although, again, civil commitment is still possible.

The insanity defense is not limited to murder cases. Lorena Bobbitt argued that she was temporarily insane when she severed her husband's penis with a kitchen knife, and a Virginia jury agreed; she was released after psychiatric hospitalization.

The insanity defense looms large in Otto Preminger's 1959 classic, *Anatomy of a Murder*, based on the novel by Robert Traver (the pen name of Michigan Supreme Court Justice John Voelker), starring Jimmy Stewart, Ben Gazzara, and George C. Scott. Just be aware that the law on insanity has changed, as has the admissibility of evidence of a woman's dress, behavior, and reputation in a rape case.

For details of John Hinckley's trial, see law professor Doug Linder's Famous Trials website. The insanity defense dates back to 1843—writers of historicals should start their research with an article on the evolution of the defense on Professor Linder's website or the Supreme Court's historical review in *Clark v. Arizona* (2006). I've also linked to a Find Law state-by-state summary. (See Book Links.)

4

...and Punishment

SO YOUR FICTIONAL CRIMINAL HAS BEEN INVESTIGATED, CHARGED, arrested, tried, and convicted. Now what? We'll shed some light on criminal sentencing, looking at the philosophy, possible ranges, and nontraditional options. We'll distinguish parole from probation, deferred sentences from suspended sentences, and consecutive and concurrent sentencing, and we'll look at what probation officers do. After your character is released from prison, he may be subject to restrictions on voting or gun ownership, or required to register as a sex or violent offender. Or he may have a juvenile record follow him. We'll also talk about plea agreements and Son-of-Sam laws. Finally, we'll consider several issues related to the death penalty.

A character in my story is convicted of assault. What is the philosophy of sentencing and what are the possible ranges for his sentence?

Debates over criminal sentencing have raged for centuries. It's now generally accepted public policy that punishment, retribution, and rehabilitation should all be considered, along with the effect of the crime on both victim and community. Since the 1970s, state and federal sentencing reform has aimed at increasing uniformity, predictability, and judicial accountability, all of which are critical to preserving constitutional rights and enhancing deterrence. However, while lawyers, judges, and defendants now have a better idea of potential sentence ranges, results in particular cases can still be puzzling.

Time behind bars is not always necessary, nor appropriate. Department of Justice figures for 2006 (the latest data published) show that of felons convicted in state courts, about 70 percent were sentenced to confinement—40 percent in prisons and 30 percent in local jails. Prison sentences averaged almost five years, with about eight years for defendants convicted of violent felonies and three years for non-violent felonies. About 30 percent were sentenced directly to probation or other sentences, with no time served. Courts ordered more than 35 percent of convicted felons to pay a fine or restitution, receive treatment, or perform community service. (Obviously, some also served time.)

Some states prescribe a range of sentences for each class of crimes, while others set a range or upper limit of punishment for each specific crime, and a few set mandatory minimums. Some use guidelines written by a sentencing commission rather than the legislature.

A pair of illustrations: Montana statutes establish maximum sentences for each individual crime. The maximum sentence for simple assault, whether intentional or negligent, is up to 60 days in the county jail, a fine of $500, or both. The sentence for aggravated assault—where the offender "purposely or knowingly causes serious bodily injury"—is two to twenty years in the state prison and a fine up to $50,000. In contrast, Washington State sets statutory maximums for each class of crime, not the individual crimes. Negligent assault is called third degree and a Class C felony; intentional assault is second degree and Class B; and aggravated assault, first degree and Class A. The maximum for Class C is up to five years in a state correctional facility, a fine up to $10,000, or both; for Class B, up to ten years, $20,000, or both, and for Class A, up to life, $50,000, or both.

So, on the surface, punishment appears stiffer in Washington State than in Montana for similar crimes, although other factors may level out the sentencing a bit. And, some inmates may earn "time off for good behavior" if they follow prison rules, comply with sentencing conditions, and cause no trouble inside. "Good time" credit can reduce a sentence significantly. It's been eliminated in some systems, though, so check your story state.

What factors might a judge consider in imposing sentence?

In choosing from a range of sentencing options, the judge might consider:

- Whether facts of the case put it on the lower or higher end of the scale for that crime.
- The defendant's criminal record, including juvenile convictions;
- Use of a dangerous weapon.
- Victim impact and the desires of the victim or victim's family.
- Knowledge that the victim was particularly vulnerable, e.g., a child, disabled, or elderly.

- A hate or bias motivation for the crime or choice of victim. Some states increase sentences for hate crimes, while others decline to treat bias as an aggravating factor, viewing such treatment as punishing thought, not action.

- Knowledge of the risks his actions created. In the negligent homicide case of a doctor who drove drunk and killed two teenage girls, the judge put great weight on the defendant's history of drinking problems and his professional knowledge of the risks he'd created. Who knew better, the judge reasoned in imposing the maximum sentence, than an emergency room doctor?

- Genuine expressions of remorse. A defendant who refuses to accept responsibility and express regret may not fare as well as one who expresses remorse. Sounds reasonable. But a judge may not impose a harsher sentence simply because the defendant continues to maintain his innocence. Nor may a judge increase the sentence because the defendant chooses to remain silent, either at trial or in sentencing.

- Fines and restitution. Judges may order restitution for victims' expenses, court costs, or extraordinary costs such as meth lab cleanup. Payments to victims are made through the court or a state victims' compensation fund. Defendants faced with financial obligations may be more likely to comply with other conditions of their sentences as well.

  > Judges may order restitution for victims' expenses, court costs, or extraordinary costs such as meth lab cleanup.

- Factors specific to the case. In sentencing a legal secretary for embezzlement, the judge considered the trust placed in her. The employer knew before hiring that she'd been convicted of embezzling from a law firm in another state, but offered her a second chance because she'd desperately needed to leave her abusive husband. Her abuse of that trust, and lingering questions about where the money went, triggered the maximum sentence.

- A plea agreement and prosecutor's recommendations.

- The sentence most likely to punish or rehabilitate.

- The defendant's cooperation at each step in the process.

TIP: Use factors like these to change the circumstances of the crime and increase or decrease the sentence your character faces.

What sentencing guidelines apply in the federal system?

Federal judges use the United States Sentencing Commission's guidelines. As a result of a 2005 Supreme Court decision, the guidelines are now advisory, not mandatory. Guidelines are intended to reduce the risk of unwarranted disparity and unpredictability in sentencing, while still giving judges flexibility to tailor individual sentences. Federal judges may impose exceptional sentences—greater than the maximum—when the facts warrant. Examples include hate crimes, deliberate cruelty, or evidence of additional crimes. On the other end of the spectrum, in a pre-2005 decision, one federal judge complained that mandatory guidelines forced him to impose a higher sentence than he thought appropriate on a defendant convicted of bank fraud, in light of the man's limited role in the crime, his loss of a professional license, and the fact that he was raising young children alone. Under advisory guidelines, the judge could have imposed a sentence more suited to the circumstances.

Guidelines are controversial, at both the state and federal level. Some legislators favor them as a way to prevent sentences that appear too lenient. Judges chafe at restrictions that seem like political interference with professional discretion. Guidelines can lead to inequities when very different incidents earn the same grade of seriousness, as in New Jersey where the act of opening a bottle of ketchup in the grocery store and putting it back on the shelf was rated the same as a charge related to a fist fight. Use the controversy to add conflict if your story involves a very public crime, a particularly appealing defendant, an ambitious legislator, or a cranky judge.

> Guidelines are controversial, at both the state and federal level.

Resources include the United States Sentencing Commission's guidelines and the National Association of State Sentencing Commissions. (See Book Links.)

When a criminal defendant is convicted, does he begin "officially" serving his sentence—and knocking off time—while other matters, such as appeals, are pending?

Depends. When a sentence includes time in custody, the sentencing order typically credits the defendant for all "time served"—that is, all time spent in custody on these charges. That includes time served before the formal sentence.

For example, a defendant may be held in the county jail all or part of the time between his arrest and the end of his trial. If he has been released on bail pending trial but is convicted, he may be taken into custody right away, even though formal sentencing may not happen for several weeks. Or he may be released on bail pending sentencing—not typical, but not uncommon. If the sentence involves jail or prison time, he'll likely be taken in to custody as soon as the sentence is imposed. But all time already spent inside on these charges is "time served" that may be credited against the eventual sentence.

Release on bail pending post-trial hearings, other than sentencing, or on appeal is not common. Requests for bail pending appeal must usually demonstrate a good chance of reversal or other extraordinary circumstances. They're far more likely in to be granted in cases of "white collar" crime than in violent crimes, but are not automatic. Martha Stewart was released on bail pending appeal of her 2004 conviction for conspiracy, making false statements, and obstruction of justice, but chose to go ahead and serve the five-month prison sentence already imposed. Good choice, in her case, as the prison time was already behind her by the time her conviction was affirmed.

My protagonist is dating a probation officer, a regular character in the mystery series. What information goes into pre-sentence reports?

In most felony convictions, the judge orders a pre-sentence investigation (PSI), which provides background information on the offender. Reports are usually prepared by the probation office, although the department name may vary by state. Investigations may take several weeks.

What's in the report?

- criminal history, including juvenile and out-of-state records, if available;

- a social history, including education, employment, health, finances, and family information;

- the facts of the crime—both the official version and the defendant's account;

- a summary of harm to the victim, the victim's family, and the community, plus an itemization of the victim's expenses and financial losses;

- special costs, e.g., drug lab cleanup, or in a financial crime, forensic accountants' fees;

- summaries of reports of physical or mental exams, and substance abuse evaluations, if ordered;

- sentencing and treatment options and recommendations, including whether the defendant is a good candidate for programs like community pre-release centers instead of prison time; and

- time already served for this crime.

Reports are provided to the prosecutor, defendant, and defense attorney. The prosecutor may reveal the contents of a PSI to the victim, but reports contain private, confidential details and are not public. After sentencing, the PSI follows the prisoner to any jail, prison, or other institution. Probation officers use PSI reports in planning an offender's treatment, evaluation, and release.

I'm not sure whether my character should be on parole or probation. What is parole?

Parole is a prisoner's release into the community before the end of his or her sentence, subject to conditions, supervision, and revocation. Eligibility depends on the crime and sentence, and it doesn't usually begin until at least one-quarter of the sentence has been served, although other factors like "good time" credit may come into play.

Parole may be granted if:

- the prisoner has followed prison rules;

- release will not diminish the seriousness of the offense or promote disrespect for the law; and

- release will not jeopardize public safety.

The trial judge, prosecutor, and defense attorney may make recommendations. Most states allow victims and their families to comment. If parole is denied, the prisoner is not generally eligible for a rehearing for a specified time. In the federal system, for example, prisoners must wait at least eighteen months.

Some states have abolished parole, substituting early or mandatory supervised release programs.

Some parolees are released into pre-release centers or treatment programs. Others live on their own but report regularly to parole officers. Supervision continues until the original sentence ends. If a parolee violates conditions of release or commits a new crime, parole may be revoked.

Parole has several purposes:

- to provide help with common problems in readjusting to life after release, such as employment, housing, and finances;

- to prevent a return to crime by helping former prisoners re-establish themselves in the community; and

- to reduce or limit imprisonment of those not likely to commit further crime.

Because parolees generally work and community supervision is less expensive than incarceration, parole also helps states save money.

In most states, a parole board appointed by the governor makes initial release decisions. A state Department of Corrections agency supervises parolees. Some states have abolished parole, substituting early or mandatory supervised release programs. Agency names and authority vary. The American Probation and Parole Association maintains a directory of state services. (See Book Links.)

In the federal system, parole was abolished for all crimes committed after November 1, 1987. The U.S. Parole Commission reviews requests and supervises parolees in the federal and D.C. systems, some military justice offenders, citizens convicted abroad but serving their sentences here, and state probationers and parolees in the federal witness protection program.

All fifty states belong to an Interstate Compact, which allows parolees to move across state lines. Parole to another state is likely if the prisoner has roots and family there to ease the transition. A state corrections agency or division tracks and supervises interstate parolees.

Parole practices have changed, so if your story involves crimes committed in the past, check the system in use at the time.

What is probation?

Probation is a period of supervision in the community imposed by the court as an alternative to imprisonment. All or part of a sentence may be probationary. For example, an offender may be sentenced to five years, with all but thirty days suspended. After serving thirty days in jail, the offender is released on probation until the five-year sentence ends. If he violates the conditions of his probation, or commits a new crime, probation may be revoked, requiring him to serve at least part of his remaining sentence.

At the end of 2008 in the United States, 5.1 million adults were under some form of community supervision, including probation or parole, compared to 1.6 million in jail or prison. Community supervision numbers are likely to increase, especially for non-violent offenders, as the high cost of incarceration drives states to more community-based alternatives.

> At the end of 2008 in the U.S., 5.1 million adults were under some form of community supervision, including probation or parole.

The judge in my story wants to encourage a character convicted of a minor crime to stay out of trouble in the future. Can the sentence be deferred?

Yes. A judge has discretion to defer or postpone imposing sentence for a specified time, with conditions, in exchange for a guilty plea. Essentially, the judge reserves authority to impose sentence. At the end of the deferral period, charges are dismissed if the offender has met all conditions. In most states, the conviction then becomes confidential, with information available only to courts and law enforcement. But if the offender fails to meet the conditions—say he commits another offense or fails to complete a treatment program—the judge may revoke the deferral and impose sentence.

Deferrals are usually limited to traffic offenses, misdemeanors, or first-time, nonviolent felonies. Actor Macaulay Culkin received a deferred sentence and a fine for possession of anti-depressants without a prescription and marijuana.

Or should the sentence be suspended?

Suspension of a sentence is another possibility. A judge may impose sentence but suspend a portion, e.g., a ten-year sentence with all but two years suspended. The offender must serve the two years, although in many states, time served can be reduced for good behavior. During the suspended period, the offender remains under supervision, with conditions. The rest of the sentence may be reimposed if the offender violates the terms of release or supervision. The suspended term hangs over the offender's head as an incentive until the full sentence expires.

Typical conditions of suspension include some jail time, work release, payment of court costs, fines, and restitution, treatment, community service, and house arrest. The goal is a combination that rehabilitates the offender and protects the victim and society.

If the offender violates a condition, the prosecutor in the county where the case was originally handled files a petition to revoke the deferred or suspended sentence. A revocation hearing is held to determine whether conditions were violated. The prosecutor's burden of proof is usually "by clear and convincing evidence," lower than "beyond a reasonable doubt," the standard for conviction of a crime.

If a violation is found, the judge may continue the original sentence, modify the conditions of release, or impose all or part of a suspended sentence.

A character has been convicted of several related crimes. Will he be sentenced on each crime separately or jointly, and how is the length of the sentence calculated?

When a person is convicted of multiple offenses, the judge imposes a separate sentence for each offense. Sentences may be served concurrently—at the same time—or consecutively—one after the other.

The factors a judge considers include:

- Did all offenses arise from the same conduct? Concurrent sentences are typically imposed on offenses arising from the same incident, where the defendant's actions violate multiple statutes. Example: a woman convicted of theft by forging her employer's signature on a check is also convicted of forgery for the same act. Concurrent sentences are likely.

- Did the defendant intend to commit separate crimes? Our forger also destroyed a bank letter notifying the employer of an overdraft triggered by the forgery. In covering up her theft, she committed a second crime, mail destruction. Consecutive sentences are likely.

- Is the defendant under any previous incomplete sentence? If she was already on probation, consecutive sentences are likely. In addition, her probation will be revoked, requiring her to complete her prior sentences.

- Were multiple incidents committed against the same victim? If our embezzler forged multiple checks over a period of months, she clearly had time to contemplate her actions and stop, making consecutive sentences likely.

Particulars vary. Some states mandate consecutive sentences for certain offenses, e.g., DUI and vehicular homicide (or any crime charged as the result of a death or injury caused while intoxicated—remember that states name similar crimes differently). As always, primary considerations are the nature of the crime, its impact on the victim and community, and the defendant's criminal history.

And, as in any two-for-one deal, the higher sentence controls. That is, if two-year and five-year sentences are imposed concurrently, the defendant remains subject to state control for five years.

Life sentences may be consecutive, and a sentence for another offense may be consecutive to a life sentence. This reflects a public policy of imposing the sentence appropriate to the crime, regardless of the defendant's ability to actually serve the sentence. This policy promotes the philosophical purposes of sentencing: punishment, retribution, rehabilitation, and deterrence.

The judge in my story is looking for a creative sentence to avoid imposing prison time while sending the defendant a message. What can you suggest?

Community service is a common element of sentences, especially for nonviolent offenses. The reasoning? Crime damages society, and community service allows defendants to repay their debt to the community. Some learn lessons in humanity, while others learn useful skills for use in their post-conviction lives.

Judges may dictate the type of service to be performed or leave it to the probation officer's discretion. Community service assignments are typically tailored to the crime committed, or to the defendant's skill and training. Drivers convicted of driving under the influence may be required to talk to high school students about the dangers of drinking and driving. A person convicted of poaching game may be required to work in a food bank or on improving wildlife habitat. A person with special skills may be required to use them, such as a carpenter put to work on a Habitat for Humanity house or the office of a local non-profit organization. Other types of volunteer service, such as coaching or roadside cleanup, are common. A probation officer may insist a defendant work with an organization willing to provide supervision or an accounting of hours worked.

> Community service assignments are typically tailored to the crime committed.

Some sentences are designed to get the offender's attention. A speeder may work with school crossing guards for a few days. A Florida judge offered a man convicted of reckless driving a choice: take a fine and have a record, or photograph ten roadside memorial markers within a month. The driver thought the homework "a crazy assignment," even morbid, but the project served the judge's goal: The driver came to appreciate the risks he had created, and he developed a better understanding of survivors' emotions.

Judges get creative in balancing the interests of the victim and the public with the defendant's rights and interests, particularly in juvenile cases. A Seattle judge's sentences often include book reports, to focus youthful defendants' attention on social issues and boost literacy and school performance. In Florida, teens in smoking cases write essays on the dangers of tobacco, followed by quizzes. Teen speeders photograph roadside shrines or clip newspaper stories about traffic accidents, highlighting the names of the dead or injured.

But creative sentencing has limits. Two state appeals courts recently rejected sentences prohibiting offenders from returning to the county where their crimes were committed after their release from prison. Why? Banishment violates the constitutional right to travel, and no evidence indicated they posed a continuing threat to their victims. One offender was developmentally disabled; banishment would have kept him from receiving the family help he needed. The other, in his late 60s, simply wanted to go home.

Corporations convicted of environmental crimes have been required to take out newspaper ads apologizing for their actions. The Ninth Circuit upheld a sentence requiring a mail thief who had served jail time to stand outside a San Francisco post office for a day wearing a signboard reading "I stole mail. This is my punishment." He argued that it violated the ban against cruel and unusual punishment. The majority held the punishment "reasonably related to the legitimate statutory objective of rehabilitation." The dissenting judge passionately objected that "public humiliation or shaming" has no legitimate role in sentencing. Debate continues.

> Corporations convicted of environmental crimes have been required to take out newspaper ads apologizing for their actions.

Here are a few other examples of judicial creativity:
- a juvenile in Washington State was turned over to his Indian tribe for traditional punishment and education;
- a football fan convicted of theft was required to donate her Green Bay Packers tickets to a local charity;
- an Ohio couple was required to take out a newspaper ad apologizing for a public sex act; and
- a man convicted of fleeing police was ordered to participate in a fund-raising fun run held by the police officers' association.

Creativity also influences treatment recommendations. A Florida judge regularly requires drug addicts to undergo addiction therapy involving acupuncture.

Above all, creative sanctions must be fair, consistent, and advance public safety. Alternative sentences can prevent crime, reduce recidivism, and provide a cost-effective means of punishment. Greater justice may be possible when sentences address individual situations and needs. Alternatives to prison can help defendants rehabilitate themselves by keeping them in the community, employed, and responsible, and help keep families together and financially independent. But the safety of crime victims and the public must be protected.

My story includes allegations of election fraud involving votes cast by felons. What are the rules on felon voting?

Forty-eight states and the District of Columbia bar inmates convicted of felonies from voting; Maine and Vermont are the exceptions. (A federal suit challenging Washington State's ban as racially discriminatory is pending.) But what happens after an offender finishes his sentence and is released?

In thirty-five states, felons on parole may not vote; thirty also disenfranchise probationers. Two states impose a blanket, lifetime ban, while nine impose a lifetime ban on some felons, depending on their crime, even though they have served their complete sentences. Limited exceptions are available if a person is pardoned or a conviction expunged, complicated processes that are rarely invoked. Numerous states have overturned or reduced their bans in recent years. Congress has considered but failed to pass several proposals to ensure voting rights in federal elections for persons with felony convictions who are not incarcerated or who have completed their sentences; supporters will probably continue to introduce proposals.

The Sentencing Project, a national organization promoting sentencing reform, estimates that the ban keeps 5.3 million Americans from the polls, including 2.1 million who have completed their sentences, and makes 13 percent of black men ineligible to vote.

Supporters call the ban a tool in fighting crime, enforcing punishment, and ensuring that full sentences are served, including payment of fines and restitution. Critics say it impedes re-entry and re-integration into society. A person barred from voting is less likely to feel part of the community and may have less respect for its laws; one study showed higher re-arrest rates for nonvoters—27 percent compared to 12 percent for voters. To an ex-felon determined to put the past behind him, the ban is a continuing obstacle to rehabilitation. A criminal sentence represents the defendant's debt to society; once it's served, critics of the ban say, the debt is paid and full civil rights should be restored automatically. Once again, political controversy equals plot potential. (Statistics drawn from The Sentencing Project. See Book Links.)

Ex-felons' votes were a major issue in Florida in the 2000 presidential election; the ban was upheld, but verification of felon lists became a political hot potato in 2004, and, in 2007, the law was changed to restore rights for many nonviolent offenders and ease the reinstatement process for others. Felon lists also played a role in the litigation that followed Washington State's disputed 2004 governor's race, and led to legislative changes.

Federal convicts are barred from gun ownership for life.

Other rights limited in some states include gun ownership, jury service, and holding public office. Federal convicts are barred from gun ownership for life. Some states permit a felony conviction to be considered a negative factor in employment or in licensing.

Crime writers can use the bans in political thrillers or to heighten the complications for an ex-felon seeking to re-establish a normal life. What happens when a man who wants to keep his troubled past a secret tries to explain to his new wife or his children why he can't vote, serve on a jury, or take his son hunting?

I'm thinking of setting a short story in a suburban neighborhood whose residents get upset when a convicted sex offender moves in. Is he required to register somewhere? What information is made public?

All fifty states, the federal government, and the District of Columbia are required by law to maintain sex offender registries. Native American tribes may set up their own registries, or they may delegate responsibility to a state.

The public notification of a sex offender's release into a community first occurred in Washington State in 1987. Within the next few years, several states started registries. Public awareness grew in 1994, when New Jersey enacted Megan's Law, named for a girl abducted, raped, and murdered by a convicted sex offender. The federal registry was also created that year. In 1996, Congress enacted the federal Megan's Law, requiring states to make information about registered sex offenders public.

Registration allows law enforcement to meet two goals:

- To track where sex offenders live, making future investigations and arrests easier. The laws require offenders to notify the government of their address, usually within ninety days of a move. Failure to provide an update may be a crime in itself.

- To give the public notice when necessary. Some states make the entire list public, while others provide limited information, based on the degree of risk an offender presents. Risk is assessed based on the crime originally committed or on a pre-release evaluation.

State systems vary in other ways:

- Some require registration and public notice for a laundry list of sex offenses and non-sex crimes against children. This may include so-called "victim-less crimes," such as viewing pornographic material online. Others limit public notice only to offenders who present a high risk of re-offending and pose a "substantial" public threat. In some states, the decision to notify the public is determined by local law enforcement, case by case.

- Most registries include out-of-state convictions, but ensuring compliance is difficult.

- About thirty states require juvenile offenders to register.

- How long an offender must register varies, usually by the type of offense or the risk assessment. Some states do not require registration by offenders convicted before the registration statute was adopted. Specified offenses may require lifetime registration.

- Some public notice methods may include: an official website, public service announcements through the media and schools, or door-to-door contact within a neighborhood.

- Some include photographs of all registrants, while others post photos only of sexually violent predators, offenders at risk to re-offend, or non-compliant offenders whose registration is not current.

Use of registries to harass an offender or carry out a vigilante campaign is a crime. Listings can't be used to refuse employment, insurance, loans, scholarships, and other services.

> Use of registries to harass an offender or carry out a vigilante campaign is a crime.

Notification laws have been challenged on constitutional grounds and some have been revised as a result. Still, problems exist. Similar names create a risk of misidentification. The public may assume registered offenders are predatory rapists or child molesters, but lists may include one-time offenders, teens who plead guilty to underage sex, and others who pose minimal threat. Offenders complain that registration adds to their sentences and subjects them to sanctions within the community, even though they have done their time.

TIP: No database is ever perfectly accurate or up-to-date. Use errors and omissions to confuse or misdirect your amateur sleuth.

Do registration and public notification reduce sex crime, either generally, or by the registered offenders? It's easy to assume they do, but an evaluation requested by the Washington State legislature concluded that research is too limited to reach definitive conclusions. Other studies show a small drop in recidivism, not necessarily linked to mandatory registration and community notification, and that offenders convicted of failure to register were more likely to commit new sex crimes than those who registered. Some analysts—

A common complication with registries is that one offender may be listed under several names. The total number of listings for my small community was staggering—until I noticed that one man was listed five times for the same offense and another four times. Name variations triggered multiple listings. Ken was also listed as Kenneth, again with his middle initial, and yet again with variations of his middle name. A man using a hyphenated last name was listed under each name, although each listing included "also known as" names. Eliminating duplicates cut the list by more than half.

including prosecutors—believe registration requirements and restrictions on where offenders may live or work actually increase the risk of repeat offenses by keeping offenders from treatment and family support.

An increasing number of states also maintain violent offender registries.

Both sex and violent offender registries can be political issues. Your fictional legislator may advocate broad registration requirements because she thinks that will reduce crime—or because she wants to portray her opponent in the next election as soft on crime. (For resources, see the Book Links.)

My character has a juvenile record, and I'd like the villain to find out and use the details to blackmail him. Is this realistic?

Maybe, depending on the state and crime. We often assume juvenile records are automatically sealed when the offender turns eighteen. But there's no blanket rule. While the trend is toward increased availability, most states allow the offender to request records be sealed. In most states, statutes govern sealing and expunging juvenile records, so check your story location.

Open or shut?

Here are some areas where state laws vary. (For a state-by-state summary of current laws, see the Book Links.) Keep in mind that most changes in statutes are not retroactive, so records might be available for recent convictions but not in older cases, and vice versa.

- Official records of juvenile cases may be open to the public, including the media, with additional information sealed.

- Under some juvenile diversion programs, no formal judgment is entered if the offender successfully completes a probation-style program with no further offenses. (The worst offenders are not eligible for diversion.) Records may be sealed automatically or the conviction may be completely expunged—that is, wiped from the slate.

- In states that treat anyone under twenty-one as a juvenile, offenses committed between eighteen and twenty-one may be merged with the adult record.

- In most states, an offender may petition the court to seal his record after a specified time.

- Records are sealed only if the offender fully serves his sentence, pays restitution, and keeps his nose clean.

- Records of juvenile offenses handled in adult court are not sealed.

- Records of sex offenses are not sealed, with the possible exception of very young offenders.

Limited access still permitted:

- Sealed records are available to law enforcement officers and to judges for sentencing on later convictions.

- Sealed records may be opened to detention and corrections officers, social service agencies, the military, school authorities, and researchers. This might give your bad guy the opening he needs.

- A few states allow victims full access to sealed records.

- A few states allow access by employers and licensing agencies.

Search and destroy:

- Some states destroy court records of "status offenses"—resisting parental control, curfew violations, truancy—five years after sealing. Court records of other juvenile crimes may be destroyed at a specific age, or on petition. Destruction laws and orders do not apply to records held by police, probation, and other agencies, unless they themselves choose to destroy their records.

- When records are destroyed, identifying information, such as photos, fingerprints, and DNA, is retained for use in future investigations.

Sealed proceedings are treated as if they never occurred. If your hero's juvenile conviction is sealed, he can truthfully say he has no criminal record and has not been convicted of a crime.

Should an adult with a juvenile record petition for seal? A seal allows for a clean slate. A record can affect the ability to enlist in the military, get a scholarship, a job, housing, or a gun. Some former juvenile offenders say they're always looking over their shoulders, waiting for the past to catch up with them. A sealed record can provide a chance to start over. But for the writer, an unsealed record—or a chance to get access—can offer wonderful story complications.

The prosecutor is my story needs to explain to the victim's family why she agreed to a plea bargain. What reasons might she give? And what does the defendant agree to?

Prosecutors and defense counsel often negotiate plea agreements. Typically, the prosecutor agrees to recommend a specific sentence in exchange for agreement to plead guilty to some or all charges, or to lesser charges. Or a prosecutor may agree not to oppose the defendant's sentencing request.

Why agree? While the public sometimes disparages plea agreements, they save time and money in a heavily-pressured judicial system. Prosecutors trade the risk of acquittal for certainty, and defendants exchange the risk of conviction for time and liberty. Increasingly, victims are being given a more active role in plea negotiations. Some states limit plea agreements for some offenses. For example, New Jersey restricts plea agreements for driving under the influence.

A plea agreement isn't risk-free for the defendant. The judge may reject an agreed-on recommendation and impose a stiffer sentence. Defendants are advised, usually in writing, that the prosecutor can't guarantee a particular sentence and that the defendant can't withdraw his plea if the judge rejects

> Prosecutors trade the risk of acquittal for certainty, and defendants exchange the risk of conviction for time and liberty.

the recommendation. Judges typically question defendants before accepting guilty pleas, and may refuse a plea if the defendant denies guilt or appears to misunderstand the process. A judge may also refuse a plea if he believes the seriousness of the case, or the defendant's criminal history, does not justify dismissing or reducing charges.

A typical written agreement includes the defendant's acknowledgment that:

- the plea is voluntary and not the result of force, threats, or promises;

- defense counsel has explained the effect of waiving the right to trial; and that he:

- is satisfied with the services of defense counsel, has been properly represented, and has had ample time to prepare a defense; is not suffering any emotional or mental disability and is not impaired by drugs, alcohol, or prescription medication; and

- fully understands what he's doing.

A plea may be withdrawn before judgment is entered on a showing of "good cause," e.g., the judge's misstatement of the maximum sentence or the defendant's lack of proper mental capacity. Pleas may be withdrawn after judgment only if new, exculpatory evidence emerges. Examples: A credible confession by another person, which we discussed in the appeals section, or testimony from a previously unknown witness. Physical evidence such as newly-discovered photographs or a bullet dug out of a wall during remodeling a crime scene. A court might also allow a defendant to withdraw a plea if he pled guilty and was sentenced before DNA testing became available, if physical evidence was preserved, grounds exist to request a test, and results exonerate him.

Can a convicted criminal write about his life and experiences?

Yes. What he can't do is profit from telling his story.

New York enacted the first restriction in 1977, after accused murderer David Berkowitz, known as "Son of Sam," tried to sell his story. Similar anti-notoriety laws—often called Son of Sam laws—now exist in about forty states and the federal system. The goal is to prevent criminals from profiting through books or movies about their crimes while their victims suffer financially—and also suffer from the added publicity.

The criminal may still write a book or sell his story to a magazine or a movie producer. However, instead of paying the criminal, the publisher or producer pays the state where the criminal was convicted. Systems vary. In some states, the author's victims must sue him in civil court for money damages; judgment in hand, they file a claim with the state against the money received. In others, payments are routed through the state crime victims' fund; money not paid to the victims may be returned to the criminal, applied to the state's costs of trial, or used to compensate victims of other crimes.

In 1981, Simon & Schuster published *Wiseguy: Life in a Mafia Family*, by Henry Hill, the pseudonym of a man under federal witness protection. (Ray Liotta played Hill in Martin Scorsese's 1990 movie, *Goodfellas*.) Hill's book readily acknowledged his participation in crimes for which he was not prosecuted. New York attempted to force the publisher to pay the state everything Hill earned. In 1991, the Supreme Court held that the law unconstitutionally infringed on freedom of speech because it applied not only to convicted criminals, but also to persons accused but not convicted and to persons who admitted an unprosecuted crime. The Court agreed that New York has a "compelling interest" in depriving criminals of the profits of their crimes and in using those profits to help victims. But the state can't confiscate payment for works that only tangentially refer to a crime. Since then, laws have been rewritten to target convicted criminals who write or sell a story primarily about their crimes.

Other examples: several political figures wrote biographies admitting involvement in Watergate, but were never convicted of crimes. They can keep their profits. An ex-President who makes a passing reference in a memoir to having inhaled can keep the profits. And, Son of Sam laws don't affect a felon who writes about how prison changed his life but only incidentally mentions the crimes that landed him there, because the focus is his personal transformation.

QUESTIONS ON THE DEATH PENALTY

My story involves a high-profile homicide, and the killer may be eligible for the death penalty. I'd like the sentence to be controversial. Can you give me some background on the death penalty?

The U.S. Supreme Court struck down the death penalty in 1972 in a landmark case called *Furman v. Georgia*. The Court held that a punishment is "cruel and unusual" under the Eighth Amendment to the Constitution if it:

- is too severe for the crime;
- is arbitrary;
- offends society's sense of justice; or
- is not more effective than a less severe penalty.

A 5–4 majority ruled that the state of Georgia's statute could result in arbitrary sentencing because it gave the jury complete discretion to impose the death penalty.

The decision effectively voided death penalty statutes in forty states. As a result, the sentences of 629 death row inmates around the country were commuted to life in prison. States began revising their statutes to comply with *Furman* and to provide guidelines for juries. The Supreme Court reinstated the death penalty in 1976, when it upheld the first amended statutes.

Currently, juries deciding whether to impose death must follow guidelines and consider aggravating and mitigating factors. In states that give the sentencing judge discretion to impose death, the jury, not the judge, must decide whether sufficient aggravating factors exist. Other state variations include:

- bifurcated trials, with guilt and punishment decided in separate phases by the same jury;

- automatic appellate review of the conviction and sentence when death is imposed; and

- proportionality review, allowing courts to compare cases to identify and eliminate sentencing disparities.

The first post-*Furman* execution occurred in 1977, when Utah executed Gary Gilmore by firing squad. Gilmore did not challenge his execution, the subject of Norman Mailer's dramatic 1979 book, *The Executioner's Song*. Since then, more than twelve hundred executions have occurred. As of October 1, 2009, 3,263 people sat on death row across the country, with 44 percent in three states: California, Florida, and Texas. The number of death sentences imposed has dropped significantly in the last ten years, from 284 in 1999 to 106 in 2009.

As of June 2010, thirty-five states and the federal and military systems allow the death penalty. Of those, one-third rarely impose it and another third rarely executes. Nearly 80 percent of executions occur in the South. Nationwide, support for the death penalty has been dropping, and proposed legislation in several states would abolish it.

TIP: Family members of murder victims may be split over the death penalty, and some may actively support the killer's plea for a life sentence or challenge to a death sentence. Use that activism or conflict to deepen your plot and characterization.

Since 1973, more than 130 people have been released from death row based on evidence of innocence. From 2000 through 2004, thirty-five death row inmates were exonerated.

The United Nations Commission on Human Rights advocates abolition of the death penalty. Other countries imposing death sentences include China, Vietnam, Iran, Saudi Arabia, Egypt, and Pakistan. More than half of all other countries—including Canada and all of Europe—have abolished the death penalty and refuse to extradite to the U.S. suspects who might be given death sentences.

> More than half of all other countries—including Canada and all of Europe—have abolished the death penalty.

Statistics are drawn from the Death Penalty Information Center fact sheet; the DPIC also provides extensive state-by-state information. (See Book Links.)

What crimes are punishable by death?

In *Kennedy v. Louisiana* (2008), the Supreme Court struck down the death penalty for the rape of a child, holding that death for any crime against an individual that does not "take the life of the victim" violates the Eighth Amendment. Crimes against "the state"—that is, all of us—that do not involve murder, such as treason, espionage, and terrorism, may still be subject to the death penalty; that question was not decided.

States that allow the death penalty don't all apply it to the same crimes, but since *Kennedy*, those crimes must involve a death. For particulars, check the laws for your story state.

A wide variety of federal crimes can result in a death sentence, although federal cases account for just over 1 percent of death row inmates. Some examples that might occur in fiction as well as real-life are:

- civil rights offenses resulting in death, as was the case in the dragging death of a black man in Texas;

- murder related to smuggling aliens;

- murder committed during a carjacking, a drug-related drive-by shooting, or by using a gun during a violent crime or a drug trafficking crime;

- assassination or kidnaping resulting in the death of the President or Vice President;

- murder of a federal judge or law enforcement official, court officer, juror, law enforcement official aiding in a federal investigation, state or federal correctional officer, or foreign official;

- retaliatory murder of a law enforcement officer's immediate family members;

- murder of a member of Congress, an important executive official, or a Supreme Court Justice;

- murder committed in a federal government facility or an international airport. A fictional example: the murders of travelers in the Orange County Airport in season five of the television show *24*;

- murder with the intent of preventing or retaliating for testimony;

- murder by a federal prisoner or an escapee already sentenced to life imprisonment;

- murder during a bank robbery, kidnaping, or hostage-taking;

- use of the mail resulting in death, as in the Unabomber case;

- death resulting from aircraft hijacking or willful train-wrecking;
- the terrorist murder of a U.S. national abroad;
- murder by use of a weapon of mass destruction;
- genocide; and
- murder involving torture.

By federal law, the death penalty may also be imposed in drug kingpin cases (cases of large-scale trafficking); the Supreme Court did not decide whether that statute is still valid.

What are aggravating and mitigating factors in death penalty cases?

Aggravating factors, used to impose a death sentence, may include:

- a particularly depraved crime;
- multiple victims;
- a financial motivation;
- whether the offender was in official custody;
- previous convictions for deliberate homicide;
- use of torture or ambush;
- murder as part of a scheme to kill more than one person;
- murder during the course of certain types of sexual assault;
- whether the victim was a law enforcement officer performing his or her duties; or
- the death of a kidnaping victim.

The Joseph Duncan case, previously discussed, involved at least five aggravating factors.

Mitigating circumstances that might merit leniency in an individual case include:

- no significant history of prior criminal activity;
- the defendant's personal history, including childhood abuse and neglect;
- the role of mental illness;
- whether the crime was committed under extreme duress or substantial domination by another person;
- diminished mental capacity; or
- relatively minor participation in an offense committed by another.

Prosecutors may agree to waive the death penalty in exchange for a guilty plea, as in the cases of Unabomber Ted Kaczynski and the Green River Killer, Gary Ridgeway. But, as with Zacarias Moussaoui, aka the Twentieth Hijacker, they are not obliged to do so.

Can juvenile defendants be executed?

No. In *Roper v. Simmons* (2005), a Missouri case, the Supreme Court struck down the death penalty for persons who committed their crimes before turning eighteen.

The Court upheld the execution of juveniles in 1989, but reconsidered the decision because of growing national consensus against the practice. Between 1976 and 2005, twenty-two defendants were executed for crimes committed as juveniles. By 2005, thirty states had passed laws barring the execution of juveniles, although some set a limit of age sixteen or seventeen. The evolution of public opinion has played a major role in the change of heart and law.

The Court held that the death penalty for juveniles violates the Eighth Amendment ban on cruel and unusual punishment and is "disproportionate" in light of the general immaturity of youth. The Court acknowledged that some juveniles commit brutal crimes, but wrote that their "susceptibility ... to immature and irresponsible behavior means their irresponsible conduct is not as morally reprehensible as that of an adult. From a moral standpoint it would be misguided to equate the failings of a minor with those of an adult, for a greater possibility exists that a minor's character deficiencies will be reformed." The majority also concluded that juvenile executions do not serve the goals of retribution or deterrence.

> The Court held that the death penalty for juveniles violates the Eighth Amendment ban on cruel and unusual punishment.

Can the mentally disabled be executed?

No. In 2002, in *Atkins v. Virginia*, the Supreme Court reversed a 1989 decision and held that execution of "mentally retarded" defendants violates the Eighth Amendment ban on cruel and unusual punishment. Eighteen states had already banned such executions. At least thirty-five mentally disabled defendants were executed from 1976 to 2001. (Most statutes and court decisions use the term mentally retarded, not mentally disabled.)

Why the ban? Mentally disabled persons may not fully understand their actions and the consequences, and they may be less able to control their behavior than persons of normal intelligence. They are often more suggestible and likely to falsely confess. The ban implements the philosophy that execution of the mentally disabled, regardless of guilt or innocence, is unacceptable in a civilized society.

State processes for determining mental retardation vary. So does the definition, but it generally means a disability, originating before age eighteen, that includes significantly below average intelligence (e.g., an IQ of seventy or less) and significant limitations in adaptive behavior, primarily in reasoning and impulse control.

Other variations include whether mental capacity is decided by the judge or jury, whether determined before trial or during sentencing, and whether the state should pay for the defense expert.

What methods of execution are used?

Lethal injection was first used in 1982. It's now the primary method in thirty-six states and the federal system, although some using lethal injection use other methods as backup or allow prisoners a choice. Other methods include gas, electricity, and, in Utah, the firing squad.

What are some examples of problems that can occur in executions?

Each method can malfunction and the results are horrific, if not cruel and unusual. A 1979 Alabama electrocution took three cycles of 2600 volts before the prisoner died, nearly twenty minutes after the first jolt. In 1992, in Arizona, the gas chamber asphyxiation of a triple murderer took eleven minutes. Witnesses cried, the attorney general vomited, and the prison warden vowed to resign rather than repeat the experience. Arizona then changed its method to lethal injection, although prisoners sentenced before the change could choose gas. In 1999, one did, hoping the courts would find gas cruel and unusual and stay the execution. He lost. Newspaper accounts say he coughed and gagged for several minutes before slumping forward and dying. He was pronounced dead eighteen minutes after the cyanide pellets were dropped into a pan of distilled water and sulfuric acid below his seat.

In 1996, in Washington State, an inmate who weighed at least 425 pounds—the highest the prison scale would go—argued that his weight made hanging cruel and unusual punishment. The Ninth Circuit rejected his argument because the state legislature had just changed the presumptive method of execution from hanging to lethal injection. (His sentence was reversed on other grounds and the new jury gave him life in prison, where he died in 2005.)

In several recent cases, courts held that lethal injection is cruel and unusual punishment because the mix of drugs used might result in extreme pain while the prisoner was still conscious. In *California v. Morales*, a 2006 federal case, the judge ordered the state to have an expert present to ensure that the inmate became unconscious from a sedative or replace the state's three-drug sequence with a single lethal dose of a barbiturate. The appeals court ordered that the physicians must personally administer additional drugs if the prisoner remained conscious or in pain. The doctors who had agreed to participate then withdrew—active participation, rather than monitoring, raises ethical concerns for physicians—and the execution was postponed. The Supreme Court upheld Kentucky's protocol in *Baze v. Rees* (2008) and held that prisoners challenging lethal injection in other states need to show a risk of severe pain that could be avoided by readily implementable and feasible alternatives. Other states are now revising their medical protocols because of concerns about the drug combinations used.

In 2009, in Ohio, guards spent more than two hours unsuccessfully trying to find a suitable vein, with the defendant's assistance, before postponing his execution. At this writing, his claim that the psychological impact of the botched attempt would make a second try cruel and unusual is still in the courts; he remains on death row.

Death penalty resources

Statistics on capital punishment come from the Death Penalty Information Center annual Fact Sheet. The DPIC website includes a directory of death penalty laws and a list of state and federal crimes punishable by death. The DPIC's excellent history, with references, is particularly useful to writers of historical mysteries and crime novels. (See Book Links.)

Several state department of corrections websites list past executions and prisoners on death row, including details of their crimes. Arizona's website describes last meal requests. Consult your story state's DOC site.

For a physician's insight into the ethical issues, a description of the physical processes, and fascinating interviews with physicians who assist with executions, see "When Law and Ethics Collide: Why Physicians Participate in Executions," by Atul Gawande, M.D., M.P.H., *New England Journal of Medicine*, Vol. 354:1221–1229, March 23, 2006.

For a lawyer-novelist's view, based in part on serving on Illinois's Commission on Capital Punishment, charged with examining how the death penalty might be more fairly administered, take a look at Scott Turow's *Ultimate Punishment: A Lawyer's Reflections on Dealing with the Death Penalty* (2003).

And, for a profile of one lawyer's work with death row inmates in North Carolina, see John Temple's *The Last Lawyer: The Fight to Save Death Row Inmates* (2009); several chapters focus on intelligence testing.

Other popular books and movies include John Grisham's 1994 novel, *The Chamber*; Helen Prejean's memoir, *Dead Man Walking: An Eyewitness Account of the Death Penalty in the United States* (1994), made into the 1995 movie starring Sean Penn and Susan Sarandon; and, of course, the classic, Truman Capote's *In Cold Blood*, a 1965 book and a 1967 movie with Robert Blake and John Forsythe.

5

Civil Matters

WHILE MOST LEGAL PROBLEMS IN FICTION INVOLVE CRIME, the civil side of the law can be equally mysterious. First, we'll discuss the pretrial phase known as the discovery process. Then we'll look at medical malpractice, some issues related to life insurance, and that old bugaboo, the oral contract.

What is the discovery process?

The discovery process is the curious name given to the formal exchange of information in a lawsuit. Although it's used to a limited degree in criminal cases, it's often central to civil litigation. The most common methods are written discovery requests and depositions.

Written requests include interrogatories, requests for production, and requests for admission. Interrogatories are written questions seeking specific information—names of witnesses and medical providers, insurance information, and details of damages claimed, for example. Requests for production cover documents, photos, and other physical things. Requests for admission ask the other side to admit certain facts, such as the location of a slip-and-fall accident, that a required payment was not made, or that a deed was not timely recorded.

A party responding to requests for production must thoroughly search its own records, including all electronic files, whether on computers, servers, or cell phones, and produce all responsive documents. While paper records are still common, document production now typically includes CDs of electronic files, photos, and scanned records. In much litigation, counsel rely on each other to produce all relevant documents, especially in cases like auto accidents where most documents—medical records, wage loss information, and so on—are in the control of one party or her witnesses and the defense has limited records. However, the requesting party still has the right to review a party's records itself, sending young lawyers or legal assistants to plow through a store-room full of boxes of dusty documents or conducting a forensic search of the other side's electronic files. What isn't produced may be as important as what is. For example, a service tech testified that he kept detailed records of all ser-

> In much litigation, counsel rely on each other to produce all relevant documents.

vice done on a generator that failed and caused an expensive loss of frozen fish, but no such records were found. The omission raised more questions: Was the service in fact performed? Is the witness unreliable? Did the company, or its lawyer, fail to make a thorough search? Or did it destroy important records, whether intentionally or inno-cently, called spoliation of evidence?

A party who fails to respond to discovery requests, thoroughly and on schedule, may be sanctioned. Most common is an order to pay the other side's fees for bringing the dispute to court. The judge may also rule that late-produced evidence, including expert testimony, can't be introduced at trial. If a party repeatedly refuses to respond to discovery in a suit for money dam-ages, the judge may enter a "summary order" finding liability, leaving only the amount of damages for trial.

Depositions are sworn testimony, taken by the opposing lawyer in front of a court reporter. Who is deposed depends on the nature of the case and may focus on liability witnesses, damage witnesses, or both. Some witnesses are neutral, although if one side intends to call them at trial, the other might depose them to find out what they will say.

The deponent list usually includes the plaintiff and defendant, and lay and expert witnesses. In an auto accident, it might include eyewitnesses, friends and relatives to testify about changes in the plaintiff since the accident, treat-ing physicians, possibly an accident reconstructionist, medical experts, and an economist or vocational counselor to testify about wage loss and employment prospects. In a product liability case, witnesses might include the manufac-turer, distributor, and designers, design experts, and experts in fields related to the specific claims: a metallurgist in a claim involving a chain that broke and hit a young man in the eye, or experts on chemicals and chemical sensitivity in a hairdresser's claim against a product manufacturer. In a case alleging sexual harassment on the job, potential witnesses include the parties, other employees who witnessed the harassment or who will deny it happened, and the plaintiff's doctor or therapist to testify about the psychological impact on her.

Depositions are critical to both sides in finding out the facts of a case and evaluating liability and damages. They also offer the opportunity to assess a witness's credibility and jury appeal. Many a case has settled before trial because a lawyer realized in deposition that his client would not make a good impression. Depositions can be used at trial if a witness dies or is unable to testify in person for reasons specified in the rules of court, or to impeach a witness—that is, to attack her credibility by showing that she previously gave contradictory testimony.

Depositions are often filmed if the witness might not be available for trial, e.g., she's elderly or terminally ill, has travel plans, or lives out of the area. It's common to play video or DVD depositions of doctors at trial, usually because

> Many a case has settled before trial because a lawyer realized in deposition that his client would not make a good impression.

of the expense of bringing them to trial, especially if they have to travel. Some deps have an informal feel, while others are contentious.

When a lawyer walks into an expert's deposition, the first thing she does is ask to see the expert's file. This is fair game, although an appraiser I once deposed didn't think so, becoming so irate that he started yelling, stood, and lunged across the table at me. Fortunately, his arms weren't long enough. The court reporter was so alarmed that she knocked her machine over. Opposing counsel was able to calm him down and explain that I had the right to look at his file to see what data he had relied on, any changes from earlier drafts of his reports, and even his notes and billing records. (When he called a few months later to ask me to represent him in a divorce, I declined.)

TIP: A plaintiff's lawyer should also make a point of looking at the client's doctor's records in person. In doing so, we once discovered that clinic staff had not produced the complete file we asked for, deciding we only needed records they considered related to our client's back injury from an auto accident. We also learned that the plaintiff had neglected to tell us about prior surgery and that his doctor suspected the man of taking narcotics prescribed for his wife. Better to learn those things sooner than later.

Discovery may also include a site visit, such as a guided tour of a house in a construction defect case.

Discovery disputes may be resolved between counsel or go to the judge on a motion—a written request to order that specific records be provided, require the plaintiff to undergo an independent medical exam, or impose sanctions for failing to produce documents. Most are routine—a little testy, perhaps, but not ultimately affecting the outcome of the case. Some do, though, as in the cases of the service tech's log and the medical records. Failing to timely identify an expert or produce his report may mean the witness won't be allowed to testify.

A judge might sanction a defendant for failure to produce critical records by entering default judgment on liability, leaving the jury to decide only what damages will compensate the injured party.

My character is a doctor being sued for malpractice by a greedy lawyer. What standards apply? Can the doctor countersue the lawyer?

Medical malpractice claims requires proof that the doctor violated the standard of care. That is, did he use the skill and care that doctors in that field agree should have been used in such a case? Expert testimony is almost always necessary. Proof of a bad result is not enough to show malpractice.

> Proof of a bad result is not enough to show malpractice.

To prevent unnecessary malpractice suits and encourage "fair and equitable" settlements of well-founded cases, some states have established mandatory review panels. An abbreviated version of the case is first presented to a panel of doctors and lawyers, which considers whether there is "a reasonable inference" of negligence. Only after that process is complete can suit be filed. Panel decisions aren't binding, but give each side a good idea whether the case will succeed, and they often lead to early settlements.

People angry over being sued often ask if they can file claims of their own. In a "med mal" case, the answer is almost always no, because the patient will not typically have breached a duty to the doctor, unless it's to pay him. The term "countersue" refers only to suits against the person who filed the suit, and doesn't apply to a suit against the lawyer. There again, grounds don't usually exist. But if the suit was truly frivolous, your fictional doctor may be able to obtain sanctions under Rule 11 of the Federal Rules of Civil Procedure; most states have similar rules. He'll need to show that the lawyer had no reasonable factual or legal basis for filing the suit, or brought it for an "improper purpose," including harassment. Sanctions include paying the other side's attorneys' fees and litigation expenses, or paying a penalty to the court, as a deterrent.

The classic portrayal of a med mal suit is *The Verdict*, starring Paul Newman as Frank Galvin, a washed-up alcoholic lawyer who takes on a loser of a case and discovers that buried in the boxes of medical records is evidence of appalling hospital malpractice and a cover-up by the Catholic church. Galvin cleans up, dries up, falls down, falls off the wagon, and eventually redeems himself and wins the case. Along the way, he's seduced by a beautiful woman, who is sent to set him up and trick him up, and it almost works. For drama, it's hard to beat.

Can a character buy a life insurance policy on someone else, without that person's knowledge?

By federal law, insurance is left to state regulation, and, of course, local laws vary. In most states, the owner of the policy—not the beneficiaries, but the person who buys it and pays the premiums—must have an "insurable interest" in the named insured, unless the named insured or his estate is the beneficiary. An "insurable interest" typically means either being financially dependent on the named insured, or if owner and insured are closely related by blood or law, having "a substantial interest engendered by love and affection." Other financial relationships may also qualify, such as a debt from named insured to policy owner. The obvious purpose is to eliminate motives for buying insurance and knocking off the named insured to collect the booty.

A corporation can buy life insurance on its officers and directors, called "key man" insurance, and provide life insurance as part of an employee benefit package. Film producers often insure their stars, because their contractual relationship gives the producers an economic interest in the actors' life and health. In some states, charities may buy policies on named insureds who consent, as a way of providing a benefit to the charity when the insured dies, if the insured pays the premiums. A person always has an insurable interest in himself or herself.

However, the insurable interest requirement is sometimes treated as just a box to be checked on a form. In 2008, two elderly Los Angeles women, Olga Rutterschmidt and Helen Golay, were convicted of first

> Film producers often insure their stars, because their contractual relationship gives the producers an economic interest in the actors' life and health.

degree murder and conspiracy to commit murder for financial gain in the deaths of two homeless men they met at shelters, Kenneth McDavid and Paul Vados, by staging fatal accidents. Suspicion focused on the women when investigators saw similarities between the two hit-and-run deaths, which were six years apart, and discovered that the same women had purchased multiple life insurance policies on the men, collecting $2.8 million. On the applications, one woman claimed to be the man's cousin and the other his fiancée. The prosecutor described the case as "like *Arsenic and Old Lace*, except that it doesn't have Cary Grant," and the media nicknamed the two women "Black Widows."

In most states, if a married person wants to buy life insurance on his or her spouse, the spouse must sign the application or be given notice of it. Again, the public policy reason—that is, the legislative goal—is to protect the person insured from being killed for the payout. In real life, many insurance companies require medical exams or other information directly from the person to be insured. But that's the kind of plodding detail that often sinks a plot. Leave it out and let your black widows—or widowers—spin their webs.

Is an oral contract binding?

Generally, yes. The main problem with oral contracts is proof of their terms. Witness testimony, notes, and the parties' actions may be used to prove what was agreed.

Some contracts, though, are required to be in writing, by laws called the Statute of Frauds. The term is a bit of a misnomer, as the purpose of the requirement is to prevent fraud. Covered contracts include real estate sales and leases for more than a year, contracts that will not be performed within a year of agreement, agreements to guarantee another person's debts, and others. Montana requires agreements "made upon consideration of marriage other than a mutual promise to marry" to be in writing; I still haven't figured out what an agreement like that might be.

6

Some Terms of the Art

LIKE ALL FIELDS, THE LAW HAS DEVELOPED ITS own phrases that insiders use without a second thought, sometimes forgetting how strange and confusing they sound to the uninitiated. However, the legal tongue can also be fun. Here are a few common terms that, when used appropriately, will give your fiction a sense of authority and realism.

Some common terms and phrases defined

Dismissed with—or without—prejudice: When a civil or criminal complaint is dismissed, the order of dismissal expressly states that dismissal is "with prejudice" or "without prejudice."

"With prejudice" means the plaintiff or prosecution has no right to refile the case. In civil litigation, that most often occurs after the parties settle and sign releases resolving all disputes between them. The lawyers then sign a stipulation for dismissal, and the judge enters an order. In a criminal case, the prosecution rarely dismisses charges with prejudice.

"Without prejudice" means the claims can be refiled. In either a civil or criminal case, that might happen when it's clear there's insufficient evidence against the defendant right now, but discovery and investigation are continuing and the plaintiff or prosecutor wants to protect the right to refile if stronger evidence surfaces, within the time limits allowed by law.

Double indemnity: A provision in a life insurance policy that the insurance company will pay double the policy value or "indemnity" if the named insured dies in an accident. Also called an accidental death clause, the provision might be stated in the policy itself or be added by a "rider," for a premium. Accidental deaths are not common, so coverage is relatively cheap. Why buy it? It's a way to increase—double—coverage without doubling the premium, and it can be advantageous to a breadwinner with a risky occupation or hobby.

If the cause of death is unclear, particularly if it looks like suicide or murder, the insurance company may refuse to pay until an autopsy or investigation is complete. Either the insurance company or the policy beneficiaries may file a civil lawsuit to determine whether benefits should be paid.

And, of course, *Double Indemnity* is the title of the terrific 1944 movie starring Barbara Stanwyck as the woman who lures life insurance salesman Fred MacMurray into helping stage her husband's death in a fall from a train. The plot unravels as insurance investigator Edward G. Robinson gets closer, and MacMurray turns the tables on Stanwyck. It's pure noir—Raymond Chandler and director Billy Wilder wrote the screen play, based on James M. Cain's novel—and great fun.

Double jeopardy: The principle that a person may not be tried twice for the same crime, based on a clause in the Fifth Amendment to the United States Constitution:

> *...nor shall any person be subject for the same offense to be twice put in jeopardy of life or limb; ....*

Jeopardy here means risk. The bottom line is that a person who's been tried and acquitted may not be tried again on the same charges.

Note that the ban only arises when there is a "final judgment." If a mistrial is declared, e.g., for misconduct by the prosecutor or jurors, or the jury is "hung," that is, unable to agree, the accused can be retried because no judgment acquitting or convicting him was entered. The second trial is a continuation of the original proceedings. For the same reason, double jeopardy is not an issue if a conviction is reversed on appeal and the case is "remanded" (sent back) for a new trial. A judgment is not final until any appeals are completed.

> The bottom line is that a person who's been tried and acquitted may not be tried again on the same charges.

So what happens if a person is accused, tried, and acquitted, and later, clear evidence of his guilt surfaces? There are no second bites. A prosecutor's only option is to bring other charges for other crimes. If the defendant was acquitted of murder, does the new evidence establish conspiracy or kidnaping? Did a crime spree cross state lines, allowing prosecution for other crimes in another state? If the first trial was in state court for assault, charge him in federal court with civil rights violations, as with the Los Angeles police officers who beat Rodney King. Cases arising from the Civil Rights Movement, where initial charges were dropped during trial or acquittals resulted from racial bias, have been successfully revived by bringing different charges.

A strange case from Illinois, *Aleman v. Judges of the Circuit Court* (1998), shows the limits of double jeopardy protection. Harry Aleman was tried in 1977 for the 1972 murder of William Logan. Aleman waived his right to a jury, bribed the judge, and was acquitted. In 1993, two men in the Federal Witness Protection Program—a former Chicago cop and a former lawyer—testified that Aleman killed Logan and another man, and bribed the judge with $10,000. Aleman was a Mafia tax collector, and the victims had refused to pay street taxes for protection of their illegal bookmaking operations. Based on this testimony and other evidence, Illinois indicted Aleman for both murders. Aleman claimed he could not be retried on Logan's murder based on double jeopardy. The courts rejected his argument, holding that the bribery made his first trial a sham. Because the trial was fixed, Aleman had never been "in jeopardy." There had never been a risk of conviction, so the Fifth Amendment protection did not apply.

On a side note, the former lawyer testified that, during trial, the judge learned that an eyewitness had also been bribed with $10,000, and demanded more money, with no luck. In 1989, after an FBI agent informed the then-retired judge that the lawyer had become an informant and given the FBI a recording of their conversation discussing the bribery, the judge shot and killed himself.

Writers of historicals should take note that the Fifth Amendment guarantee against double jeopardy was not extended to state courts until 1969, although your story state's constitution may have provided the same protection.

Habeas corpus: This Latin phrase (HAY-bee-us KOR-pus) means "bring me the body," and it is the process allowing a person held by the government to challenge the legality of his or her custody. The right to *habeas corpus* is an important check on governmental power. It is guaranteed by the United States Constitution, Art. I, Sect. 9:

> *The privilege of the writ of habeas corpus shall not be suspended, unless when in cases of rebellion or invasion the public safety may require it.*

Historically termed "The Great Writ," *habeas* originated in English common law and arose from the rights to personal freedom recognized in the Magna Carta (1215). Parliament adopted the Habeas Corpus Act in 1679. President Lincoln suspended *habeas* during the Civil War, in order to permit the detention of rebel soldiers.

Habeas is commonly used to assert constitutional violations at trial, such as inadequate counsel or violation of the right to due process. Some states allow *habeas* challenges when bail is denied, if the denial cannot be appealed. Prisoners use it to challenge denial of good time, loss of jailhouse privileges, or lack of access to medical treatment, and in some extradition proceedings.

Habeas is used to challenge detention where there has been no criminal conviction and sentence, or to challenge the physical conditions of detention. It may not be used to attack the validity of an indictment, conviction, or sentence, unless constitutional issues are raised.

Habeas may also be used in civil proceedings involving child custody, though this is rare.

The procedure generally goes something like this:

- A person in custody files a petition seeking a writ—which is a court order commanding a government official to take specific action.

- The court reviews the petition for legal sufficiency, that is, whether the restraint would be illegal if the facts alleged are proven.

- If so, the writ is issued and the custodian must bring the petitioner to court for a hearing on the facts.

- The judge determines whether detention is illegal or conditions are unreasonable.

- The judge may order release or modify any restrictions on custody.

There may be statutory time limits for filing petitions. Abuses such as raising the same issues repeatedly have led some courts to limit the exercise of the right.

A state prison inmate participated in a demonstration and disobeyed direct orders from corrections officers. Restrictions were imposed as discipline. He petitioned for *habeas corpus,* seeking to lift the restrictions. Although he got his hearing, relief was denied because the restrictions were not "cruel and unusual" under the circumstances and officials had latitude in policies used to preserve order and discipline among inmates.

Habeas corpus petitions were filed in two much-publicized cases arising after 9/11. Both ultimately reached the U.S. Supreme Court. In *Hamdi v. Rumsfield* (2004), an American citizen taken into custody in Afghanistan challenged his detention as an "enemy combatant." The Court held that he was denied due process of the law when he was not told the grounds for his detention or given a fair opportunity to challenge it. Similarly, in *Rasul v. Bush* (2004), the Court held that

Habeas has also been sought by reporters jailed for contempt of court for refusing to disclose their sources to law enforcement or other government officials.

non-citizens from countries not at war with the United States have the right to challenge their detention and assert constitutional violations through petitions for *habeas corpus.*

Habeas has also been sought by reporters jailed for contempt of court for refusing to disclose their sources to law enforcement or other government officials.

Negligence and breach of duty: In a civil case, negligence simply means failure to use reasonable care, by acts or omissions. What is "reasonable care"? It's what an ordinarily prudent person would do under the circumstances. For example, a person may have an obligation to act in a particular way—such as the duty a driver owes his passenger to drive safely. If he fails to do so, he "breaches" his duty.

Criminal negligence, appropriately, demands proof of a higher standard. It occurs when a person consciously disregards a risk that certain things will happen—for example, if he pulls kids on an inner tube behind his truck on an icy street, the tube will hit a bump and a child will fall off and be seriously injured. Disregard for the risk becomes criminal when, by the nature of risk, disregarding it is a "gross deviation" from the standard of conduct that a reasonable person would observe in that situation. In other words, it's far greater than lack of ordinary care, the standard for civil negligence.

Pro bono: Short for *pro bono publico,* "for the public good," meaning free or reduced-fee legal services. Most state bars encourage lawyers to provide twenty to fifty hours a year of *pro bono* legal services to low-income people or groups that serve them. Some large law firms keep *pro bono* lawyers on staff, or give lawyers leave to handle significant cases *pro bono.* For example, several firms provided lawyers and staff assistance to work for the release of Guantanamo Bay detainees. Others assist projects that aid applicants for

> Some large law firms keep *pro bono* lawyers on staff, or give lawyers leave to handle significant cases *pro bono.*

asylum or prisoners seeking exoneration for wrongful convictions. *Pro bono* work also includes activities to improve the legal system and profession and to educate the public.

Pro se **or** *pro per:* Meaning "for one's self," or representing yourself. Civil plaintiffs and civil or criminal defendants can always represent themselves. Only lawyers can represent other people in judicial proceedings, although some tribal courts allow trained advocates in certain types of cases. Alternate terms are *pro per* and *in propria persona.* Check the usage in your story state.

Why do it? In civil cases, the motive is usually lack of money, or unwillingness to part with it. Often, a *pro se* plaintiff has not been able to find a lawyer who believes in the case, and the cause it espouses, as much as he does. And, sometimes, a client chooses to go it alone when he disagrees with his lawyer's advice, or thinks he's smarter.

In civil cases with a low dollar value, as in small claims court, self-representation makes sense. Judges in those courts are used to dealing with the parties directly. Think of Judge Judy's courtroom, without the cameras or melodrama.

In criminal cases, a defendant who can't afford a lawyer is entitled to a public defender. But some defendants choose to represent themselves for philosophical reasons. In the late 1980s and 1990s, anti-government folks and militia members like "the Freemen" frequently chose to represent themselves, grinding their axes by refusing to cooperate with a system they opposed.

However, in higher value disputes and in criminal cases, self-representation can be a minefield. The biggest drawback is that lay people often don't understand important legal points or some of the law's finer distinctions. As a result, making cogent arguments can be tough. *Pro se* parties get more emotional than lawyers—a good potential source of drama for writers. Imagine a custody dispute where a father pleading for a change of custody makes his own case, or a child welfare proceeding where a *pro se* mother argues that she's conquered her drug addiction and is now rehabilitated and should get her children back.

Widespread cutbacks in county law libraries make research difficult, and official on-line sources can be hard to navigate. Non-official on-line sources abound, but are not always reliable. Some sources aimed at adherents of a particular philosophy perpetuate misinformation that resurfaces over and over. Persons representing themselves often don't recognize the differences between states' laws. They may not understand that a 1937 Vermont decision interpreting a then-current statute is virtually meaningless to a modern day court in, say, California or Florida, because the law has evolved and state statutes and precedents differ. Many state bars, law libraries, and court systems now provide paid staff who help guide *pro se* litigants to the resources they need, or provide forms and other basic information online.

Pro se briefs tend to be ramble, but they can be entertaining. My personal favorite remains a brief submitted to the Washington State Court of Appeals while I clerked there. The case involved an easement and boundary line dispute. The only authorities cited were definitions from an antiquated edition of *Black's Law Dictionary* and the Bible. Of course, Ezekiel may be an authoritative source, but before a different judge.

Most judges give *pro se* parties some leeway and guidance with procedural aspects of trial. For example, the judge may point out that a *pro se* defendant is asking his own witness impermissible leading questions and suggest another way to phrase them. However, the judge is less likely to warn against a line of questioning or suggest a topic the defendant hadn't considered. Judges may suggest that the case may be more complicated than the *pro se* party thinks and that he or she really ought to consult with a lawyer; judges often continue (that is, postpone or reschedule) a hearing to give a party time to find representation.

However, no judge will ever tolerate a *pro se* party obstructing the proceedings. If your fictional *pro se* litigant disobeys a judge's order and asks prohibited questions, raises his voice once too often, or blatantly violates decorum, a warning is likely, with a threat of contempt.

Most *pro se* defendants are well-behaved, though nervous and worried about missteps. Lawyers should take extra care communicating with *pro se* parties, and most do, but the seriously hard-nosed or ill-intentioned could take unfair advantage of an unrepresented opponent. In a suit that a *pro se* backhoe operator brought against our client, a homeowner who refused to pay in full a bill triple the written estimate, I sat in the hallway outside the courtroom after a hearing and explained the details of the judge's ruling to the plaintiff. I wanted him to understand why he lost, and not blame it on "a stacked system" or say "the defendant had a slick lawyer." The next time I saw him in town, in a coffee shop, he insisted on buying my coffee as thanks.

In felonies, especially death penalty cases, courts often appoint experienced defense counsel to assist the *pro se* defendant. In *U.S. v. Moussaoui* (aka the Twentieth Hijacker), the defendant initially accepted defense at public expense, then fired his attorneys. The judge found Moussaoui competent to represent himself—he was mentally competent and of sufficient intelligence, understanding, and language skills—and appointed his former counsel to assist him. The lawyers could help him outside the courtroom with writing briefs and planning arguments and witness examination, but their role inside the courtroom was strictly limited. They sat behind him, not at counsel table. Hence the term "standby counsel."

Ted Kaczynski, the Unabomber, also accepted public defense initially, but fired his counsel when they insisted on presenting an insanity defense. The judge found that he had the requisite intelligence and understanding, but based on several psychiatric exams, was not mentally competent to represent himself. The judge's refusal to allow Kaczynski to fire his counsel and represent himself led directly to his agreement to plead guilty in exchange for not receiving the death penalty.

You've heard the old saw "a lawyer who represents himself has a fool for a client." Does the same hold true for a non-lawyer? Your story, your call. But what possibilities!

Res ipsa loquitur: Pronounced "race" or "rez" "IP-suh LO-kwit-ur," meaning "the thing speaks for itself." This is a concept in civil claims where there is no evidence of negligence (a breach of the standard of care) but negligence can be inferred because the event ordinarily does not occur without negligence and other causes have been ruled out.

A typical example: A car flies off the road and hits a power pole, killing the passenger and injuring the driver so badly that he can't remember the accident. The passenger's widow sues. There is no evidence of physical defects in the car that would have caused it to veer off the road. The only other explanation is negligence—e.g., the driver taking his eyes off the road or speeding and missing a curve—which cannot be proven without witnesses or physical evidence. That the accident happened speaks for itself, and establishes negligence. On the other hand, if the front bumper was bloody and troopers found a freshly killed buck in the road, there is evidence of the cause of the accident. *Res ipsa* would not apply, and the jury would be asked to decide whether the driver's apparent loss of control while swerving to avoid a deer was negligence.

Res judicata: Pronounced "race" or "rez" "ju-duh-KAH-ta," the phrase means "a thing adjudged." Once a matter has been decided, it cannot be litigated again. A person who has had a full opportunity to litigate an issue, whether he took the opportunity or not, may not raise the issue in a separate case against the same parties, hoping a second bite of the apple will taste better. The rule protects persons who have been sued once from repeated suits and multiple judgments over the same matter. The rule also avoids an unnecessary waste of judicial resources, sometimes described as "promoting judicial economy."

The doctrine could be used in a mystery or crime story involving an old case that's reopened after a person has already been held liable for monetary damages. The rule has some technical limits, so check further before letting your fictional characters make a career out of a lawsuit, as in Dickens' *Bleak House*.

When a law school or bar association sponsors a 10K run, it's often called *Res Judicata*. Who says lawyers don't have a sense of humor?

Voir dire: Pronounced "vwahr deer" or "vwahr dyer," the phrase means "to see and speak." The first phase of jury selection, *voir dire* is the process of questioning potential jurors. Lawyers meld the responses with other information and their own gut reactions to decide whether to challenge or accept a potential juror.

Voir dire is also the jurors' first glimpse of the facts of a case. The judge or lawyers introduce the case with a brief summary, then start their questions, which reveal some evidence and issues. A skillful lawyer selects the facts given to subtly influence the jury, using the doctrine of primacy, the tendency to remember and believe what we heard first.

Voir dire has two core purposes:

- to root out prejudgments that might prevent a fair hearing; and

- to detect beliefs and perspectives that might affect how jurors view the evidence.

Naturally, each side wants to seat jurors likely to sympathize with their

> A skillful lawyer selects the facts given to subtly influence the jury, using the doctrine of primacy, the tendency to remember and believe what we heard first.

position and tailors questions accordingly. In a vehicular homicide case fueled by alcohol, both prosecutor and defender want to know if potential jurors have been convicted of alcohol-related driving offenses, or have lost friends or relatives to drunk drivers, but they phrase their questions differently. Prosecutors look for a sense of indignation and anger. Defense lawyers often remind jurors of reasonable doubt and the presumption of innocence. Either side may engage jurors in a conversation about beliefs and attitudes.

Jurors can be "challenged" for cause, meaning a lawyer asks the judge to determine that a juror is biased and should be dismissed. Each side also gets several "peremptory" challenges—how many varies by state—that can be used to dismiss a juror without explanation. Under *Batson v. Kentucky* (1986), peremptory challenges may not be used to dismiss a juror solely because of race.

TIP: Lawyers test their arguments by viewing them from the other side. Show your prosecutor speculating about the defense perspective of the facts, or vice versa.

In some courts, potential jurors are sent questionnaires with their summons, asking general information such as age, occupation, past jury experience, and whether they've ever been a party to a case. Customized questionnaires may be sent for complex or lengthy trials, such as a product liability suit where potential jurors were asked about their experience with plumbing failures and insurance claims, or a class action suit involving an employee stock ownership plan, where jurors were questioned in advance about their knowledge of the much-publicized dispute.

In recent years, some judges, especially in federal court, have taken more control of *voir dire*. Judges often ask general questions themselves, allowing lawyers to follow up on individual responses. The move is an attempt to control the length of trial and prevent invasive or wandering questions.

In many cases, *voir dire* is complete the first morning of trial. In complex cases, jury selection takes longer. Pretrial publicity affects the length of the process: The more attention a case receives, the more jurors will be called, and the more closely they will be questioned about their knowledge of the case. The goal is not to find jurors who know nothing about the case, but to find jurors who can keep an open mind until they've heard all the evidence and seen all the witnesses. And, if a trial is expected to be lengthy, alternate jurors are also selected.

Voir dire can be daunting to conduct, but fun to watch, and it is fascinating for a writer who wants to get the details right.

Note: *Voir dire* also refers to a short Q&A, conducted by the judge or counsel, to determine a witness's competence to testify. For example, before a witness testifies about something she saw, opposing counsel may be allowed to ask foundation questions about where the witness was standing, the lighting, and her vision. Before a young child testifies, the judge may ask questions to determine his ability to understand and tell the truth.

Why is legal terminology sprinkled with Latin phrases?

For centuries in Europe, Latin was the language of scholarship. As other languages gained importance, succinct phrases not easily translated into the vernacular were left in Latin. Pronunciation differs depending on historical influences on a particular usage, so the same words or syllables may be said differently in classical Latin than in church Latin or the Latin used in law, medicine, and science—sometimes called Anglo-Latin because it reflects the influence of English pronunciation over time.

Plus, it's cool.

Illegitimi non carborundum—don't let the bastards get you down.

7

Wills, Probate, and Adoption

DEATH AND TAXES—LIFE MIGHT BE EASIER WITHOUT THEM, but we'd have a lot fewer stories to tell. In this chapter, we'll answer common questions about wills and property distribution. We'll talk briefly about common law marriage, consider the case of the mysterious safe deposit box, look at the effect of illegitimacy on inheritance, and discuss a few legal issues arising from adoption.

My character died without a will. Who decides what happens to his property?

A person who dies without a will is called "intestate"—an odd word stemming from the Latin *testare*, to make a will. State law sets out the distribution of assets for intestate persons. If he were married without children, his surviving spouse takes everything he owned in his own name. Any assets he held with another person as "joint tenants with right of survivorship" pass directly to that other person and are not part of his estate. A common example is spouses, who often own their home as joint tenants; when the husband dies, all rights pass to the wife without becoming part of his estate or subject to probate. Joint tenancy with right of survivorship is also frequently used by an elderly parent who adds a child to her accounts to make bill-paying easier, especially in emergencies. But legal problems might arise if the child uses the joint account for personal reasons. And, when the parent dies, should the remaining funds go to the child on the account, or be split with the siblings?

Intestacy gets tricky when there is a surviving spouse and children. Typically, the "spousal share" of assets is one-half, with the remaining half split equally between any minor children. That leaves any older children nothing, which can be ugly, especially in step-families. Marital property is handled differently in the nine community property states: Arizona, California, Idaho, Louisiana, Nevada, New Mexico, Texas, Washington, and Wisconsin.

"Community property" means each spouse has an undivided half-interest in earnings or property acquired by either spouse during the marriage. If your story is set in a community property state, keep in mind the differences; typically, half immediately goes to the surviving spouse, while the remaining half and any separate property are subject to intestacy laws.

If your intestate character left no surviving spouse or minor children, the estate is divided among other heirs as set out by state law: first degree relatives (parents and children) first, if they survive him, then grandparents and grandchildren, siblings, nieces and nephews, cousins, and so on. Distant relatives may sue to establish their right to inherit. How distant a relationship qualifies for inheritance varies, but the premise of those spooky gothic novels isn't too far off—it is entirely possible to inherit from a relative you didn't know existed.

> The premise of those spooky gothic novels isn't too far off—it is entirely possible to inherit from a relative you didn't know existed.

A state or county usually has a public administrator who handles estates without a legally appointed PR (personal representative, called an executor or administrator in some states) or known heirs to take control of the assets, find heirs, and handle claims against the estate, such as unpaid debts or ongoing litigation. By statute, if a stranger or someone without known heirs dies in your house, you must also give notice to the public administrator.

Assets go to the state—called "escheat"—only if there are no legal heirs, either by will or by the intestacy statutes. Potential heirs may still make a claim, usually within two to seven years. Some states, such as Washington, allow a stepchild who has not been legally adopted to inherit if doing so will prevent escheat. The idea is that the intestate person would probably have preferred the stepchild to inherit, where there are no living blood relatives, rather than give his assets to the state. States typically hold funds for potential claimants for a time specified by statute; real or personal property may be auctioned. After the time expires, the state keeps the funds for a purpose specified by statute. In some states, funds go to a trust or permanent fund for the public schools, in others to the general fund.

Do lawyers actually conduct readings of the will?

No. A will-reading scene adds drama, but not realism. The lawyer for the estate typically sends copies to the named PR and beneficiaries, although he might make copies available on request instead if there are numerous beneficiaries and the estate is small. The estate's accountant receives a copy. And copies should be sent to anyone who might challenge the will, such as relatives still living who were named in previous wills but not in the current one, or who were explicitly disinherited, to start the time clock on their right to file a challenge.

Once a probate file is opened, the will becomes part of the public record, which anyone can see—unless the judge orders it sealed, which is rare.

The wills of many famous people, including Michael Jackson, Princess Diana, Walt Disney, and Richard Nixon, are reproduced online. Janis Joplin left $2,500 for a party "as a final gesture of appreciation and farewell" to her friends. Jerry Garcia distributed his guitars. Napoleon Bonaparte got political in his will, calling his death a premature assassination "by the English oligarchy and its tool," labeling the acts of his enemies treason and calling on "the posterity of France [to] forgive them as I do," and pardoning another for a libel "replete with false assertions and falsified documents." He left his son his personal items, including his field-bed, saddles, spurs, chapel-plate, and books, and pleaded with him "never to forget that he was born a French prince," or to allow himself to be used "to oppress the nations of Europe." Richard Nixon left a large bequest to his official library, along with historical and commemorative items; he left his notes and diaries to his daughters, with instructions that they not be published, sold, or made public, and for their ultimate destruction.

The British National Archives website includes the wills of Shakespeare and Jane Austen, and a searchable website of historical wills, starting in 1348. (See Book Links.)

My character's vindictive stepmother lied to get him cut out of his father's will. How can he get his share?

He'll have to file a claim with the PR, and if it's denied, contest the will in probate court. He'll need to prove he was left out of the will through undue influence on his father or his father's mental incompetence. If the challenge succeeds, the entire will may be invalidated, or just a portion of it. The father's property will then be distributed according to the terms of an earlier valid will, if there is one, or by the laws of intestacy. Strict timelines and procedures apply.

Wills sometimes include a penalty clause, denying a person who contests the will any right to inherit. In most states, penalty clauses are unenforceable if the person had good cause for the challenge.

My character's vindictive stepchildren want to deny her any right to her husband's estate. How can she get her share?

It depends. If he left a will naming her but the children filed a challenge to exclude her or limit her share, she'll need to show that the will expressed his true intent and that he was of sound mind and not unduly influenced when he signed it. She'll need a good lawyer, her husband's medical records, and any other relevant writings (such as a letter or journal entry stating his intent to provide for her in his will). Do any witnesses support her claim, e.g., the lawyer who drafted the will, his tax and financial advisors, friends or relatives?

If he left a will excluding her, was it written before or after the marriage? In some states, a will written after marriage must state intent to exclude the spouse. The person writing the will is called the testator, sometimes testatrix for a female. He might have left her out because she had her own money, or he might have provided for her separately by gifts or a trust. Those are important facts as well.

> The person writing the will is called the testator, sometimes testatrix for a female.

And, in either case, the Uniform Probate Code, adopted with variations in most states, provides a spousal elective share. A surviving spouse may choose or "elect" to "take against the will," giving her a percentage (of up to 50 percent) that depends on the length of the marriage. In other words, she could elect to take a percentage in lieu of other rights she might have to his property.

If he left no will, of course, state intestacy laws govern. Their provisions are mandatory and neither she nor those nasty kids can get more than the state legislature provided.

What is undue influence on the terms of a will?

"Undue influence" means pretty much what it sounds like—that a person used his or her relationship to the testator to induce him to leave property a certain way. If undue influence is found, a judge can invalidate the entire will or a specific provision. However, the key here is "undue." Undue influence occurs when someone uses a confidential relationship or position of authority to take unfair advantage of the testator, effectively substituting his or her intent for the testator's. The judge considers the nature of the relationship, the testator's mental and physical condition at the time, his ability to withstand influence, whether the will or provision distributes assets in a way that shows influence or mental unbalance, and any other relevant circumstances, like education, literacy, and isolation. A close relationship between a testator and a beneficiary not related by blood or law is not enough to show undue influence. The person challenging the will has the burden of proving undue influence.

Here's a typical scenario: an elderly widow executes a will leaving her property equally to her two children. A few years later, while living with her, her son takes her to a new lawyer to write a will leaving everything to him. After her death, the daughter challenges the second will, claiming undue influence. Her doctors, nurses, and friends testify that she suffered severe dementia and physical problems, no longer remembered that she had a daughter, and did not know how much property she had. The court finds undue influence and accepts the previous will. In other cases, unscrupulous friends and relatives have taken advantage of people with dementia, paranoia, deteriorating ability to understand English, and other vulnerabilities to get them to change their wills, increasing a small bequest or leaving everything to someone not previously named in the will and excluding close relatives. Tragic, but not uncommon. In short, a writer's dream.

What does "of sound mind" really mean?

A testator must have sufficient mental capacity at the time he signs a will to generally understand the nature and extent of his property, what making a will means, and the names and his relationship to the people affected by his will. Such people are sometimes referred to as "the natural objects of his affection," such as relatives by blood or law (that is, by marriage or adoption). To challenge a will on grounds of mental capacity, your character will need to show the testator was lacking in at least one of those areas.

For example, can she show that because of Alzheimer's disease or a brain injury, her father no longer knew he had a daughter or had formed inaccurate ideas about her that led him to exclude her from the will? She'll need evidence from his doctors, caregivers, friends, or other relatives. Did the lawyer who drafted the will and the witnesses lack knowledge of his mental status? A person may appear competent at some times but not at others—the question is whether he actually was competent at the time he signed the will.

> A person may appear competent at some times but not at others—the question is whether he actually was competent at the time he signed the will.

My character's late husband did not rewrite his will after they married. What rights does she have as surviving spouse?

In most states, if a testator remarries after executing a will, the surviving spouse will be entitled to inherit, as if he had died intestate, any assets not specifically left to a child who is not a child of them both. An illustration: Art wrote a will leaving two-thirds of his estate to his only child, Brian, and one-third in various individual and charitable bequests. Art then married Connie, who is not Brian's mother. Art died without changing his will. Brian's share of Art's estate is untouched. The laws of intestacy apply to the remaining one-third. How much of that third Connie receives depends on state law, including whether it's a community property state.

But if Art specifically left everything to Brian, Connie's only remedy would be to elect the spousal share we talked about above. If you want her left with nothing but anger and a motive for revenge, tie up Art's property in other ways or leave so little cash that she feels destitute.

Who can witness a will?

Anyone over eighteen and legally competent can witness a will. In some states, a beneficiary can't be a witness; in other states, that's not a problem. Some testators bring friends with them to serve as witnesses. Often, law office staff are called in to listen while the lawyer reviews the will with the testator or asks questions to establish that it's his will, his intent, and so on. The testator's signature block looks something like this:

> I, ..., the testator, sign my name to this instrument this ......
> day of ...., 20..., and being first duly sworn, do hereby declare to the
> undersigned authority that I sign and execute this instrument as my
> will, that I sign it willingly (or willingly direct another to sign for me),
> that I execute it as my free and voluntary act for the purposes expressed
> in it, and that I am 18 years of age or older, of sound mind, and under
> no constraint or undue influence.

Most wills are "self-proving," meaning that when the will is admitted to probate, it's not necessary to call the witnesses to testify that the testator signed the will in front of them, and so on. The witness signature clause includes a statement like this:

> We, _____, and _____, the witnesses, sign our
> names to this instrument, being first duly sworn, and do hereby declare
> to the undersigned authority that the testator signs and executes this
> instrument as the testator's will, that the testator signs it willingly (or

willingly directs another to sign for the testator), that each of us, in the presence and hearing of the testator, hereby signs this will as witness to the testator's signing, and that to the best of our knowledge the testator is 18 years of age or older, of sound mind, and under no constraint or undue influence.

The signatures should be notarized.

Are handwritten wills enforceable?

A handwritten will is enforceable in about half the states if it meets all the requirements of a will—that is, it's in writing, signed, and witnessed. In other words, a will need not be typed to be valid. The handwriting need not be the testator's, so long as he signed it or directed its signature for him. The same rule applies to revocations or amendments, often called codicils.

Under the Uniform Probate Code, a handwritten will is valid if the material provisions, which specify who gets what assets, are written and signed by the testator. No witnesses are required. Some states previously required a handwritten will not witnessed to be entirely in the testator's handwriting, and a few still do. These wills are called holographic, meaning all in one handwriting. Some people mistakenly refer to any handwritten will as holographic.

Some states recognize handwritten wills only if the testator is on active duty military and for a specific period of time (usually a year) after his return from duty. A few states that usually don't recognize handwritten wills do so if the will was executed in a state that does recognize them.

Handwritten wills and codicils are often executed in emergencies. Real-life examples include miners trapped underground, airplane crash victims who survived the crash but died before rescue, and others who reach death's doorstep rapidly. Veteran broadcaster Charles Kuralt handwrote a letter to the woman with whom he'd had a secret, thirty-year relationship, from the hospital, saying he would "have the lawyer visit the hospital to make sure you inherit" certain property. He died two weeks later, without calling the lawyer. His estate characterized the letter as a statement of future intent, but the court recognized it as a valid codicil intended to amend his earlier will and gave her the property.

How is a provision in a will leaving money for the care of a pet carried out?

Obviously, pets can't inherit directly. It's hard to manage money when you've got a paw instead of a thumb. The most common method to provide for a pet after the testator's death is to designate a caretaker and make a specific bequest to that person for the pet's care. Make sure, though, that the caretaker has agreed to take the animal, so the pet isn't left in limbo during probate. The PR may advance funds for the pet's routine or special care while probate is still pending—that is, before the estate "closes" and final distributions are made.

If the will says, "I leave $2,500 for the care of my Rottweiler, Bruno," without designating a caretaker, the PR will need to find one. The PR may choose to pay the bequest directly to the caretaker, especially if it's small, or to set up a trust if it's a large sum. If the animal predeceases the testator, or dies before the estate is closed, the PR must leave any unused funds in the estate, to be distributed by its terms, unless the will designates that any unused funds go elsewhere, such as to an animal charity.

Alternatively, the testator could set up a trust for the pet's care, independent of the will. That way, funds are available immediately. "Pet trusts" are an emerging area of the law. California's pet trust statute took effect in 2009, and allows for the creation of legally enforceable trusts for the life of the pet. In other states, a traditional trust is created, with a trustee who manages the funds and a caretaker who is the designated beneficiary; they may be the same person or not.

Numerous shelters now specialize in caring for animals who have been provided for. It's a situation ripe for humor, but also, alas, for potential abuse.

Hotelier Leona Helmsley, sometimes called "the Queen of Mean," left $12 million in trust for her Maltese dog, Trouble, when she died in 2007, although a judge later reduced Trouble's share to $2 million. She also specified that he be buried next to her in the family mausoleum. She designated a large chunk of a charitable trust to animal welfare groups; the trustees reduced that amount to $1 million, mostly for service dog training, and gave the remaining $135 million of her estate to other charities, prompting a lawsuit by several animal welfare groups seeking half.

In my story, a husband and wife were killed in a double homicide. Their wills left all their property to each other. What happens to the property?

Most wills include a survivorship clause providing that if the spouse does not survive the testator by a specified length of time, e.g., twenty-four or seventy-two hours, the testator's assets will be distributed as if the spouse had predeceased him. In most states, by statute, any heir (not just a spouse) who does not survive the decedent by a specified time is treated as predeceasing him; the statute kicks in if the will does not include a survivorship clause or there is no will.

So, in this case, if there was a survivorship clause and both spouses died within the time specified in the clause, each spouse's property passes according to the terms of his or her will, as if he or she had no spouse. Many couples own their homes and primary bank accounts in joint tenancy with rights of survivorship; in this case, her half of the jointly owned property goes to her legal heirs, along with all her separate property, e.g., bank accounts, cars, real or personal property, business interests held in her own name. Likewise for him. The result is the same in community property states.

If the wills had no survivorship clause, or they left no wills, the state statute controls.

What looked like a double homicide turns out to be a murder-suicide. How is the property distributed then?

Same result. Most states have statutes prohibiting a murderer from inheriting from his victims, but don't prohibit a murderer's heirs from inheriting from him. An illustration: Jason and Kara are married. Jason kills Kara, then turns the gun on himself and dies a few hours later. Both wills include a survivorship clause. Since neither survived the other for the requisite time, their assets are distributed according to their wills but as if unmarried. So, say Kara's will left half her assets to Jason, one-quarter to her daughter Lindsay, who is not Jason's child, and one-quarter to her daughter Meghan, who is Jason's child. Because Jason is treated as predeceasing Kara, her assets are split evenly between her daughters, Lindsay and Meghan. Jason's will left half his assets to Kara, one-quarter to Meghan, and one-quarter to his sister Nicole. Meghan and Nicole split the pot.

Either Lindsay or Meghan could sue Jason's estate for wrongful death on behalf of Kara and for personal injury on behalf of themselves. If Lindsay files suit and proves that Jason killed Kara, she may be awarded both her mother's damages, such as lost income and pain and suffering between the time of the shooting and death, and her own, for loss of the relationship with her mother and her own grief. If Lindsay is a minor, her damages will be greater than if she were an adult. Damages awarded to her come out of Jason's estate, reducing or even eliminating the amount available to Meghan and Nicole. Meghan could also sue Jason's estate for her mother's death and her own losses; any damage award would likewise reduce the value of the estate, including both her own inheritance and Nicole's.

What are the duties of a personal representative?

A personal representative (sometimes called an executor or administrator) is the person legally appointed to settle an estate. Although a testator may name a PR, the judge ultimately makes the appointment. If the named PR and alternate are unable or unwilling to serve, or no will was left, state law may specify the order of priority for appointment, e.g., the spouse, the parent of any minor children, an adult child, a parent, or a sibling.

Minimum requirements vary by state, but minors and felons may not serve. PRs must have sufficient mental and physical capacity. Some states require residency, while others don't. Banks and trust companies may be appointed if authorized in that state. Attorneys often serve as PRs.

If your character leaves a will, he should name as PR someone able to handle legal and financial matters fairly and efficiently. The PR must protect the beneficiaries' interests, resolve any conflicts, organize documents that may be hard to find or which have been left in disarray, and understand financial matters and make decisions. Hard feelings sometimes arise when a family member PR makes decisions that seem unfair to other relatives, who may not understand that the PR is required to enforce the terms of the will and follow the law, whether the results seem fair or not. Choose the responsible businessman son or the detail-loving paralegal daughter over the drug-addicted spendthrift, even if he was once a CPA—that is unless you are looking to set up family conflict. Be sure the PR agrees in advance to serve to avoid problems later, unless those problems will further your story.

In essence, an estate is a legal entity and the PR runs it. The estate is responsible for all the decedent's financial and legal obligations. The PR locates the will and other important documents, like bank records and insurance policies. She may open a checking account to pay final medical bills, utilities, and other expenses—and provide for the immediate needs of dependents. She'll need to carry out specific bequests made in the will, making sure Stacy gets Grandma's wedding ring and Sarah gets the ruby necklace, that $5,000 goes to the local Humane Society to build a new cathouse, and that money left for a party be spent on a party. She'll need to deal with personal property not addressed in the will. If the testator owned a home or other real estate, getting it cleaned out and sold can take a lot of time. The PR becomes the temporary overseer of businesses the testator owned, and may need to make arrangements for their sale or transfer, while supervising their continued operation.

> In essence, an estate is a legal entity and the PR runs it. The estate is responsible for all the decedent's financial and legal obligations.

A major part of the PR's responsibilities is to ensure that taxes are properly paid. She'll probably work with an accountant and estate lawyer. She may also need to bring or continue litigation on behalf of the estate; particulars depend on state law. For example, if the decedent was killed in an auto accident, the PR may file a wrongful death action on behalf of the decedent and a survival action on behalf of the heirs. If the decedent was already party to a lawsuit, the estate is substituted as a party, and the PR makes the necessary decisions.

The PR also handles the statutory obligations of probate while working with the estate lawyer, such as publishing notices to potential creditors, making the initial determination whether to accept or deny claims against the estate, and responding to any legal challenges to the will.

Wills should specify how the PR is to be paid, make a bequest in lieu of payment, or refer to the institution's standard fee schedule for banks or trust companies. If no provision is made, state law governs payment. It may be a percentage of the value of the estate, an hourly rate, or some other "reasonable fee" set by the court. A PR may be paid extra for additional services, such as running a business. If the PR is a beneficiary, she may be better off declining payment and avoiding income tax.

What is a common-law marriage, and is it legal?

Be careful about that "common-law" characterization. Many people have the misconception that if a couple lives together for a certain number of years, they magically become married in the eyes of the law. Common-law marriage has specific requirements. It is recognized in Alabama, Colorado, Iowa, Kansas, Montana, Rhode Island, South Carolina, Texas, and Utah, and in the District of Columbia. About two dozen states have abolished it, and some have never recognized it.

Generally speaking, common-law marriage requires that each person intend to be married and have legal capacity to marry—that is, they are of legal age and not already married. Some states require cohabitation, representing themselves as married, or consummation. Intent is demonstrated by the circumstances as a whole—e.g., holding a ceremony, referring to each other as husband and wife, wearing wedding rings, using the same last name, and so

> Common-law marriage requires that each person intend to be married and have legal capacity to marry.

on, although there's no one definitive criterion. As one court said, marriage can't just sneak up on you.

Common-law marriage isn't distinct from legal marriage—it's simply another way to become legally married. The traditional way, with a license and a proceeding before a judge or clergy member, is called solemn, ceremonial, or statutory marriage. If a couple forms a common-law marriage in one state and then moves to another, they are legally married in the second state, even if it does not allow common-law marriages to be formed there. Similarly, a couple who formed a common-law marriage in a state that later abolished it (e.g., Ohio, which abolished it in 1991, or Pennsylvania, in 2005) is still legally married in all states.

Intent to be married will not create a marriage the state would not recognize. So, it's not a way for same-sex couples to legally marry in states that do not recognize same-sex marriage.

Common-law marriage typically becomes an issue after one spouse dies and the other tries to establish the marriage and claim a share of the estate. Other beneficiaries, such as the decedent's adult children, may protest. New Hampshire allows common-law marriage claims only in that situation.

By the way, there is no common-law divorce. To legally end a common-law marriage, a couple must go through regular divorce proceedings. Of course, many don't, but it can be necessary in resolving property and custody disputes.

(For sources of specifics on state marriage and divorce laws, see Book Links.)

My character finds a safe deposit box key in her late aunt's desk drawer. How can she find the box and get access to it?

Most keys, and the cute little envelopes they come in, don't identify the institution where the box is held, for the box holder's safety. The best tracing method is the process of elimination. Start with banks or credit unions where you know the person had an account, then move out geographically to places where she could have kept an account. If no luck locally, where did she last live? Did she travel to another community regularly?

Of course, most institutions will confirm that a person had a box only to the legally appointed PR of an estate or guardian of a person still living, or to their lawyer. Access requires signatures, so the PR will need a court order showing her appointment in order to allow the institution to transfer ownership and access to her. But a character certainly might try to obtain access, using a clever cover story.

My firm once handled the estate of a migrant orchard worker who died intestate. Initially, he appeared to have little more than a few cherry-stained clothes and a white pickup—and a key to a safe deposit box, which contained the key to another, which contained another, and on it went. Ultimately, we discovered several wives, numerous children, and real property in three states. Of course, truth is stranger than fiction because fiction has to make sense, but if you're alert to the technical details, estate and probate problems can make riveting plots.

Are adopted children treated differently by the laws of inheritance than biological children?

Generally, no. Once an adoption decree is entered, the child has a full legal relationship with the adopting parents and no longer has a legal relationship with the biological parents. This means that an adopted child inherits from the legal—that is, adopting—parents, grandparents, and other relatives just as any biological relative would.

Despite that, some states allow adopted children continued inheritance rights from biological relatives. Kansas, Louisiana, Rhode Island, Texas, and Wyoming allow adopted children to inherit from biological parents after the decree is entered, but bar the biological parents from inheriting from the children. Alaska, Idaho, Illinois, and Maine allow all inheritance rights to continue if provided in the adoption decree. In Pennsylvania, adopted children may inherit from biological relatives other than parents—a biological grandparent or aunt, for example—if the relative has maintained a familial relationship with the child, as in open adoptions and stepparent adoptions. About a dozen states provide that a child adopted by a stepparent may still inherit from the biological parent whose relationship is terminated by the adoption. For example, Alan and Becca have a child, Cari; they divorce and Becca marries Dan, who adopts Cari. Cari may inherit from Alan, Becca, or Dan, if any of them dies intestate.

Most states' statutes provide that children not named in a will because adopted (or born) after the will was signed will be treated the same as children born earlier. If the will says "all my assets go to my children, Ethan and Frank," the after-adopted (or after-born) child Ginger will get an equal share, unless it's clear from other evidence that Ginger was left out intentionally or was provided for outside the will.

For state-by-state specifics on adoption, child abuse and neglect, and child welfare laws, consult the amazing database on the U.S. Department of Health and Human Services Child Welfare Information Gateway site, or the Cornell University Legal Information Institute tables. (See Book Links.)

How can my adopted character get access to adoption records and find out who her biological parents are?

State laws and procedures on access to adoption records vary widely, have changed considerably over time, and may depend in part on how records were kept at the time of adoption.

Nonidentifying information is usually given to the adopting parents at the time of adoption. It may be a one-page checklist, or as for a friend adopted in California in the early 1950s, a lengthy social services report, prepared at the time of adoption. The report summarizes her birth parents' "social history," including race, ethnicity, and religion, gives a general physical description including age and eye and hair color, and summarizes their education, employment, family background, relationship, and medical histories. It also gives a summary of the pregnancy and birth, and presents the reasons given for placing her for adoption. All names had been redacted. In small communities, or where the adopted child has other information, such as photographs, letters, or other relatives' names, the report may provide enough to start a successful investigation.

If not provided at the time of adoption, a parent or child can request the information later, though some states do not allow requests by minors. A handful—California, Idaho, Nevada, and New Jersey—restrict requests to adoptive parents. If your character's adopting parents are no longer alive, she may need a court order to give her access; if they are alive but oppose her search, she'll need to try another route. Some states maintain registries to handle all requests for information. A few require a court order. Others allow adoptive parents to ask the registry to contact birth parents for additional medical information when necessary. All contact is confidential, unless the two sets of parents agree otherwise.

Identifying information is available in most states through registries and may contain names, a copy of the original birth certificate, unredacted social and medical information, and last known contact information, including any changes in the birth mother's name. The birth parents may consent to have contact information provided if the child requests it. Of course, it may not be current, leading the child on a hunt. If there's no record of consent, the child may seek a court order allowing release of files; typically, that requires "good cause," such as a need for medical information or another compelling reason that outweighs the right to confidentiality. Some states maintain mutual consent registries, where adopted children and birth parents sign up voluntarily, indicating whether they are or aren't willing to have contact information provided if ever requested. Other states default in favor of disclosure, unless nondisclosure is specifically requested. Some use confidential intermediaries to make contact and convey disclosure requests.

A few states, including Arkansas, Mississippi, South Carolina, and Texas, mandate counseling for adopted children who request information about the possible consequences of search and contact with the birth family. About two-thirds also allow biological siblings access to records. For links to state laws, see Book Links.

Can my character's illegitimate grandchild inherit his fortune?

Yes. Illegitimacy is no longer a bar to inheritance. Obviously, questions about paternity may arise, and are answered by the usual suspects: testimony, written records, and, if necessary, DNA evidence.

In a series of decisions ending with *Trimble v. Gordon* (1971), the U.S. Supreme Court held that state statutes preventing illegitimate children from inheriting violated the children's constitutional rights to equal protection. In *Trimble*, the challenge was to an Illinois law allowing illegitimate children to inherit from their mothers, but not from their paternal line. The Court held that limiting children's inheritance rights did not reasonably serve the state's purpose of promoting legal family relationships. In other words, punishing children does not prevent parental sins. Many states had already reached the same conclusion and changed their laws. For stories involving earlier inheritances, check when your story state changed its law.

TIP: Family secrets often emerge at deathbeds, funerals, or reunions. A previously undisclosed adoption, a claim of incest, or a claim that a much-younger child is the illegitimate child of an older child can surface unexpectedly, creating new conflicts and motives.

Illegitimate children had more rights at some times and in some countries than in others. Questions about legitimacy and inheritance can be important elements of plot in historicals—think of many of Shakespeare's plays. Henry Fielding's *The History of Tom Jones: A Foundling* (1749) is the story of an illegitimate child left on a rich man's doorstep. Legitimacy also plays a part in Jane Austen's *Emma* (1815), Nathaniel Hawthorne's *The Scarlet Letter* (1850), Charles Dickens' *Bleak House* (1853), Dorothy L. Sayers' *The Nine Tailors* (1934)—perhaps reflecting Sayers' own experience as an unmarried mother—and John Irving's *The World According to Garp* (1982). And the real-life story of Hank Williams' daughter Jett combines an adopted child's search for information, an illegitimate child's fight to establish the right to inherit, the rights of a posthumously-born child, and fraud, by relatives who intentionally suppressed a written agreement Hank made to take care of the baby and who kept all information about it from her and her adoptive parents.

8

Legal Miscellany

IN THIS CHAPTER, WE DISCUSS SEVERAL ISSUES WITH great story potential: what hospitals can reveal about injured persons, missing persons and those who return from being missing, public records, and the legal obligations of real estate sellers and agents to disclose the criminal history of a house and neighborhood. We'll also look at diplomatic immunity—a spicy ingredient in international thrillers as well as local crime stories—and wrap up with a look at repressed memories.

Can hospitals give law enforcement officers personal information about the condition of victims and suspects injured in a crime?

Hospitals can provide medical information to law enforcement officers in several specific situations. The federal law called HIPAA—the Health Insurance Portability and Accountability Act—sets strict rules for privacy in medical records and information. Hospitals may disclose private information about patients to law enforcement officers without authorization *for law enforcement purposes*, but not to the public or media. Disclosures may include a patient's name, age, sex, race, birth date and Social Security number, physical or mental health condition (including blood alcohol content or BAC), what health care has been provided, and where the patient is hospitalized.

"Law enforcement purposes" include:

- information required by law, including court orders, warrants, and subpoenas—this information may later become part of the public record if charges are filed;

- information needed to identify or locate a suspect, fugitive, material witness, or missing person;

- information about a victim or suspected victim of a crime—this can aid investigations and help prosecutors determine what charges to file, e.g., whether the injuries warrant charging felony or misdemeanor assault;

- alerting law enforcement of a death, if the hospital suspects that criminal activity caused the death;

- when the hospital believes the information is evidence of a crime that occurred on its premises; and

- in a medical emergency not on hospital premises, such as when nursing staff leave the hospital on a rescue helicopter mission, if this is necessary to inform law enforcement about a possible crime, or the location, victims, or perpetrator of a crime.

Disclosures to law enforcement officers are to be limited to the minimum necessary. Hospital staff can rely on officers' statements about what information is needed.

Federal law provides a minimum, or floor-level, of protection of individual privacy. State laws are preempted unless they provide greater protection. An example: State law might preclude disclosure of a sexual assault victim's "survivor kit" or "rape kit" without written consent from the victim or the parent of a minor victim—an issue not addressed by HIPAA.

When can a missing person be declared dead? And what if he comes back to life?

State law sets out the requirements for declaring a person dead without a death certificate. This can happen in several ways:

- Where there is a certified or authenticated copy of a record of a governmental agency, domestic or foreign, that a person is dead, e.g., an Indian police report documenting that a specific American was killed in an attack on a Mumbai hotel. The record is *prima facie* ("at first appearance") evidence of the death, but can be rebutted with contradictory evidence.

- Where there is clear and convincing evidence—the civil standard of proof—of death. That is, the facts, direct or circumstantial, show that the person is probably dead. After the September 11, 2001 attacks, New Jersey changed its laws to allow death certificates to be issued in any case certified by the governor as a catastrophe involving loss of life, if the person's subsequent absence is not otherwise explained. Pennsylvania and Virginia made similar revisions, referring specifically to the 9/11 attacks. In New York, the change occurred by court ruling. Other states have made similar changes to address apparent death from future catastrophes. In other cases, death has been declared based on evidence of a specific "peril" likely to have killed the person, as with adventurer Steve

Fossett, who flew alone over the Nevada desert on September 3, 2007, and was declared dead on February 15, 2008.

- A person is presumed dead if he is absent for a specified time (seven years in most states, five in others, and four in Georgia and Minnesota), has not been heard from, and his absence has not been satisfactorily explained after a diligent search and investigation. He is presumed to have died at the end of that period, unless there's good reason to presume death occurred earlier; this affects life insurance, Social Security benefits, and other payouts.

The procedure for declaring a person dead, called "death in absentia," generally starts with a petition by an "interested person," such as a spouse or life insurance company, to a court in the state where the person is last known to have lived or is believed to have died. The petition states the facts and attaches supporting documentation, such as the governmental report if that's the proof, other evidence establishing or suggesting death, or the investigation supporting a presumption of death. All information must be admissible, i.e., certified copies of public records, affidavits of persons with knowledge, and so on.

The investigation should thoroughly probe the circumstances of the disappearance, including contacting everyone likely to have heard from the missing person—friends, relatives, or business associates, a review of financial records for recent or suspicious activity, and checking out any reported sightings or other contact.

Notice of the proceeding is published in the newspaper of record for the place where the person last lived or disappeared, that is, the newspaper legally designated for publishing official notices. Contradictory evidence can also be submitted, e.g., sightings, communications, or behavior by beneficiaries that suggests the missing person disappeared by choice. A life insurance company, for example, might contest a request for a declaration of death by showing that the missing insured was a fugitive or had marital or money troubles, a boat or airplane disappeared with him, or he had untraceable foreign assets.

> A life insurance company might contest a request for a declaration of death by showing that the missing insured was a fugitive or had marital or money troubles.

"Death in absentia" procedures provide a way to solve the legal and financial limbo caused when someone disappears. Is the wife a widow? Can she claim Social Security benefits for herself and any minor children? Legally remarry?

Claim his life insurance benefits? What happens to civil or criminal actions against him? What happens to his business, debts, real estate, and other assets? Once a person is declared dead, his estate is distributed as if he were dead, i.e., by will or intestacy.

But what if the evidence was flawed, or the wrong conclusions were drawn, and the once-dead returns? He must prove he's who he says he is and obtain a court order revoking the declaration of death. If his "estate" has already been distributed, there might be little left for him to claim, although in some states, heirs must repay what they received. If he's suspected of fraud—faking his death to obtain money, escape a debt, or the like—he can be charged criminally or sued civilly. In the movie *Cast Away*, with Tom Hanks, the protagonist should have died, but didn't, and persevered to not only survive but find his way home. In real life, people who have faked their own deaths (committed "pseudocide") have returned voluntarily to visit a sick parent or child, tired of greener pastures, or been located by determined law enforcement or private investigators.

> People who have faked their own deaths (committed "pseudocide") have returned voluntarily to visit a sick parent or child.

"The living dead," as Tulane University law professor Jeanne Carriere calls them, walk among us. The NCIC, the FBI data clearinghouse, receives hundreds of thousands of missing persons reports each year; while many are ultimately resolved, many are not.

Thomas Perry's *Dance for the Dead* opens with a proceeding to declare a missing child dead, but Jane Whitefield knows he's alive, and she intends to keep him that way.

Numerous books offer guidance on disappearing and creating new identities. A sample probate court petition for declarations of presumed death, from Georgia, is listed in the Book Links section. If your story involves a claim for insurance benefits after a disappearance, take a look at "The Missing Insured and the Life Insurance Death Claim," by a retired insurance company executive. (See Book Links.)

What public records can my character find legally? What's online?

Your character may be an amateur or semi-pro sleuth, or a private investigator, digging for dirt on a person, a company, or a piece of property. Make sure she stops at the local courthouse and goes online at state and local government agency websites. Department names vary, but here's a sample of records typically available:

Local government records:

Clerk of Court's office:

- files for current civil and criminal litigation, unless sealed, including divorces, custody proceedings, and probates. Check courts of both general and limited jurisdiction (described in Chapter 1). Some state courts make filings available online. Federal court records are available online through the PACER system.

- closed files, usually archived but available on request;

- restraining orders;

- child support liens filed against real or personal property. Support liens against motor vehicles are filed with the state Department of Motor Vehicles.

- marriage licenses issued and divorces and annulments granted;

- daily dockets for each judge, listing scheduled trials and hearings.

Clerk and Recorder's office:

- registered judgments;

- liens, including mortgages, against real and personal property;

- plat rooms, home to official certificates of survey, subdivision plats, easements, and records of property ownership and transfer. In many counties, older records are still kept in oversized, leather-bound, dust-covered ledgers with faded ancient penmanship.

Property Tax Department (often part of a county treasurer's office):

- property tax info—owners of record and mailing addresses, appraised or assessed value, taxes paid or owing. In all but a few states, sales prices are also public.

- delinquent real and personal property taxes.

Planning and Zoning office:

- GIS maps, showing subdivisions, zoning, information about individual parcels (assessor numbers, owners, size, tax records), districts (zoning, school, fire, water/sewer, transportation, voting, and so on), geographic features, and more;

- applications for subdivision approval, zoning changes, building permits and inspection records where required, and supporting documents. While a list of applications and permits may be on line, physical files typically require in-person review.

Law enforcement (sheriff or police department):

- public jail roster, adults only (name, booking date, charges);
- outstanding warrants;
- "most wanted list": suspects who can't be located, bail jumpers, and more.

Health Department:

- food and beverage health inspection reports.

Other local records:

- Agendas and minutes of official meetings of councils and boards, e.g., City Council, Planning Board, Board of Adjustment, Sanitation Board, and records of their actions;
- business licenses, where required.

State records:

State Department of Corrections:

- Sex and violent offender registries;
- prisoner database with release dates.

Secretary of State:

- business entities: name, type (corporation, partnership, etc.), status (e.g., active, inactive, voluntarily dissolved, administratively dissolved), relevant dates, where incorporated, registered agent name and address. Ownership, names of officers, and articles of incorporation are also available in some states.
- Uniform Commercial Code (UCC) filings on secured transactions.

Insurance Commissioner's Office:

- licensed sales agents and producers;
- insurance carrier rate and revenue filings and other mandated reports;
- current and resolved legal actions against agents and carriers.

Auditor's or Securities Office:

- licensed securities dealers and firms;
- current and resolved legal actions against dealers and firms, including cease and desist orders.

Board of Pardons and Parole:

- pardon and parole dispositions;
- parole violators at large, including date of warrant and crimes.

Other state records:

- winning Lottery numbers;
- hazardous waste sites and cleanup status;
- appellate court dockets and records, including briefs and attached documents, and opinions. Some other court records may be available.
- registered contractors;
- professional and occupational licensing, including disciplinary action;
- delinquent taxpayer list (state taxes);
- unclaimed property search services.

Department and agency websites also include forms and information requests of all kinds.

TIP: Your private investigator may subscribe to specialized databases that provide additional info or compile public records for easy searching. Some restrict access to licensed investigators and claims adjusters, mortgage lenders, lawyers, and law enforcement personnel.

As always, check your locale for specifics. In my experience, the staff in these offices are some of the most helpful people around.

Are real estate sellers and agents required to disclose crimes committed in the house? What about known sex offenders living nearby?

General principles of contract law require sellers and real estate agents to disclose to prospective buyers any knowledge they have about the property that would be "material" to a buyer, that is, information likely to affect a buyer's decision. Obvious examples might include a leaky roof, a faulty septic system, a toxic spill from a prior commercial use that's never been addressed. What about knowledge that a neighbor is a convicted pedophile, or that a previous owner committed suicide in the house? Yes, it's material and should be disclosed because it presents a risk, involves a "creep factor," and might create a stigma affecting property values. However, disclosure applies only to known information, not suspicion or rumor.

As we discussed in Chapter 4, the demand for public disclosure of registered sex offenders grew in the 1990s. The federal version of Megan's Law, enacted in 1996, requires all states to make information about registered sex offenders public.

So, how do sellers' and agents' disclosure obligations mesh with registries? Real estate agents can't know every detail about a property, and it's not reasonable to require them to continually check registries to see if an offender has moved into a neighborhood where they have a listing. And, agents shouldn't face potential liability for conveying registry information that might not be accurate, inadvertently costing a client a sale or harming a neighbor's reputation. Many states solve these problems by requiring agents to provide notice that information about sexual and violent offenders is available through government registries. But if an agent has actual knowledge of information related to that property, from a registry or another source, he or she is obligated to speak up.

Owners and managers of rental property may be required to make similar disclosures.

Some states require sellers, when listing property, to disclose any deaths that occurred in the home, whether natural or violent.

> Some states require sellers to disclose any deaths that occurred in the home, whether natural or violent.

Be aware that not every state has addressed this issue. In states requiring disclosure, and in some that don't, standard forms for listings, buy-sells, and leases now include disclosures.

Registries inevitably contain errors and gaps. Some buyers or tenants may rely on them and cross a property off their list, while others might mistakenly think they've avoided danger. Or a home may be stigmatized by inaccurate or out-of-date information.

Do disclosure requirements limit sales or rentals? No doubt. I would not have rented an isolated basement apartment had I known the attack on one of my law school classmates the year earlier occurred in an apartment up front, one with immediate neighbors and more visibility. A male renter might not have been concerned. The legislatures made the policy judgment that the benefits of disclosure outweigh the potential harm.

Susie Salmon of Alice Sebold's *The Lovely Bones* might never have met her killer had registries and disclosure requirements existed in 1973. How will changes in the law change your story?

In my story, a foreign national affiliated with his country's embassy is suspected of murder. Can he claim diplomatic immunity?

His right to claim immunity depends on the circumstances of the crime, his position, and the relationship between the host and home countries. If the alleged crime is connected with official business, his home country will likely invoke immunity and recall him, although he may be tried at home. If the crime is clearly outside the scope of his work, the home country may still invoke immunity and recall him, or it may waive immunity and allow the host country to try him.

Diplomatic immunity is grounded in the need to protect official representatives of foreign countries from harassment. The U.S. State Department emphasizes that "[t]he purpose of these privileges and immunities is not to benefit individuals but to ensure the efficient and effective performance of their official missions on behalf of their governments." Diplomatic immunity is governed by the Vienna Conventions of 1961 and 1963; some countries have additional bilateral treaties. The conventions and treaties bar host countries from forcing diplomatic staff to appear in court, although they require staff to obey host countries' laws. Host

> Diplomatic immunity is grounded in the need to protect official representatives of foreign countries from harassment.

countries must also protect diplomatic personnel and property, as Iran failed to do when the American embassy was invaded and hostages were taken in 1979.

Degrees of protection vary. According to the State Department chart of diplomatic and consular privileges and immunities, "diplomatic agents" and administrative and technical staff and their immediate families cannot be arrested, detained, subpoenaed, or prosecuted, although they can be issued traffic tickets. Service staff, on the other hand, are protected only from prosecution for official acts, and their families have no immunity. Consular officers and employees, whose presence is not for diplomacy but to assist fellow citizens in the United States, cannot be prosecuted or subpoenaed for official acts, but they have few other protections. Diplomatic-level staff of international organizations have some protection, but lack full immunity. (See the State Department chart mentioned in Book Links.) By one estimate, about 18,000 foreign nationals in the U.S. have full immunity, with less than two dozen facing felony or misdemeanor charges involving violence and half a dozen expelled each year.

But humans being humans, stuff happens, and immunity is called into question whenever there's a highly publicized case or a controversial decision. In 1997, the Georgian deputy ambassador to the U.S. killed a teenage girl and injured four others while allegedly driving drunk in Washington, D.C. He was initially released, but Georgia later waived immunity and he was tried and convicted of manslaughter; after serving three years in federal prison, he was sent home, where he served two more years. In a 2001 Canadian accident, on the other hand, Russia invoked immunity and recalled its diplomat, trying, convicting, and imprisoning him at home. In the home country, of course, an individual is familiar with the legal system, has greater access to family, and faces no language barrier; governments may also take into account added risks their nationals might face in foreign prisons.

If the foreign national is a member of the military, the home country typically invokes immunity and handles the matter internally. When an American Marine guard at the U.S. embassy in Romania was involved in an accident that killed a popular musician in 2004, the U.S. invoked immunity; in a court-martial, a military jury acquitted him of negligent homicide but convicted him of other felony charges.

In 2005, a Virginia sheriff's department sting snared a diplomat from the United Arab Emirates who solicited sex from a thirteen-year-old girl on the Internet and arranged to meet her in a mall. The girl was actually a male sheriff's deputy. The diplomat, who oversaw UAE students in the United States, left the country before an official request for waiver of immunity could be made; a warrant assures his arrest if he returns.

In 2007, the Kuwaiti government refused to waive immunity and allow prosecution of a diplomat and his wife for abuse of three Indian women employed as domestic staff; the State Department then expelled them. The ACLU then raised similar claims against several other embassies. Allegations include extreme low pay and high hours, little time off, no ability to leave their employers' homes or communicate with their families, loss of their passports, physical and emotional abuse, and invasion of privacy. Domestic staff are typically hired abroad, and they can be particularly vulnerable to abuse because of their distance from home, limited English, and isolation. American labor laws don't apply, and foreign laws can't be enforced here. Additional protections have since been enacted.

Diplomats generally reside in Washington or New York, but consuls live in major and minor cities. Mexico, for example, maintains a consular office in Boise, Idaho, to help Mexican citizens, many of them migrant farm workers, in the northwest. As a result, law enforcement across the country can encounter immunity issues. The State Department maintains a 24-hour hotline to verify immunity status and provide guidance on the rights of foreign nationals, diplomatic and otherwise.

Some exceptions to immunity offer fictional possibilities. Immunity does not extend to diplomats engaged in commercial activities, nor does it protect a diplomat married to an American citizen in divorce court. Nor does it apply to civil actions involving motor vehicle accidents not involving an official purpose, meaning a diplomat's wife who runs a red light and causes an accident on the way to the grocery store cannot be charged with a crime, but she could be sued for property damage and personal injuries.

New York City's Commission for the U.N. Consular Corps and Protocol provides information for U.N. staff and foreign government personnel. Take a close look at immunity if you're setting a thriller or mystery series in New York or Washington, D.C.

Diplomatic immunity plays a role in *Lethal Weapon II*, episodes of *Law & Order*, and on *The West Wing*, where the president yells at an ambassador over the phone about unpaid parking tickets.

Can a psychiatrist testify about repressed memories?

A repressed or recovered memory is a memory that the witness has only recently brought to mind or consciously recognized. Repressed or "delayed-recall" memories usually involve severe early childhood trauma, such as experiencing sexual abuse or observing a brutal killing or assault, but they may also involve adolescent or adult experiences, or events like self-mutilation or a suicide attempt. Other cases involve combat, natural disasters, torture, or the Holocaust and other genocides.

Questions abound: Can lost memories be recovered? Are they sufficiently reliable to be admitted in court to prove first, that the event occurred, and second, that the person accused was the perpetrator? In the 1980s, the number of reported cases of recovered memories increased significantly. Was the increase due to greater awareness and identification of previously undiagnosed cases, or was it due to over-diagnosis through the influence of mental health practitioners on highly suggestible patients? And, if the latter, were the practitioners overly-enthusiastic, poorly trained, manipulative, or downright malevolent?

> Questions abound: Can lost memories be recovered? Are they sufficiently reliable to be admitted in court?

The Diagnostic and Statistical Manual of Mental Disorders, Fourth Edition, published in 1994 by the American Psychiatric Association, with text revisions in 2000 (*DSM-IV-TR*), includes a diagnosis of "dissociative amnesia," diagnostic code 300.12. The *DSM-IV-TR* states:

> *The essential feature of the Dissociative Disorders is a disruption of the usually integrated functions of consciousness, memory, identity, or perception of the environment. The disturbance may be sudden or gradual, transient or chronic.*

The essential feature of dissociative amnesia, formerly called psychogenic amnesia, is:

> ...*an inability to recall important personal information, usually of a traumatic or stressful nature, that is too extensive to be explained by normal forgetfulness. ... This disorder involves a reversible memory impairment in which memories of personal experience cannot be retrieved in a verbal form (or, if temporarily retrieved, cannot be wholly retained in consciousness).*

In other words, the patient may have a memory gap or series of gaps for traumatic events, but the gap may later fill in.

Dissociative amnesia may coincide with other mental conditions, such as dissociative identity disorder, previously called multiple personality disorder, or posttraumatic stress disorder, but doesn't have to. Diagnosis requires a finding that the memory gap is not caused by drugs or alcohol, or by a neurological or other medical condition, such as Alzheimer's disease or traumatic brain injury. A recovered memory merits a *DSM* diagnosis only if it causes "clinically significant distress or impairment in social, occupational, or other important areas of functioning;" not all do.

In cases involving new scientific methods or theories, courts must first determine whether the method or theory is scientifically valid. There is usually a phase of uncertainty—a few years, maybe longer, depending on the theory and the amount and conclusiveness of supporting and contradictory evidence—before the theory is largely accepted or largely discounted. Publication of diagnostic criteria in the *DSM* largely resolved the dispute over whether evidence of rediscovered memories is admissible at trial.

Whether the theory applies in any particular case depends on the facts. If the judge decides there is enough evidence to support the claim of a recovered memory, then the jury weighs the evidence and decides whether it is reliable. Numerous factors may influence the decision:

- What triggered the memory? Triggers might be a specific incident, an article or a TV show, a reminder from a person who knew of the incident, or something that surfaces in therapy. Or there may be no apparent reason.

- How detailed is the memory? Has all of it returned, or do gaps persist?

- Is there any corroboration? Consider testimony from other witnesses, diaries or letters written by the accused or the victim, medical records, reports of similar incidents, or a confession by the accused. If part of a memory is corroborated, the jury may be more inclined to believe the rest. For example, a thirty-year-old woman claims she was molested at the circus by an uncle when she was six, but that she did not remember the incident until a month ago when the uncle asked to take her six-year-old niece to the circus. She now describes the incident in detail, including what she was wearing. The accuser's mother confirms that she went to the circus with her uncle when she was six; when they returned, she cut up her new pink seersucker dress, threw it in the garbage, refused to wear pink again, and when asked why, said only that she hated both dress and color. A photograph found in the uncle's home, taken that day, shows him at the circus with the crying girl, in her pink-striped dress. The mother's testimony and the photograph are partial corroboration that lends support to the rest of the victim's testimony.

- The presentation of expert testimony by psychiatrists, other medical providers, and therapists is often considered highly credible. While experts can't necessarily offer an opinion on a witness's reliability, they may testify about their diagnoses and professional opinions and the bases for them, including the patient's disclosures.

- And of course, "Exhibit A" is always the accuser herself. How credible is she? How certain is she of the recalled memory? Has she made similar accusations against other persons? Whether she claims to be the victim or a witness to a crime against another, what would she gain by false testimony?

Keep in mind that statutes of limitations require both civil and criminal actions to be filed within a specific time. They may be suspended—"tolled"—while the victim or witness is a minor, and if a mental disability such as a repressed memory prevented earlier assertions.

Recalled memories are occasionally recanted. A handful of persons acquitted of a crime or accused but not charged have filed civil suits accusing therapists of planting false memories.

> **Recalled memories are occasionally recanted.**

Amy Bishop claims she does not recall shooting her faculty colleagues at the University of Alabama-Hunstville in February 2010, killing three and injuring three others. Was it a case of the mind protecting itself from a traumatic memory, a psychotic episode indicative of mental illness, or a cover-up?

The mysteries of memory, its gaps, and the protective power of the mind offer rich material for fiction. Examples include Sandra Parshall's *The Heat of the Moon*, Elizabeth George's *A Traitor to Memory*, and Sue Grafton's *U Is for Undertow*.

For more on the diagnostic criteria for dissociative amnesia, see the *DSM-IV-TR* and casebooks, published by the American Psychiatric Association. The *DSM-V* is scheduled for publication in 2012; draft criteria are available online. Psychiatric journals include many reports of cases and discussions of diagnosis and treatment, and several books have been written on the subject. The *Writer's Guide to Psychology: How to Write Accurately About Psychological Disorders, Clinical Treatment and Human Behavior* by Carolyn Kaufman (2010) is an excellent resource for all things psychological. For other references, see Book Links.

9

Thinking Like a Lawyer

WHETHER LAWYERS ARE MAJOR OR MINOR CHARACTERS IN your story or script, you'll want to understand what drives them, what their working life is like, and some of the influences on their decision-making. In this chapter, we'll look at legal education, admission to "the bar," and law firms and professional organizations. We'll tackle the conundrum of representing "those people," consider how "the case" can affect relationships, and talk about the public image of the profession.

What's law school like?

Three years of hard work. It's a mental and intellectual challenge and, very often, a financial one to boot.

No specific undergraduate study is required, although degrees in political science, history, business, and English literature are common. Science and engineering degrees are good background for patent lawyers. Any degree that teaches critical reading, thinking, and analysis, along with research, writing, and communication skills, is good preparation.

Students study principles applicable nationwide and, in theory at least, are prepared to take the bar exam and practice in any state, learning local variations after they enter practice. The core curriculum typically includes evidence, civil procedure, torts (civil law), criminal law and procedure, contracts, constitutional law, research and writing, business organizations and transactions, property, federal tax, trial practice, and ethics or professional responsibility. Common electives include labor and employment, environmental law, probate and family law, bankruptcy, and international law; less common choices are courses in legal matters concerning oil and gas, agriculture and water law, nonprofits, American Indian law, copyright, patent law, and insurance. Some schools offer specialized programs, such as environmental law, public policy, or international law, drawing on the expertise of regular and adjunct faculty.

Students spend a lot of time learning to research and write. They learn to read statutes and delve into legislative history, i.e., the impetus and intent behind a bill, the debates that led to adoption of specific language, and amendments. Using casebooks and the Socratic method of questioning and debate, they learn to analyze court decisions (aka opinions), often using the IRAC structure to identify the Issue, governing Rule, Analysis employed, and Conclusions drawn. Students analyze so many decisions that the method becomes instinctive.

Reading decisions also teaches analogizing, meaning to compare one case to another and use similarities and differences to understand nuances between them. This skill is critical in daily practice. A seemingly small distinction between the facts of two cases may completely change the issue, governing rule, or analysis—and the outcome—while other distinctions make no difference. A case presenting an issue not yet decided in that jurisdiction is called "a case of first impression," while a case nearly identical to one under consideration is said to be "on all fours." Students study how lawyers and judges apply the basic principles from prior decisions to new issues and problems.

> A seemingly small distinction between the facts of two cases may completely change the issue, governing rule, or analysis.

While much research is now computerized, students still spend countless hours with the books. They learn to use treatises, commentaries, and other references. They also study and practice persuasive writing skills, and learn to draft pleadings, research memoranda, contracts and other documents, and to prepare briefs.

"Making law review" is a prestigious achievement for students with a high first-year GPA. Some schools also hold a writing competition, allowing a few students to "write on" to the staff. Organizations are student-run, using faculty advisers as guides. Law reviews publish scholarly articles by professors, practicing lawyers, judges, and students on a wide range of topics. Articles may advocate changes in a particular area, propose a solution to an emerging or contentious issue, or highlight a recent decision and its potential consequences. Some schools publish both a general law review and specialized law reviews; for example, Harvard publishes *The Harvard Law Review* and more than a dozen other publications, including journals on environmental law, law and gender, and human rights. The selection process for specialized law reviews varies.

Many schools also run clinics, offering real-world opportunities to work with individual clients on civil and criminal matters, or with nonprofit organizations, courts, and local governments. Students may also participate in moot court competitions, writing briefs and arguing hypothetical cases.

School culture varies greatly. Some are friendly and cooperative, while others are more competitive. Early in the first year, students are typically assigned a research project designed to move them around the library, in order to discover the basic resources. The project usually includes finding a citation for a specific case. Rumor has it that at some schools the book has gone missing or the page has been torn out. At my law school, classmates who'd found the volume earlier had left a bookmark in it. School atmosphere also depends on size, whether it's public or private, the culture of the university, and the location, as well as the mix of locals with out-of-area students, the number of "returning" or older students, and whether there are night classes and part-time students.

According to the American Bar Association, which accredits law schools, of the nearly 143,000 students enrolled at two hundred schools in 2008–09, 53.1 percent were male and 46.9 percent female. Minority enrollment during that period reached 21.9 percent, the highest ever. Average tuition was $16,836 for residents and $28,442 for nonresidents at public law schools and $34,298 at private schools. The average amount borrowed was $59,324 for public schools and $91,506 for private schools, up nearly 30 percent from the 2001–02 school year. That tremendous debt prevents many students from taking lower-paying jobs in the public and non-profit sectors; loan repayment or forgiveness programs exchange debt for public service work.

What are the requirements for taking the bar exam and being admitted to practice?

Each state sets its own criteria for admission. In most states, applications are reviewed by a state board of bar examiners, which may be an agency of the state's highest court or it may be run by the bar association. Licensing requires proof of competency, character, and fitness.

To establish competence, applicants must show they are graduates of an approved law school. Most states accept graduates from any school

> Bar exams are usually given in February and July. Some states use national tests, while others administer their own.

meeting the ABA's accreditation requirements; graduates of the handful of unaccredited schools, mostly in California, have fewer options. New grads must pass the bar exam. Lawyers admitted elsewhere may be required to pass the exam, although some states allow admission through reciprocity agreements.

Bar exams are usually given in February and July. Some states use national tests, while others administer their own. Most states also require an ethics exam, again either a multi-state exam or one developed in-state.

The character and fitness review is critical to protecting the public. As one state's rules put it:

> *The primary purposes of character and fitness screening before admission to the Bar of Montana are to assure the protection of the public and safeguard the justice system. An attorney should be one whose record of conduct justifies the trust of clients, adversaries, courts and others with respect to the professional duties owed to them.*
>
> *The public is adequately protected only by a system that evaluates the character and fitness of practitioners as those elements relate to the practice of law. The public interest requires that the public be secure in its expectation that those who are admitted to the bar are worthy of the trust and confidence clients may reasonably place in their attorney.*

Lawyers owe their clients and the system a high duty of care, and they deal with some of the most important and vulnerable areas of clients' lives, with the potential to do substantial harm through error or misrepresentation. Review is based on a lengthy application, typically requiring a birth certificate, college and law school transcripts, fingerprints, information on any academic discipline and involvement in civil or criminal proceedings, character references, employment history, military discharge forms, and information on any illness or condition that might affect fitness to practice law. Applicants must also provide details of prior rejected applications, in any state. Lawyers admitted elsewhere must submit certificates of good standing and disciplinary history from other state bars and courts.

Felony convictions are generally presumed to establish a lack of moral fitness, at least until the sentence and probationary period ends, although some felonies permanently establish lack of good moral character. Admission to the bar has also been denied based on a history of debt collection and financial problems, tax liens and failure to file returns, drug convictions and illegal drug use without sufficient evidence of rehabilitation, failure to show resolution of problems leading to prior disbarment, prior malpractice claims showing a pattern of misconduct, and failing to be truthful in the application or hearings. Matt Hale, leader of the white supremacist World Church of the Creator, was denied admission to the bar in Illinois and Montana, based on character and fitness reviews.

> Felony convictions are generally presumed to establish a lack of moral fitness.

Review committees have investigatory powers, allowing them to dig deeper into an applicant's history when necessary. They can also hold hearings to review or reconsider an application. In most states, the highest court holds ultimate authority over bar admissions.

Each state also has rules for admission *pro hac vice*, meaning for a particular case, used by an out-of-state lawyer who wants to represent a local client.

For the American Bar Association's list of approved schools, statistics, and other information on legal education, and more information on bar admission requirements and a sample form for character and fitness examination, see the Book Links.

Can a person still read for the bar the way Lincoln did?

In Lincoln's day, would-be lawyers "read" for the bar, studying for several years with experienced lawyers. Law schools did not become the norm until late in the 19th century, when the ABA began pushing for state regulation of legal education and control of bar admissions.

Only a few states still have an apprenticeship process, such as Washington State's Law Clerk program. Applicants must have a four-year degree, pass a moral character review, and work full-time for four years with a lawyer or judge, who serves as primary tutor and provides weekly supervision focused on case analysis, discussion of the law, and writing. There is a specific course of study, and regular exams are required. Law clerks must apply for bar admission and take the bar exam. For details, see the Book Links.

Why is the legal profession called "the bar"?

In most courtrooms, a partition or railing near the front separates the public from the area occupied by the judge, court staff, lawyers, parties, and jurors. Witnesses enter that area when called to testify. Like many legal terms, the origin is English—the divider was called a bar, and lawyers who tried cases took the name "barrister." Over time, the term came to refer to the profession as a whole.

How is a law firm typically structured?

Most law firms are technically partnerships or professional corporations, although single-owner sole proprietorships are also common, especially in small communities and specialized practices. A handful of firms have two or three thousand lawyers in dozens of offices around the world. Many more have

> A handful of firms have two or three thousand lawyers in dozens of offices around the world.

several hundred lawyers in multiple locations. In large firms, a third to half of the lawyers may be partners or shareholders, including equity and non-equity partners, with the rest being associates. Large firms typically have a managing partner or management committee, assisted by professional staff. Some managing partners continue to practice, while others focus on firm business.

Large firms include "practice groups" of lawyers who specialize in one area, such as estate planning, land use and environmental law, or mergers and acquisitions. It's not uncommon for large firms representing corporations to keep a small group of lawyers to help clients with estate planning, family law, and other personal legal matters. Think of the movie *Michael Clayton* without the drama, and without George Clooney.

Firms may employ other professional staff, including engineers, economists, tax advisors, investigators, or nurses who assist with medical malpractice and personal injury cases. Marcia Muller's character, Sharon McCone, started her literary career as an investigator for a legal services cooperative and, in later books, runs her own business. And Sharon McCrumb's forensic anthropologist, Elizabeth MacPherson, works as an investigator for her brother's law firm in *If I'd Killed Him When I Met Him*.

In large firms, professional management typically handles daily management, HR, accounting, payroll, and IT. Some firms maintain a marketing staff to manage the firm's website, blogs, and advertising; others contract the work. Firms also employ receptionists, legal secretaries, and legal assistants or paralegals.

Smaller firms may limit their practice, e.g., to personal injury plaintiffs' or defense work, intellectual property, land use, or criminal defense. Or they may consist of lawyers with diverse practices who benefit from sharing clients and provide a sounding board and collegiality.

Firms of all sizes hire associates, lawyers either fresh out of school or with some experience, also called "lateral hires." Time to be considered for partnership varies, but typically ranges from three to seven years. Associates not offered partnership may be asked to leave, in an up-or-out system, or offered non-equity partner status, giving them job security but no voice in firm business or share of profits. Another alternative is the permanent associate, an employee who is neither a partner nor a partner-track associate. Non-equity partners and permanent associates are often lawyers who don't want the risk and demands of partnership, but are known quantities who offer valuable experience and talent. Some work part-time. Many are women with young families, or lawyers who want to keep practicing while following other dreams, like painting, music, or writing fiction.

"Of counsel" status often refers to a semi-retired lawyer who works with a few existing clients or assists others in the

> Time to be considered for partnership varies, but typically ranges from three to seven years.

firm. In recent years, more younger lawyers have taken "of counsel" status to maintain their business association while cutting back their practice temporarily for personal reasons, e.g., while ill or on parenting leave. "Of counsel" lawyers are neither partner (or shareholder) nor associate; payment, liability, insurance coverage, and other issues are negotiated case-by-case.

Many firms hire student law clerks part-time during the school year or full-time during the summer. These internships give both firm and student the chance to size each other up for future employment. Clerks spend most of their time researching, but they also shadow other lawyers in depositions, negotiations, or at trial.

A common alternative to the self-contained law firm is office-sharing. Solo practitioners may share space, each with their own office, clientele, and secretary, sharing a receptionist, library, and conference room. Benefits include camaraderie, referrals, and cost savings.

No novel better portrays the perils of legal employment, or its potential upside, than *The Firm* by John Grisham. Perri O'Shaughnessy's Nina Reilly is a typical solo practitioner, and several of Lisa Scottoline's books portray small-firm practice.

What professional organizations do lawyers belong to?

Thirty-two states and Washington, D.C., have unified bars, meaning the state bar association is authorized by law or court order to regulate the practice of law, and membership is mandatory. In eighteen states, lawyer licensing and regulation are managed by the state, through the court system or a separate agency; bar association membership is voluntary.

State bars provide a variety of services, including continuing legal education, education for the public, assistance to courts on funding, rules, and related projects, lobbying on policy and legislation, and promoting and coordinating *pro bono* services. Most offer sections for practice specialties, monthly publications, job search services, and Lawyers Assistance Programs for lawyers with drug, alcohol, or mental health problems. State bars typically employ ethics counsel who respond to questions from lawyers and the public, provide written opinions, handle complaints, and make recommendations for discipline.

A variety of voluntary professional organizations provide educational and other services. The largest national association is the American Bar Association (ABA), which has numerous sections for specialties, such as criminal justice, dispute resolution, taxation, trial practice, and insurance. The ABA also sponsors research and publications on a wide range of subjects, evaluates judicial candidates, and accredits law schools. Other organizations include national African American, Native American, Hispanic, and Asian Pacific bar associations, the Lesbian, Gay, Bisexual and Transgender bar association, and local chapters. During the 1970s, women lawyers' associations sprung up across the country; some state and local bars have women's sections.

Local bar associations may serve a city, county, or region.

Many associations organize by practice specialty. The American Association for Justice, formerly the American Trial Lawyers Association, and state affiliates primarily serve the plaintiffs' bar. The Defense Research Institute and various state Defense Trial Lawyers associations serve the civil defense bar. Others focus on criminal defense or prosecution, bankruptcy, agricultural law, and other specialties.

How can a lawyer defend someone accused of a reprehensible crime, or defend a client he knows is guilty?

This goes to the heart of what lawyers do, and it is the source of much misunderstanding and wise-cracking. Lawyers serve justice, not just their clients. The principle that everyone accused of a crime deserves a competent defense underlies the Supreme Court decisions in *Gideon* and *Miranda*, as we've discussed, as well as many other decisions.

> Lawyers serve justice, and not just their clients.

Ideally, lawyers work for justice without bias, although being human, that doesn't always happen. However, justice is hard to define. As the late Supreme Court Justice Potter Stewart said of pornography, "I know it when I see it." So, as a country and society ruled by law, we have to rely on process, making sure that the accused get the due process and fundamental fairness guaranteed by the Constitution. Which means lawyers take on unpopular causes and defend those the community condemns.

Not only is everyone innocent until proven guilty, but some accused persons actually are innocent. The role of lawyers is, in part, to make sure the government proves every element of its case beyond a reasonable doubt, based on the evidence, not assumptions and prejudice.

Further, people often think they know something, when, in fact they're making assumptions. They may draw perfectly logical conclusions based on a misunderstanding of the facts. A lawyer often has to act while basing his actions on uncertain or incomplete evidence. "Everybody" might "know" the defendant crossed the center line and hit an oncoming vehicle, pronounce him guilty, and be prepared to throw away the key to his jail cell. But they may not know that the other vehicle had been in his lane and crossed back over at the last possible second, after the defendant had already decided that going left was preferable to going right, into an icy river. When that fact emerges, the case changes, although public opinion may not.

> A lawyer often has to act based on uncertain or incomplete evidence.

Fiction writers can play up this conflict, showing how it affects the conversations between lawyer and client, between co-counsel, and between lawyer and spouse—and how it keeps the lawyer awake at night. What snide remark does the barista make about representing "those people," when he hands a public defender her morning latté? How does the chatter in the locker room, or the book club, change the morning after her client has made the nightly news once again?

Will the defense lawyer typically ask the client if he "did it"?

Many criminal defenders don't ask a client if he committed the crime. Why? Because knowing the answer limits their flexibility in pursuing available defenses and presents too much risk of influencing their decisions, small and large, in ways potentially harmful to their client. Those who do tend to ask "the question" believe knowing prevents them from unwittingly putting on a false defense—strictly prohibited by the Rules of Professional Conduct (RPC).

Of course, the client may volunteer a confession. But the truth is not always crystal clear. He may be lying to protect someone else, or to prevent discovery of another crime.

Remember that the question for trial is not what the defendant did, but what the prosecution can prove. Defense counsel who knows her client did what he's charged with can't ethically argue that the client "didn't do it"—and neither should a defender who deliberately didn't ask. Instead, both should focus on reasonable doubt. They probe for weaknesses in the state's case, demonstrate witness bias, expose any mistakes in the investigation, and challenge the credibility or logic of witnesses and the state's theory of the case. The defendant is legally guilty only if the government proves its case.

But what about justice, and the interests of the community and the victim in seeing criminals caught and punished? In our system, the rights of the accused are just as important as the state's interest in justice and a conviction. The old saying is "better a hundred guilty men go free than an innocent man hang." Use that tension to heighten the conflict in your story.

What rules govern how a lawyer handles a client's money?

Lawyers have a fiduciary relationship to their clients, meaning the relationship is one of trust and the lawyer owes the client the highest duties of honesty and good faith. To flesh that out, each state has its own Rules of Professional Conduct governing handling clients' money, such as retainers (advance payments for fees), other money received from clients (e.g., funds to be paid to satisfy a judgment or fulfill a contract), or money received on behalf of clients (e.g., money received in settlement or payment of a judgment).

What about contingency fee agreements for personal injury claims? Typically, the lawyer takes one-third of any settlement received before trial, and 40 percent if the case goes to trial or appeal. Costs advanced—witness and deposition fees, trial exhibits, and the like—are reimbursed and medical liens paid before fees are calculated and proceeds disbursed to the client. Lawyers often compromise fees in small cases, such as personal injury cases where insurance limits are too low to fully compensate the plaintiff, in order to make sure the client ends up with some money after the medical bills and other expenses are paid. It's good practice to make sure the client ends up with at least as much as the lawyer does. In most states, contingency fee agreements must be in writing, a sound practice whether mandated or not. It's also smart to document hourly fee arrangements with a fee agreement or engagement letter. The American Bar Association's Model Rules of Professional Conduct, which are the basis for most state codes of legal ethics, recommend it, and some state variations require it.

Fee disputes often trigger malpractice claims: The lawyer sues for fees, and the client counters with a malpractice claim. A leading professional liability insurer advises against suing for fees for just that reason; mediation or arbitration is less likely to trigger a retaliatory lawsuit.

Lawyers must keep client funds in a trust account, separate from their business accounts. The retainer held in a trust account can be drawn on as fees are earned. Interest on lawyers' trust accounts (called IOLTA) is used in some states to fund indigent legal services, although a large sum can be deposited into a separate account so the client receives the interest. Trust accounts are at the center of a large percentage of lawyer discipline cases. State bars can audit accounts randomly or in response to a complaint.

Most state bars also maintain a Lawyers' Responsibility Fund, funded by mandatory assessments on all lawyers admitted in that state. In fact, the legal profession may be the only one that assesses itself to compensate persons injured by the dishonesty of its members. Applications are reviewed by a panel authorized to make gifts from the Fund to reimburse clients, at least partially. The most common claims involve disbarred lawyers who abscond or are "judgment proof" (meaning broke) and took the client's retainer without performing the services, or failed to pay the client money received on the client's behalf. The Funds do not consider fee disputes, malpractice claims, or cases where restitution has been made.

How can lawyers fight each other in the courtroom and be friendly out in the hall?

The case belongs to the clients, not the lawyers, who face each other repeatedly. Everyone is best served by professionalism. That doesn't mean lawyers have to be chummy, but it does require civility and basic courtesy. Still, during a trial or depositions, lawyers typically lunch at different restaurants to avoid being overheard and to limit client discomfort.

Clients sometimes want their lawyers to take an overly hard line with opposing counsel, but most understand that hostilities between the parties should not spill over to their lawyers. Good client control means educating the client about the importance of cool heads and cordial relationships with opposing counsel, witnesses, the court, and court staff. This is just as important in big cities as in small towns. It's only right. And it can be good for business. It's not unheard of for a party to a lawsuit to decide in the future that he would rather be represented by the lawyer who once opposed him.

That said, it's not always easy to be friendly in the hall, let alone civil in the courtroom. In tense moments, tempers can flare. Some people are just plain difficult. Disputes that should be resolved between counsel may escalate and end up before the judge. The sharp exchanges between Jimmy Stewart and George C. Scott in *Anatomy of a Murder* are brilliant examples of innuendo and personal animosity woven into questioning; in reality, few of us are so articulate or controlled when we're angry. A lawyer in doubt about her ability to be civil may simply wait for her opponent to clear the building before leaving the courtroom, and trust that tempers will cool to a manageable level the next day.

But that's no fun for reader or writer, is it? Spice things up when you need to—just be aware that's the exception, not the rule.

Why does it seem that the public hates lawyers?

It's like congressmen—people love their own, but hate those other bastards.

Seriously, public distrust of lawyers is real, and it has many sources. Simply put, lawyers complicate things. Except for adoptions and the occasional real estate or business purchase, people don't go to lawyers for happy reasons. They call lawyers when they have problems.

Lawyers cause trouble, or bring it to light, which can amount to the same thing. "We fired that employee for good reason, and he found a lawyer to say we didn't." "Nobody had any problem with us dumping in the stream until the damn lawyers came along." "Thirty years in business and nobody ever sued me until now."

Lawyers often represent unpopular people or causes, and lawyers are frequently in the middle of very public controversies. Many government officials are lawyers, and the ebb and flow of government distrust that's part of our country's history may also heighten distrust of the profession and the judicial system lawyers represent.

> Lawyers often represent unpopular people or causes, and lawyers are frequently in the middle of very public controversies.

The law isn't always clear. How it is applied depends on the facts of the case and on precedent (decisions in past cases). That can make it hard to predict. Results sometimes seem arbitrary. Nonlawyers can be frustrated by differences of opinion or outcome.

And the law isn't always evenly or fairly enforced.

Legal language can be confusing. Writer and lawyer Helen Sandoval points out that while the language of the law sometimes seems convoluted, it's evolved to deal with complicated situations, provide flexibility, and allow for the unanticipated. For example, a statute might simply say killing is murder. But what about self-defense? Shouldn't the law recognize a distinction between accidental and intentional killings? And so more definitions are added to deal with the many variations.

Legal fees can add up. The plaintiff in an auto accident case or a slip-and-fall usually has a contingency fee arrangement with counsel, and liability insurance typically provides a defense to the driver or store owner and pays any judgment. But you'll need to pay a lawyer out of your own pocket to enforce a contract or establish rights to an easement, to contest the property division in a divorce or obtain child custody, to prevent the PR from siphoning off the assets of an estate, to evict a balky tenant or fight an unfair eviction. Small business owners need lawyers to draft employee handbooks and contracts. And, of course, private criminal defense is expensive. Legal fees can be difficult to estimate, and some lawyers don't explain fees clearly. The legal process can be long and slow, and it's hard to pay a bill when you don't see a lot of progress, especially if the case isn't going well. Mandatory mediation in divorce and custody cases and mandatory arbitration in low-dollar personal injury claims has cut fees and sped up the process. It's also taken the wind out of the sails of some of the bullies who make threats to attempt to gain leverage, like demanding full custody to bargain for a larger share of assets; the claims may be groundless, but fighting them is expensive, and emotionally draining.

An old, but not necessarily good, adage says if the law is against you, argue the facts. If the facts are against you, argue the law. If both are against you, pound the table.

TIP: To some extent, lawyers' positive and negative traits can be mirror images. Assertiveness can become aggression; strength of convictions can become uncompromising; hardworking can look greedy; and creative thinking can look indecisive or unprincipled. Use this duality to add layers to your lawyer-characters.

The phrase "adversary system" simply means that disputes are worked out through opposing arguments. However, some lawyers take the phrase too far, refusing reasonable extensions in emergencies, badgering a witness, filing unnecessary motions, or arguing over every little thing. None of that helps anyone.

Lawyers can make things easy, or difficult. Krista Davis, author of the Domestic Diva mystery series and previously a lawyer under her own name, notes that there is no contract or business deal without a weakness. A good lawyer learns to solve problems and make the deal go forward, while poor ones point out the flaws and let the deal fall apart.

At least one subset, the trial lawyers, is also a political lightning rod. Trial lawyers represent both plaintiffs and defendants, but the term usually refers to lawyers for injured persons. A few high-dollar cases have created the impression that verdicts are too high and litigation is a money grab. Medical malpractice and product liability cases are particularly suspect. Some are quick to blame litigation for the high cost of services, even though the Center for Justice and Democracy reports that the cost of defending medical malpractice claims is a very small percentage of total health-care costs and has no effect on insurance premiums. While statistics vary, a Rand Institute for Civil Justice study reports that only 2 percent of people injured seriously enough to incur economic loss file lawsuits. If a case goes to trial and ends in a high verdict, it's usually because injuries in such cases can be catastrophic, and juries may punish defendants who flagrantly disregard serious risks of injury. Plaintiffs' lawyers who bring these cases often bring about changes that benefit all of society. Think of the lawsuits over the exploding Ford Pinto that brought the manufacturer's cost-benefit analysis to light, or suits that exposed dangers in strollers, car seats, Vioxx, and other drugs.

> A few high-dollar cases have created the impression that verdicts are too high and litigation is a money grab.

(The National Center for State Courts reports a 21 percent drop in tort filings (personal injury claims) from 1996 to 2005, although contract disputes rose during that same time.)

In truth, lawyers don't always behave well, professionally or in their private lives. Lawyers sometimes appear willing to argue any side for money; that's an oversimplification, but lawyers who don't properly investigate claims before filing suit can cause expense, stress, and aggravation that can't always be laid on the clients. Lawyers who take their clients' disputes too personally and become unpleasant or behave badly harm the entire profession, and maybe their own karma.

Is there a bit of professional envy? Maybe. The image of lawyers as educated and successful may push the jealousy button at times. Most make at least a decent living and some do extremely well. A few have made themselves lightning rods for criticism, deserved or not. However, as in any profession, lawyers run the gamut of commitment, competency, success, and honesty.

"First thing we do, let's kill all the lawyers," Dick the Butcher said in *Henry VI, Part II*. There's some debate whether Shakespeare intended to skewer the profession or point out its value in a free and fair society. Probably both. Lawyers were just as human then as now. And, then and now, they make great characters.

What's your favorite lawyer joke?

Did you hear the one about the lawyer who quit his practice to write a novel, because he wanted to make a lot of money?

10

Thinking Like a Judge

JUDGES—FAIR-MINDED, REASONABLE DISPENSERS OF JUSTICE, or secretive, power-grabbing tyrants? Whether appointed or elected, as we discussed in Chapter 1 on the basics of the judicial system, judges are typically the least well-known public officials. Here, we'll look at what the job involves, courthouse security, and the sensitive question of judicial bias.

Why would a person want to be a judge?

There are as many answers as there are judges, but some common reasons are belief in the rule of law and respect for our justice system; the confidence that one has the intelligence, perception, and sense to understand the issues, deal fairly with lawyers and litigants, and make sound decisions in difficult cases—that one possesses a "judicial temperament"; the ability to communicate the grounds for those decisions, both orally and in writing, and to withstand criticism and keep learning; an opportunity to serve the community and help people change their lives; intellectual challenge; and variety—each case is different. Some lawyers choose the bench as a career. Others seek it only after years of private or government practice or teaching, having accomplished what they wanted in their practices and welcoming the next challenge. And, being a judge simplifies the professional wardrobe.

Judges can suffer professional isolation. When a small-town lawyer takes the bench, he usually gives up regular lunches and golf games with other lawyers to avoid bias and "the appearance of improriety." When I clerked at the Washington State Court of Appeals, the judges usually ate with the clerks, all of us **Judges can suffer professional isolation.** fresh out of law school. Great for us, because we got to know them and hear terrific stories. However, their circle of peers was limited to the court itself. In a rural county with one or two judges, lunching alone gets old.

The job can take an emotional toll. Writer and retired Missouri judge Bill Hopkins notes that few people have much sympathy for judges, except other judges. "When you make decisions that affect other people's lives," he says, "it can get quite nerve-racking."

The best-known judge in mystery is Margaret Maron's Deborah Knott. Her judicial cases don't usually relate to her detective work, but they are always well-portrayed; some are gut-wrenching and some are pretty funny. Judge Deborah rocks.

John Grisham wrote about judges in *The Brethren* (2000), and judges appear in some of his other novels. A particularly intriguing portrayal is Rosemary Aubert's Ellis Portal series, featuring a disgraced Toronto judge who is homeless for a time.

You notice I didn't mention money. In 2010, federal statute sets the salaries of Supreme Court justices at $213,900 (slightly higher for the chief), appeals judges at $184,500, and district judges at $174,000, which is the same as members of Congress. According to the National Center for State Courts Judicial Salary Resource Center, for 2010, state court pay is highest in California ($228,856 for the chief justice, $218,237 for associate justices, and $178,789 for judges of general jurisdiction) and lowest in Mississippi (ranging from $112,530 to $104,170). (See Book Links for further details.) Many chiefs, including Supreme Court Chief Justice John Roberts, have advocated strongly for increases, pointing out that experienced and capable judges have left the bench for the higher-paying private sector. But with state budget shortfalls likely to continue for several years, future pay raises will likely be small or non-existent for a while.

And judges make great secondary characters. It's hard to beat the judges in John Mortimer's stories and novels for their quirks and their ability to drive a barrister to drink—admittedly, a short trip for Horace Rumpole.

Several recent biographies and memoirs give a close look at the judicial life: Linda Greenhouse's *Becoming Justice Blackmun: Harry Blackmun's Supreme Court Journey* (2005), and Joan Biskupic's *American Original: The Life and Constitution of Supreme Court Justice Antonin Scalia* (2009) and *Sandra*

Day O'Connor: How the First Woman on the Supreme Court Became Its Most Influential Justice (2006). Justice Stephen Breyer occasionally appears on TV to talk about the courts, and he published *Making Our Democracy Work: A Judge's View* (2010). Justice O'Connor's speeches are collected in *The Majesty of the Law: Reflections of a Supreme Court Justice* (2003). The book's subjects include how the Court works, issues that have shaped it, and a few particularly notable members, women in the law and on the bench, and the role of the law and Constitution in our country. She's a goddess in my book.

What are a judge's responsibilities, before and during trial?

Short version: maintain order and administer justice. Think back to the pretrial and trial procedure discussed in Chapter 1. The judge runs every pretrial hearing and each step of trial. Some pretrial stages, such as initial appearances and bail hearings, don't usually require much preparation. But later stages, when parties file motions asking for evidentiary or legal rulings before trial, involve tremendous work. A trial judge may handle dozens of cases at a time. Motions typically involve an opening brief, answer, and reply, which the judge reads before hearing oral argument (if there is one) and making a decision. Briefs often include lengthy attachments. Clerks review briefs first and may write prehearing memos—routine in appellate courts—as a road map of the case; the conversation with the clerk after the hearing is often critical. Judges may write their own first drafts of opinions, or work with the clerk's draft. The workload can be staggering.

> A trial judge may handle dozens of cases at a time.

During trial, the judge makes additional evidentiary rulings, usually on the spot, and listens with a sharp ear for evidence proving, or disproving, each element of the case. Later, the judge will meet with counsel to "settle instructions," deciding what final instructions to give the jury, based on what the evidence shows. The judge may need to rule on other matters, and even decide or dismiss some claims during trial. In a bench trial, the judge makes the ultimate factual decisions as well as the legal rulings, requiring him or her to assess the credibility of each witness and weigh each piece of evidence.

The judge should be alert to make sure *pro se* litigants understand what's going on. If a *pro se* party shows signs of mental instability, the judge may need to request an evaluation. In a recent case in my county, the judge grew concerned about the safety of a criminal defendant jailed while awaiting a mental health examination, knowing he had no lawyer to keep tabs on him, and ordered his transfer to the state hospital for an expedited evaluation—all this despite the defendant's repeated disrespectful treatment of her in the courtroom.

TIP: Most judges have little patience for delays, especially avoidable ones, and get downright testy about intentional stalling. Use a refusal to extend a deadline, or "continue" (postpone) or "recess" (pause) a trial to pressure your characters. Judges also keep in mind the jury's needs and comfort. They have little tolerance for delays that keep jurors waiting longer than absolutely necessary.

Judges supervise staff and may have to deal with budgets, depending on how the local courts are financed.

Most judges work hard, keep long hours, and try their best to do the right thing. But "the right thing" isn't always clear, giving writers plenty of leeway.

How do judges make their decisions? Can they take time to research or think about their decisions?

In both civil and criminal cases, the parties file pretrial motions intended to resolve some issues before trial. In civil cases, one party may file a motion asking the court to decide the case "on summary judgment," meaning to rule that there are "no genuine issues of material fact" and part or all of the case can be decided by the judge "as a matter of law." Judges decide these motions based on written briefs and, for major issues, oral argument. They don't usually rule from the bench. Instead, they "take the matter under advisement" and issue a written ruling later. They read the briefs and review their notes from oral argument—and possibly a transcript, now that most court reporters use "real time" transcription software. They may research an issue themselves or rely on law clerks to do the research and draft an opinion. Some judges rule quickly, while others are notoriously slow. If a scheduling order has been issued in the case—and one usually is, at some point—that may affect the speed of rulings. It's not uncommon for a judge to issue a flurry of decisions shortly before trial.

In civil cases, the parties prepare a joint pretrial order setting out the agreed facts, additional facts each side expects to prove, legal issues pending and those remaining for trial, and a list of exhibits, among other things. In complex cases, counsel may file pretrial briefs outlining the evidence and issues for trial so that the judge knows what to expect.

During trial, the judge makes evidentiary rulings on the spot. Examples include whether to sustain or overrule an objection and whether to admit a document or object into physical evidence. In a jury trial, the judge may call a "sidebar," asking counsel to approach the bench so he can ask questions or hear short arguments out of the jury's hearing. The judge then announces his ruling so all can hear. After the evidence is heard and the parties "rest," counsel and the judge meet to "settle instructions"—that is, go over the proposed jury instructions so the judge can decide which ones to give. In a bench trial, or on summary judgment, the judge may request proposed orders or "findings of fact and conclusions of law." Typically, both paper and electronic copies are provided. The judge can pick and choose from the proposals, or he can toss them all and write his own. In some courts, law clerks assist at every stage. In others, the judges do all the work.

Judges are expected to know the rules of evidence to a greater degree than the finest trial attorney. To achieve this ideal, judges must study on their own and also attend seminars. They do an enormous amount of reading, often more than can be done during the workday. Make sure your fictional judge has a good pair of reading glasses and a sturdy briefcase.

How do judges control courtroom behavior?

With a stern look, the weight of tradition, and a small wooden gavel, and with fines imposed on the spot for ringing cell phones.

Seriously, most people are well-behaved in court, out of respect or fear. But judges do have a few tools. One is that gavel—rapped sharply on the wooden top of the judge's bench, it gets most people's attention. The presence of a bailiff, or an armed detention officer or federal marshal, in the courtroom helps, too.

Lawyers play a huge role in controlling courtroom behavior. We're required to instruct our clients and witnesses how to behave, and we take the heat when they step out of line. Judges have no patience for a party who makes snide remarks under the breath, or whose facial expressions distract from the testimony or arguments. Judges may reprimand them directly or tell counsel to "control your client."

Another major tool is contempt of court. Contempt stems from disobedience of a court's order or authority. A criminal defendant who behaves inappropriately toward a victim, witness, or juror, or makes repeated outbursts, will be warned that he could be "held in contempt" if he doesn't stop. If necessary to restore order in the court, the judge can punish contempt on the spot, issuing a verbal order. Other cases may require a warning. In criminal contempt, sanctions are intended to punish the person and vindicate the court's authority. In civil contempt, sanctions are aimed at ensuring compliance with a court order. State-by-state specifics vary, of course. Criminal contempt must be determined "beyond a reasonable doubt" at trial, following standard criminal law procedures. A person who is ordered to be jailed may be able to avoid incarceration by paying a fine or doing the act ordered, e.g., paying a judgment or turning over disputed property.

A pair of examples of contempt: When a probation revocation hearing was properly closed, a reporter who reentered the courtroom after being ordered by the judge to leave was guilty of contempt and fined. A lawyer who defied a judge's repeated order to sit while another lawyer was speaking was held in contempt for "disorderly, contemptuous, or insolent behavior toward the judge," which disrupted the proceedings, and fined $50; that was in 1984—it would likely be higher now.

An obstreperous defendant can be removed from the courtroom, but the judge must tread carefully. In a particularly nasty case, *Montana v. Aceto* (2004), a man was accused of trying to kill his former girlfriend and her new boyfriend and kidnaping her, holding her hostage in the woods for 30 hours. At trial, Aceto represented himself. He harassed his ex-girlfriend in the guise of cross-examination, and he ignored repeated orders to stop. He blew up, swearing at her and the judge, and threw a file at her while she cowered on the stand. The judge threw him into jail. He apologized the next day, but the judge ordered him to watch the proceedings by closed-circuit TV, with standby counsel taking over in the courtroom. The state Supreme Court held that the judge violated Aceto's constitutional right to be present at all criminal proceedings when he removed Aceto from the courtroom without warning him first, and without giving him an opportunity to return. Aceto could waive the right to be present, but had not done so. On retrial for attempted deliberate homicide and aggravated kidnaping, Aceto was convicted again—but without the ex-girlfriend's testimony. Sadly, after the first trial, she committed suicide.

When it comes to unruly lawyers, retired Missouri judge Bill Hopkins says a knowledgeable trial court judge should follow a three-step rule: First, call all lawyers and the court reporter to the bench, on the record but outside the hearing of the jury and witnesses, outline the offending behavior and warn the attorney that it is unacceptable and he should stop or be punished. If it happens a second time, the judge warns the lawyer in front of everyone and on the record that the behavior must stop or he will be punished. If the lawyer commits the offensive behavior again, the judge explains on the record and in public what the lawyer has done and imposes punishment.

Nothing like a vivid courtroom scene to hook a reader.

What areas of the courthouse are public and what are private? What do judges' chambers look like?

Public areas include courtrooms, the clerk's office where papers are filed, a lobby or hallway lined with benches or chairs, and small conference rooms where lawyers can meet with clients or witnesses. The jury conference room is typically attached to the courtroom, with jurors entering through the courtroom itself; some jury rooms have a private restroom.

Private areas include offices or work stations for the court administrator (if there is one), secretaries, bailiffs, court reporters, and law clerks, as well as the judges' "chambers," or private offices. Designs vary, of course. Law libraries once took up a lot of space, and they were often open to the public and lawyers as well. They've shrunk considerably with the shift to electronic research, but most courthouses probably still include a physical copy of the "reporters"— that is, the books containing the official copies of decisions for that state, along with state codes and administrative regulations, treatises, and other resources. In chambers, judges keep copies of the court rules and many other references.

Judges' chambers are as varied as any other offices. Your fictional judge might hang her diplomas and judicial commission next to a finger painting by her six-year-old. One judge I know is an avid wildlife photographer whose work fills the walls in and around his office. Your judge may be neat or messy, with an antique desk passed down through the generations or a modern one. Her robe may hang on a hook over the door or in a small closet next to the courtroom door. I still smile at the memory of a judge in Tacoma, Washington, who hung an antelope head wearing Groucho Marx glasses over his desk; the sight reduced any tensions considerably.

Courthouses tend to be crowded and much-remodeled. Many older courthouses, especially in smaller towns and cities, are striking examples of period art and architecture. The Missoula (Montana) County Courthouse houses eight historical paintings by Edgar Paxson, a renowned western artist. Similar treasures decorate courthouses around the country.

Call the court administrator or clerk and schedule a tour for your writers' group. I can't promise antelope heads or murals of scantily-clad, blindfolded women holding the scales of justice, but I can promise you great material for courthouse settings.

Remember that courthouses, especially federal courthouses, have security measures in place. Don't try to carry anything into a courthouse that would get you into trouble, e.g., weapons (including pocket knives), pepper spray, heavy key rings, and the like. Some courthouses prohibit cell phones. Check before you go.

What courthouse and courtroom security measures should a writer be aware of?

Courtroom security measures and training have increased tremendously in recent years, in response to threats and incidents across the country. Federal courthouse security is managed by the U.S. Marshals Service. Metal detectors guard public entrances and visitors must log in. Three or four armed marshals typically staff each entrance, with others on patrol or in courtrooms, if needed.

State court security management varies. Many state courthouses use metal detectors and entry screening, either at building entrances or when visitors reach the courtroom floor. State court security is complicated by numerous factors, including the fact that local courthouses often include other county or municipal offices without the same security needs and with high daily traffic.

Court buildings may use closed circuit TV cameras, alarmed doors, and mail screening rooms.

During trial, a bailiff, frequently armed, will be in the room to assist the jury. In criminal cases, armed security is typical in any proceeding where the defendant is present. If the defendant is in custody, he'll be brought to the courtroom by armed detention officers, who stay in the courtroom—usually seated or standing along the wall near the defense counsel table, so they can keep an eye on the defendant and the public. Judges may request extra security at any time.

> During trial, a bailiff, frequently armed, will be in the room to assist the jury.

The public and private areas of the courthouse are separated by doors with intrusion alarms and security codes. In private areas, judges and staff move about freely, and the public, including lawyers, enters by invitation only.

Security extends to the parking lot or garage. Judges and other staff may have assigned parking spots for their convenience, but typically without their names indicated, removing an easy target. After the 2005 murders of the husband and mother of a federal judge in Chicago, Congress authorized payment for home security systems for federal judges, which about three-quarters of the 2,000 federal judges have requested, as of a 2006 report.

And, in many parts of the country, especially in state court, it's not uncommon for a judge to keep a loaded handgun close by.

The worst recent example of courthouse violence is the 2005 shooting spree in Atlanta, when a rape suspect grabbed a deputy's gun, shot her, then killed the judge and court reporter and a deputy attempting to stop him outside; later that day, he killed a federal customs agent and took a woman hostage. Unfortunately, there are plenty of other examples to draw on. Retired Texas District Court judge Susan P. Baker's book, *Murdered Judges of the Twentieth Century and Other Mysterious Deaths* (2004), tells some of the stories. For more on court security, consult the National Center for State Courts 2010 report on best practices. (See Book Links.)

Not all courthouse crime relates to official work. In the northwest, a rural judge's office and courtroom were destroyed by a fire set during a burglary, part of a string of business burglaries.

And it isn't just defendants who present a safety risk. Vigilante justice is alive and well, and a tasty plot prospect. John Grisham's *A Time to Kill* starts with the father of a rape victim shooting the two accused men as a bailiff is leading them through the courthouse. For your own story, imagine a witness as shooter or target, or a victim of an earlier crime who believes the defendant was wrongly acquitted and isn't about to see him get off again.

A courthouse tour is a great field trip for writers' groups. Just ask the marshal's or administrator's office. You may get a few minutes with a judge, and a chance to ask your own questions.

How can I convey that the judge in my story is biased in favor of one side or the other?

The overt signs we sometimes associate with bias (that is, pre-judgment or favoritism) like facial expressions, body language, and obvious familiarity or past friendship are not reliable signs of judicial bias. Bias does exist, although it may be a matter of judicial philosophy rather than personal leanings. Where it's most evident is in rulings: admitting evidence that doesn't directly bear on the legal issue but is unfairly prejudicial; dismissing a claim despite evidence showing a *prima facie* case; or allowing a claim to go forward despite the lack of a *prima facie* case. Of course, such rulings could simply be error—hard to show, maybe; realistic, definitely.

> Bias does exist, although it may be a matter of judicial philosophy rather than personal leanings.

Closely related to actual bias are conflicts of interest and the "appearance of impropriety." In 2009, the Supreme Court held that a West Virginia Supreme Court judge's refusal to recuse himself from a case where one party had made a large contribution to his election campaign violated the other side's right to due process, because of both the potential for actual bias and the risk that the public would perceive bias. In 2010, the Court ordered the Eleventh Circuit to reconsider whether a man on death row for rape and murder had an adequate opportunity to explore the possibility that his trial was tainted by bias or misconduct. Only after trial did he learn that the judge had failed to disclose behind-the-scenes contact among jurors and with the judge himself, and a rather odd gift. Proving that truth is stranger than fiction, jurors had given the judge and bailiff a chocolate penis and chocolate breasts.

However, the Court refused to consider, without comment, an appeal asking if a previous extramarital affair between the judge and prosecutor in a capital murder case created a conflict of interest that denied the defendant a fair trial. The Texas Court of Criminal Appeals had denied retrial, concluding the defendant waited too long to raise the issue. He contended that it had taken him nearly twenty years to establish that the rumored relationship had in fact existed. Twenty-one former judges and prosecutors and thirty experts in legal ethics signed *amicus curiae* ("friend of the court") briefs supporting the appeal. The experts say the judge should have recused herself. But people sometimes don't do the right thing to protect themselves and those they love; judges are no exception.

> Like anyone else, some judges are better than others at controlling their demeanor and reactions.

Like anyone else, some judges are better than others at controlling their demeanor and reactions. The ability to appear interested without seeming to favor one side or the other is part of that judicial temperament we discussed. So, use judges' nonverbal communication, comments, rulings, and past relationships to raise the specter of bias, and to add an additional layer of tension. Or, show actual favoritism, bias, or misconduct. Threaten a judge with true accusations, or false ones. Put a judge in a compromising position and watch the chocolate hit the fan.

11

Legal Ethics

MUCH OF WHAT LAWYERS DO, AND DON'T DO, is dictated by the rules of ethics, known in some states as the Rules of Professional Conduct or Professional Responsibility. They set out lawyers' responsibilities and govern everything from communication, confidentiality, and fees to safeguarding property, trial publicity, and responsibilities for employees. But of course, ethics goes beyond following the rules. We'll talk about some common ethical issues that might arise in fiction: conflicts of interest, representing multiple defendants charged with the same crime, and lawyer-client sexual relationships. We'll also look at the lawyer as witness, discipline, and readmission after disbarment.

Is there such a thing as legal ethics?

Yes, of course—but you knew I'd say that, didn't you?

The public sometimes perceives that lawyers lack ethics, in part because of the occasional bad apple, but also because of a failure to understand or appreciate the lawyer's role. The adversarial system means lawyers advocate for their client's position—as long as that position is supported by the law or makes a good-faith argument for extension of the law. And, lawyers often take on unpopular clients. At times, those roles put lawyers in conflict with accepted standards in society. Examples might include harsh cross-examination that casts a witness in a poor light or seeking acquittal for a client "everyone knows" is guilty.

Each state bar establishes ethical standards through rules of professional conduct, based on the ABA's model rules. The rules are meant to protect the public and individual clients and to give lawyers guidance in sticky situations. Most state bars have an Ethics Committee that reviews proposed rules changes and issues opinions on specific questions of law and ethical conduct, often with the advice of a state bar lawyer or a professor of ethics.

Of course, ethics goes beyond the written codes, which address specific recurring situations and establish, as the voice of a considered, knowledgeable group, what a lawyer should or must do. Some rules establish minimum standards, such as for communication with a client; others dictate required actions, such as rules controlling deposits of clients' funds.

Many state bars now require lawyers to take regular continuing legal education (CLE) classes on ethics. Allegations of ethical violations can't be used as a trial tactic, although lawyers do have an obligation to report clear violations to the bar. Malpractice is not of itself an ethical violation, or vice versa, though there can be some crossover.

TIP: Lawyers concerned about ethical dilemmas often consult other lawyers, state bar counsel, or professors of legal ethics. Your characters might do the same or keep their doubts to themselves, not wanting to choose between competing arguments.

What's a conflict of interest?

Simply put, it's any situation where the lawyer's interests may conflict with those of the client. The possibilities are limitless. Common situations where real and fictional lawyers need to be alert to potential conflicts:

- How do a potential new client's interests relate to those of existing or former clients?

- Business transactions with clients or those that are adverse to a client are barred. This doesn't mean a lawyer can't have dinner in a client's restaurant, just that he shouldn't invest in it, unless it's a public company.

- Substantial gifts from clients are prohibited, particularly "testamentary gifts"—that is, by will—except among relatives. A restaurateur can give his lawyer free dessert, but not a share in the business.

- Financial assistance to clients is strictly limited. You can buy your client lunch, or advance him the costs of a lawsuit, but if you want to advance him money for living expenses from a hoped-for settlement, check the rules closely.

- When a lawyer can be paid by someone other than the client is strictly controlled. Common examples include insurance companies hiring counsel to defend insureds in lawsuits, under the policy terms, or a parent who pays for representation of a young criminal defendant. The lawyer-client

> The lawyer-client relationship is with the client, regardless who pays, and all duties are owed to the client.

relationship is with the client, regardless who pays, and all duties are owed to the client.

- In settling civil cases, a lawyer representing more than one person must be extremely careful and may need to bring in other lawyers to evaluate offers and advise the clients.

- Specific rules apply to current and former government lawyers, and to former judges. When a former government lawyer joins a law firm, conflicts could be extensive. Notice and screening procedures have been established; otherwise, former prosecutors or agency lawyers might have trouble changing jobs.

Some conflicts can be waived by the client, while others can't—they're just too serious. If a conflict prevents a lawyer from representing a particular client, the conflict is "imputed" to the rest of his or her law firm, and no lawyer in the firm may take the case. Lawyers should check for potential conflicts of interest before taking a case. If a conflict surfaces later, he'll need to withdraw from the case.

Here's a twist for real and fictional lawyers who aspire to write about their cases: A lawyer may not make or negotiate an agreement with a client giving

> If a conflict prevents a lawyer from representing a particular client, the conflict is "imputed" to the rest of his or her law firm, and no lawyer in the firm may take the case.

the lawyer "literary or media rights to a portrayal or account based in substantial part on information relating to the representation," although he may do so once the representation ends (Model Rule 1.8(d)). Such an agreement would create a conflict between the lawyer's personal interests and those of his client, and could affect his judgment, because what's best for the client during the case might not be best for the story.

Conflicts of interest can become pretty technical, and dicey, ethics problems. If you plan to use one to complicate your fictional lawyer's life, look at the specifics in Model Rules 1.7–1.12, or talk to an expert about the options. Conflicts can make things real uncomfortable real fast—bad in real life, but great in fiction.

How does a lawyer withdraw from a case?

Very carefully. A lawyer representing a client in a specific transaction, e.g., a business or real estate purchase, or ongoing matters, such as advising a business on employment or tax issues, has a different task than a lawyer involved in litigation. And, of course, the reason for the withdrawal makes a difference, too. The lawyer's first obligation is to make sure that the client's interests are not harmed or neglected in the process of "disengaging." He can't simply stop work on matters with time limits because his invoices have gone unpaid. He should first communicate with the client and tell him that if the bills aren't paid by a certain date, he will withdraw. However, if a document is already prepared, he needs to file it. If it's not prepared, he may need to do the work anyway and risk not being paid, or request an extension from the court, depending on the circumstances.

Withdrawals during litigation may be governed by the Rules of Professional Conduct or by state statute. Typically, the lawyer must file a motion with the court requesting "leave," or permission to withdraw. He'll need to state the reasons, e.g., unpaid bills, inability to locate the client, lack of cooperation, or an irretrievable breakdown in communication. He must also give written notice of the client's last known address, so the court and opposing counsel can communicate directly with the former client. Leave to withdraw may be refused if trial is in progress or fast approaching, especially in criminal cases, where a waiver of the right to speedy trial may also be needed.

Most written fee agreements give the lawyer the right to withdraw if he isn't paid or if the client does not tell him the truth, withholds information, or fails to cooperate with the lawyer.

Disputes often arise over the files. Generally, the file belongs to the client and must be given to him, although the lawyer may retain any "work product," that is, material he prepared, such as research memos or strategic analyses. The lawyer can keep a copy of the entire file, at his own expense. If the disengagement is friendly, the lawyer may talk with the client's new lawyer to bring him up to speed. But if the withdrawal is because of a newly discovered conflict of interest, it's a good idea not to talk, to avoid the risk of passing on privileged information.

If withdrawal doesn't require a court order, the smart lawyer confirms the end of the lawyer-client relationship with a "disengagement letter," expressly terminating the relationship and outlining the work he'd been retained to do, what's been done and what remains, and providing any relevant deadlines or statutes of limitations.

Can a lawyer represent two people charged with the same crime?

Generally, no. When two defendants are charged with the same crimes, or with different charges arising out of the same incident, there's a good chance that one defendant will implicate the other. That would create an impermissible conflict of interest if they shared the same lawyer. While some conflicts can be waived, this isn't one of them.

Even so, some sharing of information and resources is likely. For example, in financial or environmental crimes and conspiracies charged against the officers of a corporation, the cases are often tried jointly and defense counsel coordinate their strategy. The obvious exceptions are cases where one defendant shifts primary blame to another, as in the felony murder case of the young man who lent his car to his friends and found himself charged along with them.

Does a lawyer violate something—besides common sense—if he sleeps with a client who isn't his wife?

Yes. Rule 1.8(j) of the Model Rules says: "A lawyer shall not have sexual relations with a client unless a consensual sexual relationship existed between them when the client-lawyer relationship commenced." If the conduct results in a complaint to the bar association, sanctions are possible. We'll talk more about sanctions and the disciplinary process in a minute.

Even if the personal relationship predates the professional, the lawyer should consider whether it will interfere with his independent judgment or limit his ability to represent the client properly. The rule does not prohibit sexual relationships with former clients.

Why the ban? We've talked about the lawyer's "fiduciary" obligations to the client; that is, that the relationship is built on trust. And, it's almost always unequal. A lawyer has a basic obligation not to misuse or abuse the client's trust. Whenever the relationship becomes emotional, either person's judgment can be impaired. There is tremendous potential for undue influence and for harm to the client's interests, which he or she may not recognize until too late.

If your fictional lawyer just has to do it, deepen the characterization with a moment of doubt.

Can a lawyer testify for or against a client?

Only in very limited situations. For lawyer-witnesses, silence has two sources: the attorney-client privilege and the rules of ethics. The privilege, established by statute, belongs to the client, and only the client can waive it, e.g., by authorizing the attorney to speak or by revealing the contents of the conversation to someone else. A conversation is not privileged if it occurs in the presence of a person not covered by the privilege. For example, if the client's girlfriend is in the room when he talks to his lawyer, no privilege arises, but if the third person is the lawyer's paralegal, the conversation is privileged.

If the privilege doesn't apply, the attorney may testify, subject to the second source of silence, the rules of ethics. Under the American Bar Association Model Rules, if the testimony involves information relating to the representation—e.g., what the client said about a crime, his own negligence, the sources of money he used to pay fees—the lawyer can testify in three situations:

1) only if the client gives "informed consent";

2) the testimony is necessary in carrying out the representation and therefore implicitly authorized; or

3) "to the extent the lawyer reasonably believes necessary" in the following circumstances:

- "to prevent reasonably certain death or substantial bodily harm," e.g., if the client makes a threat the lawyer thinks he's likely to carry out;

- "to prevent the client from committing a crime or fraud that is reasonably certain to result in substantial injury to the financial interests or property of another and in furtherance of which the client has used or is using the lawyer's services;"

- "to prevent, mitigate or rectify substantial injury to the financial interests or property of another that is reasonably certain to result or has resulted from the client's commission of a crime or fraud in furtherance of which the client has used the lawyer's services;"

- "to secure legal advice about the lawyer's compliance with these Rules"—e.g., when the lawyer faces an ethical dilemma and consults a colleague or expert;

- "to establish a claim or defense on behalf of the lawyer in a controversy between the lawyer and the client, to establish a defense to a criminal charge or civil claim against the lawyer based upon conduct in which the client was involved, or to respond to allegations in any proceeding concerning the lawyer's representation of the client." Examples might include a claim for fees, a malpractice claim, a criminal or civil claim alleging fraud by the lawyer and client acting together, a claim of ineffective assistance of counsel in a criminal case, or a lawyer discipline proceeding; or

- to comply with other law or a court order.

Note that not every state has adopted the Model Rules verbatim. (The Model Rules are simply guidelines, and states may review and update their own rules when they please, as they please.) Some states expand the first exception to include property crimes. Some did not adopt the second and third exceptions, which allow disclosure to prevent fraud or crime causing financial or property damage, or to address damage from crime or fraud that has already occurred, if committed using the lawyer's services. Say bad guy Gary sold good guy Harry a house, concealing his knowledge that it had been used as a meth lab and needed expensive restoration; the lawyer who wrote the real estate contract could not reveal confidential information about Gary learned in representing him unless those exceptions were in place.

How are lawyers officially sanctioned or disciplined?

State systems vary in structure and terminology. The state bar or regulatory agency has an office of bar counsel or disciplinary counsel that handles complaints, typically from clients or other lawyers, but sometimes from judges or other persons.

According to a 2009 ABA Survey on Lawyer Discipline, there are about 1.42 million lawyers with active licenses nationwide, ranging from 2,200 in Vermont to nearly 170,000 in California. The disciplinary agencies received about 120,000 new complaints. Many were dismissed for lack of jurisdiction—e.g., they involved claims of malpractice or fee disputes, an unsuccessful case, or a personality conflict, but not possible rules violations—with about 76,000 of the complaints investigated. Ultimately, 5,507 lawyers, or .3 percent, received a private or public sanction; 823 lawyers were disbarred—489 involuntarily and 334 with consent (typically, because the lawyer accepts the inevitable). That's .05 percent of all lawyers.

The investigation process varies, so check the state bar website for your story state. However, one thing is the same all over: that letter from disciplinary counsel is the scariest thing a lawyer can get in the mail, short of a box with a live snake or a severed finger.

While investigations themselves are typically confidential, that changes once discipline is imposed. Some states make public the details of an investigation resulting in public sanctions, while others identify the lawyers, rules violated, and sanctions imposed but keep the details confidential unless the lawyer consents to disclosure. Discipline may include private sanctions, such as a letter of admonishment, or public sanctions, including reprimand, censure, suspension, or disbarment. Payment of costs may be ordered, and conditions such as addictions counseling or use of an approved mentor may be imposed.

> That letter from disciplinary counsel is the scariest thing a lawyer can get in the mail, short of a box with a live snake or a severed finger.

Without a doubt, the column reporting on lawyer discipline is one of the most popular features of the state bar journal. Train wrecks are both frightening and fascinating. The sex cases make good reading for the myriad ways lawyers can exercise astonishingly bad judgment.

How are lawyers disciplined by the bar viewed by their colleagues?

With fear, terror, disbelief, repulsion, pity, sadness, love, and astonishment. The response depends upon the conduct, and on the relationship between the lawyers. A lawyer who's always been considered a bit shady and is reprimanded for a minor rules violation will be watched more closely. But if he's suspended for a serious violation, opposing counsel will be very wary of him in future cases. If the conduct that prompts the discipline is unrelated to the practice—a criminal conviction for drug possession, or domestic violence—individual reactions will vary, but professional relationships may be little changed.

Alcoholism and mental illness play a role in far too many ethical lapses. Most states now require lawyers to take continuing legal education classes in ethics, and some require "SAMI" (substance abuse and mental illness) education.

Your fictional lawyer may come back to the practice after being sanctioned, determined to redeem himself and prove that the problems of the past are past. Or, he may be unchastened and carry a grudge the size of Kansas. Mess up his marriage, his friendships, and his case load, give him one loyal client or referral source, and see what happens.

Can a disbarred lawyer ever practice again?

Yes. In most states, a disbarred lawyer requesting reinstatement goes through the same application process, including character and fitness reviews, as a new graduate. There's a waiting period, typically five years, although some states allow permanent disbarment in particularly egregious cases. The applicant must also show compliance with all requirements of the discipline, including payment of fines or restitution. If the disbarment resulted from a criminal conviction, the sentence must have

> In most states, a disbarred lawyer requesting reinstatement goes through the same application process as a new graduate.

been completed. If drug or alcohol use were involved, evidence of successful treatment is required. There must have been no subsequent professional misconduct and the lawyer must admit the wrongdoing. He'll have to show he's kept up with the law, usually by taking continuing legal education classes, although if he's been away a long time, he may need to repeat some law school classes or retake the bar exam. Any hint that he practiced law while disbarred is a serious obstacle, because it shows a disrespect for the profession that admissions committees take very seriously.

A reinstated lawyer has no obligation to inform new clients of his past disbarment. However, disciplinary results are public, even in states where the details aren't disclosed, so a savvy client could do some quick research online, or call the bar. Does someone in your story carry a grudge and spread news or false rumors of your fictional lawyer's past?

The bar commission may hold a public hearing to hear evidence for and against reinstatement. Conditions may be imposed, such as working with an approved mentor, limiting the scope of practice, practicing with another lawyer who handles the trust account, or maintaining sobriety. A lawyer disbarred in one state is typically disbarred in all other states where he's admitted through reciprocal discipline; reinstatement must be sought in each state separately.

Famous disbarments: Spiro Agnew was disbarred in Maryland in 1974 after pleading no contest to tax evasion charges. Richard Nixon resigned from the California bar, but the New York bar would not accept his resignation unless he acknowledged his lack of a defense to obstruction of justice charges related to Watergate; he refused and was disbarred in 1976. He resigned from the U.S. Supreme Court bar before any action was taken against him. Several other lawyers were also disbarred for their role in Watergate, including John Dean, Gordon Liddy, and Donald Segretti.

F. Lee Bailey was disbarred in Florida in 2001 on several charges stemming from using millions of dollars of a client's stock—which the client later agreed to forfeit to the government in his own criminal case—as collateral for personal loans. He'd been admitted in Massachusetts as a new lawyer in 1960, but was disbarred under reciprocal discipline; his application for reinstatement in Massachusetts was denied.

And in 2001, facing disciplinary action, Bill Clinton accepted a five-year suspension and fine in Arkansas. In exchange, he was not charged with perjury for lying about his relationship with Monica Lewinsky. He was suspended from the Supreme Court bar and resigned, no doubt to avoid the infamy of being tossed out.

12

Research and References

So now that you know a few general principles and more than a few specifics, how can you be your own research assistant? Here are some suggestions for researching state and federal statutes, case law, and the law by topic. (For clickable links to the websites listed, see the Book Links page on my website, **www.LawandFiction.com**.)

Some guidance for doing your own legal research

For one-stop shopping for statutes, case law, and other resources, start with **www.FindLaw.com** and its companion site for legal professionals, **lp.FindLaw.com**. The basic site includes introductory articles on a variety of subjects, along with articles on recent major developments, Q&A on hot topics, and some state court forms. The professional site links to searchable databases of federal codes and court decisions, and to some state resources. Not all state statutes or codes are linked, so you may need to search for your story state's statutes directly.

To find a state code through a search engine, start with the state name and "statute," "code," or "legislature." Searching inside the code can be daunting. If you're looking for a statute specifying the elements of a particular crime, locate the criminal sections and scan the chapter headings to see how the code is structured. Then look for the definitions of specific crimes. They should all be in the same area. They may be organized by crimes against persons (homicide, sexual assault), crimes against property (burglary, theft), and so on. Or they may not be. You may also find general definitions of common terms, usually at the beginning of the criminal code.

You may want to find the potential sentence for a specific crime. As we discussed in Chapter 4, some states specify sentences in the definition of the crime, while others classify each crime and, in another part of the code, specify sentencing ranges by class. Again, it may take you a few minutes to grasp the structure of the statutes before you can locate the answer. If your story state uses a sentencing commission to set guidelines, those probably won't be in the statutes, but should be on the commission's website or in the law library.

The U.S. Code can be searched on the official government site, **thomas.loc. gov/home/thomas.php**, named for Thomas Jefferson, by title (scroll through the list, click on a likely subject, then follow chapter headings, subchapters, and so on) or popular name (e.g., Missing Children Act). Or use FindLaw. As with any database search, the more specific you can be, the better.

A terrific source for state statutes by topic is the Cornell Law School's Legal Information Institute,**topics.law.cornell.edu/wex/state_statutes**. Topics range from Alcoholic Beverages to Water, but most importantly for writers, also include Courts, Criminal Codes, Criminal Procedure, and Family Law.

Finding specific court decisions can be tricky. If you know the court and at least one party name, use the FindLaw databases. Most state and federal courts have websites—reach them through FindLaw or the National Center for State Courts site (**www.ncsc.org**). Court websites often include only recent decisions, within the last 30 days to a year, but provide links to other sources. Some states publish searchable databases for appellate opinions; you'll need at least one party name, although a date range helps narrow the search. To find a well-known decision, e.g., *Miranda*, search the name directly. You'll likely find links to the official ("reported") opinion, and to commentaries.

State law libraries and law school libraries, both physical and virtual, are gold mines, as are state bar associations and attorneys' general offices and web-sites. Many provide helpful information designed for the public, e.g., Know Your Rights pamphlets on the state court system, criminal issues, or child wel-fare laws. Some states and local courts staff Self-help Centers with practical resources on using the courts, forms, and subject matter information; look at your story state's court system or bar association website.

And, of course, don't forget your local library and staff.

Here are a few other sources:

Bureau of Justice Statistics: Stats on criminal sentencing, victims, law enforcement, and more, and FAQs on various topics. **bjs.ojp.usdoj.gov**.

Federal Justice Statistics Resource Center: Online analysis of law enforce-ment, prosecution, the courts, and incarceration. **fjsrc.urban.org/index.cfm**.

National Center for State Courts: State court stats of all kinds, charts, and directories. **www.ncsc.org**.

National Center for Juvenile Justice: The state juvenile justice profiles and the national court data are particularly useful. **www.ncjjservehttp.org/ NCJJWebsite/main.html**.

The Crime Report: A wide-ranging news and information site sponsored by the Center on Media, Crime and Justice at the John Jay College of Criminal Justice, and Criminal Justice Journalists, a national organization. **thecrimereport.org.**

U.S. Courts: The official site. **www.uscourts.gov**.

Countless other websites provide information on the law. Some are slanted, although a focus is not the same as a bias. Absolute objectivity is impossible; what you're after is evidence of general reliability. Use the same standards you would in your own field of expertise. Is the information factual, stated clearly, and verifiable? Check who runs the site, looking at the home and "About Us" pages. Sites sponsored by universities and recognized research institutions are good places to start. If a site is sponsored by a national association you don't know, look at its stated purpose and sponsorship. Check for biographical or professional information about the founders, directors, and authors that suggests reliability, or that hints at a bias. Do the funding sources give you any clues? Has it been recently updated?

Check a site's reliability by glancing at a few links. While researching her medieval noir novel, *The Demon's Parchment*, mystery writer Jeri Westerson found a site with a perspective she hadn't encountered before on "blood libel," the allegation that Jews use human blood in their religious rituals; nothing on the site hinted at its authors' biases, but a link to a white supremacist group told her all she needed to know.

A good example of a reliable association website is the National Center for State Courts, a national organization with a specific, detailed purpose of providing information and services relating to state court systems, with a long history and well-established credentials. Look for similar sources for the greatest reliability.

In evaluating an article, be it online or in print, look at the authors and their qualifications. Does it include citations to primary sources or reliable secondary sources? A bibliography? The more willing the authors are to back up their information and arguments, the more reliable it usually is. Who publishes the journal, and has it been around a long time?

Read with potential slant in mind. You'll get a different view of gun rights and violence from the NRA than you will from the Brady Campaign. Look at both, as well as others, to get a deeper understanding of the issue. But regardless of philosophy, an organization may still provide reliable research, such as the NRA's detailed charts of state and federal gun laws.

What about Wikipedia and other online encyclopedias? They can be a good starting point, but as with any other topics they feature, articles vary in depth and reliability. Some focus on American law, while others don't. Some borrow heavily from other sources, sometimes verbatim. Some are better footnoted than others; those notes can lead to original sources and more ideas. Judge their accuracy as you would any other resources. If a specific point of law is critical to your story, follow the citations and use other tools to confirm the point.

Law professors are one of my favorite resources, especially their blogs—or blawgs. The best blawgs report and analyze recent developments in an area, providing a good view of the many sides of an issue, with links and citations to decisions and statutes. One good example is Ohio State University law professor Doug Berman on sentencing. His blog also includes numerous links to blogs and sites on other areas of criminal law and general legal interest. Go to: **sentencing.typepad.com/sentencing_law_and_policy**.

The SCOTUS blog and accompanying wiki, sponsored by a law firm, focuses on the Supreme Court of the United States: **www.scotusblog.com**.

Topics include petitions for review filed and accepted, oral arguments, decisions issued and continuing debate over the issues involved, discussion of possible successors to retiring justices, and more. Other blogs focus on specific Circuit Courts of Appeal, with summaries and analysis of important recent decisions in criminal law. One example: **www.rashkind.com/weblogs**. The ABA Journal publishes an annual "Blawg 100" list of favorites, covering just about every aspect of the law you can imagine: **www.abajournal.com/magazine/article/the_2010_aba_journal_blawg_100**.

In-print and online resources are nearly limitless, and it's easy to get lost. Keep your focus on the needs of your story. And don't forget the phone. If you have a specific local question, call a law school or criminal justice professor in your story state.

And keep in mind the goal: to write a good story, well-told, that gets the facts right.

Book Links

THESE LINKS ARE TO REFERENCES MENTIONED IN THE book. They may change from time to time; I'll make every effort to keep an updated Book Links page on my website, **www.LawandFiction.com**

Chapter 1: Trial and Error

A. *The Judicial System:*

The National Center for State Courts (**www.ncsc.org**) maintains a directory of state court websites:

www.ncsc.org/Information-and-Resources/Browse-by-State/State-Court-Websites.aspx

The National Association of Drug Court Professionals provides drug court statistics and a fact sheet:

www.nadcp.org/learn/drug-courts-work

C. *Evidence:*

A sample chain of custody form, from Montana:

www.dphhs.mt.gov/publichealth/lab/documents/chainofcustody.pdf

E. *Burden of Proof*

The Innocence Project maintains a directory of state laws requiring preservation of evidence:

www.innocenceproject.org/news/LawView4.php

For additional discussion, and one example of how the failure to preserve evidence affected an appeal in a capital case, see:

www.innocenceproject.org/Content/Preservation_Of_Evidence.php

Chapter 2: Legal Issues in Criminal Investigation

The National Center for State Courts' FAQs page on Indigent Defense gives details on current state systems:

www.ncsc.org/Topics/Access-and-Fairness/Indigent-Defense/FAQ.aspx

For a sample state extradition form, see this Minnesota form:

forms.lp.findlaw.com/form/courtforms/state/mn/mn000030.pdf

For details on international extradition in cases of child abduction or violence against family, see the State Department's International Child Abduction web page:

travel.state.gov/abduction/abduction_580.html

For state-by-state information on recording conversations, see The Reporters Committee for Freedom of the Press guide:

www.rcfp.org/taping

Chapter 3. Crime ...

Gun laws change regularly, so consult the laws for your story locale. The NRA website maintains links to federal, state, and local laws:

www.nraila.org/GunLaws

Juvenile justice: The statistics on transfers are taken from a U.S. Dept. of Justice, Office of Juvenile Justice and Delinquency Prevention Fact Sheet, published June 2009, "Delinquency Cases Waived to Criminal Court, 2005":

www.ncjrs.gov/pdffiles1/ojjdp/224539.pdf

For an overview and state-by-state summary of transfer laws, and a look at children under twelve, see "From Time Out to Hard Time: Young Children in the Adult Criminal Justice System," by Michele Deitch (2009), a project report of the University of Texas LBJ School of Public Affairs:

www.utexas.edu/lbj/archive/news/images/file/From%20Time%20Out%20to%20Hard%20Time-revised%20final.pdf

The National Center for Juvenile Justice state profiles are another excellent source of state-by-state specifics:

www.ncjjservehttp.org/NCJJWebsite/main.html

For details of John Hinckley's trial, see law professor Doug Linder's Famous Trials website:

www.law.umkc.edu/faculty/projects/ftrials/ftrials.htm

A state-by-state summary of laws on the insanity defense, unfortunately without links to the statutes, is on FindLaw:

criminal.findlaw.com/crimes/more-criminal-topics/insanity-defense/the-insanity-defense-among-the-states.html

Chapter 4. ... and Punishment

United States Sentencing Commission's 2010 guidelines:

www.ussc.gov/Guidelines/2010_guidelines/index.cfm

National Association of State Sentencing Commissions' website with links to state guidelines:

www.thenasc.org/aboutnasc.html

The American Probation and Parole Association maintains a directory of state services for community supervision"

www.appa-net.org/eweb/DynamicPage.aspx?Webcode=VB_Directory

The Sentencing Project's March 2011 report on Felony Disenfranchisement Laws in the United States provides statistics and state-by-state information:

www.sentencingproject.org/detail/publication.cfm?publication_id=15&id=131

State sex offender registry websites, from the FBI:

www.fbi.gov/scams-safety/registry/registry

National sex offender public registry, maintained by the Department of Justice with links to state registries and statutes:

www.nsopw.gov/Core/Portal.aspx

Studies from the Washington State Institute for Public Policy, a research bureau created by the state legislature, on sex offender sentencing:

www.wsipp.wa.gov/topic.asp?cat=10&subcat=55&dteSlct=0

The Reporters Committee for Freedom of the Press offers a primer on access to juvenile courts:

www.rcfp.org/juvcts/index.html

and a state-by-state summary of laws:

www.rcfp.org/juvcts/juvcts_stateindex.html

Death penalty statistics are drawn from the Death Penalty Information Center fact sheet. The DPIC also provides extensive state-by-state information:

www.deathpenaltyinfo.org

Chapter 7. Wills, Probate, and Adoption

Several websites reproduce wills of famous people—Michael Jackson, Princess

Diana, Walt Disney, Jerry Garcia, and even Napoleon Bonaparte. Search "Famous Wills."

The British National Archives website includes the wills of Shakespeare and Jane Austen, and a searchable website of historical wills, beginning in 1348:

www.nationalarchives.gov.uk/documentsonline/wills.asp

For specifics on state marriage and divorce laws, see Cornell University's Legal Information Institute tables:

topics.law.cornell.edu/wex/table_marriage

For state-by-state specifics on adoption, child abuse and neglect, and child welfare laws, consult the amazing database on the U.S. Department of Health and Human Services Child Welfare Information Gateway site, including searchable access to state laws:

www.childwelfare.gov/systemwide/laws_policies/state/index.cfm

The Cornell University's Legal Information Institute tables mentioned above also include links to state adoption laws:

topics.law.cornell.edu/wex/table_marriage

On access to adoption records, the Child Welfare Information Gateway site includes a lengthy summary of state laws.:

www.childwelfare.gov/systemwide/laws_policies/statutes/infoaccessapall.pdf

Chapter 8. Legal Miscellany

Here's a sample probate court petition for declarations of presumed death, from Georgia:

forms.lp.findlaw.com/form/courtforms/state/ga/ga000010.pdf

If your story involves a claim for insurance benefits after a disappearance, take a look at "The Missing Insured and The Life Insurance Death Claim," by retired insurance company executive Edgar Sentell:

findarticles.com/p/articles/mi_qa4023/is_200401/ai_n9391589

The National Center for Missing and Exploited Children provides resources and a list of state clearinghouses; some also track missing adults or provide links to other databases:

www.missingkids.com/missingkids/servlet/ServiceServlet?LanguageCountry =en_US&PageId=1421

See the State Department chart of diplomatic immunities:

www.state.gov/m/ds/immunities/c9118.htm

The International Society for the Study of Dissociation and Trauma website includes informative FAQs, annotated bibliographies on trauma and dissociation, and links for professionals and self-help

www.isst-d.org

For research resources on recovered memories of sexual abuse, see:

www.jimhopper.com/memory

And see the child welfare information websites mentioned in Chapter 7.

Chapter 9. Thinking Like a Lawyer

For the American Bar Association's list of approved schools, statistics, and other information on legal education, see the ABA website:

www.americanbar.org/groups/legal_education/resources/statistics.html

For the Comprehensive Guide to Bar Admission Requirements and sample form for character and fitness examination, see the National Conference of Bar Examiners:

www.ncbex.org/comprehensive-guide-to-bar-admissions

For details on Washington State's law clerk program, see:

www.wsba.org/Licensing-and-Lawyer-Conduct/Admissions/Limited-Licenses-and-Special-Programs/Non-Lawyers-and-Students/Law-Clerk-Program

Chapter 10. Thinking Like a Judge

Salary information is available on the National Center for State Courts Judicial Salary Resource Center:

contentdm.ncsconline.org/cgi-bin/showfile.exe?CISOROOT=/judicial&CISOPTR=317

For more on court building security, consult the National Center for State Courts 2010 report on best practices:

contentdm.ncsconline.org/cgi-bin/showfile.exe?CISOROOT=/facilities&CISOPTR=155

Chapter 12. Research and References

For statutes, case law, forms, and other resources, start with Find Law (**www.Findlaw.com**) and its companion site for legal professionals:

lp.findlaw.com

The official government site for statutes, proposed legislation, and lots more.

thomas.loc.gov/home/thomas.php

A terrific source for state statutes by topic is the Cornell Law School's Legal Information Institute:

topics.law.cornell.edu/wex/state_statutes

Other resources:

Bureau of Justice Statistics: Stats on criminal sentencing, victims, law enforcement, and more, plus FAQs on various topics.

bjs.ojp.usdoj.gov

Federal Justice Statistics Resource Center: Online analysis of law enforcement, prosecution, the courts, and incarceration:

fjsrc.urban.org/index.cfm

National Center for State Courts: State court stats of all kinds, charts, and directories:

www.ncsc.org

National Center for Juvenile Justice: The state juvenile justice profiles and national court data are particularly useful:

www.ncjjservehttp.org/NCJJWebsite/main.html

The Crime Report: A wide-ranging news and information site sponsored by the Center on Media, Crime and Justice at the John Jay College of Criminal Justice, and Criminal Justice Journalists, a national organization

thecrimereport.org

U.S. Courts: The official site:

www.uscourts.gov

Blawgs:

Ohio State University law professor Doug Berman on sentencing and related topics: His blog also includes numerous links to blogs on other areas of criminal law and general legal interest:

sentencing.typepad.com/sentencing_law_and_policy

The SCOTUS blog (**www.scotusblog.com**)and accompanying wiki, sponsored by a law firm, focuses on the Supreme Court of the United States.

For blogs focusing on the Supreme Court and Courts of Appeals, see the Federal Defender web ring:

www.rashkind.com/weblogs

The ABA Journal's 2010 "Blawg 100" list of favorites:

www.abajournal.com/magazine/article/the_2010_aba_journal_blawg_100

Acknowledgments

It's a thrill to see my name on the cover of a real book, but a lot of people helped me get it there. Thanks to:

The Sisters in Crime Guppy chapter, the best writers' group anywhere. Special thanks to Guppies Elizabeth Zelvin, Jeri Westerson, Helen Sandoval, and Krista Davis for discussing specific topics with me or reviewing draft Q&A, and Bill Hopkins for wading through the full manuscript and particularly for his insights as a retired trial judge. Of course, I made the mistakes all by myself.

Jeff Boxer, for reviewing the questions on guns.

Debbie Burke, long-time critique partner and friend, for listening to me talk about this project for years, and for reading the full manuscript.

My brother and personal super-lawyer, Tom Budewitz, for willingness to read any thing I write, including this manuscript.

Doug Lyle, M.D. and Lee Lofland for their encouragement, and agents Kimberley Cameron and Elizabeth Evans for helping shape the proposal.

Kent Sorsky at Linden Publishing for taking a chance on this project, and Jaguar Bennett, publicity & marketing director, for helping spread the word.

Doranna Durgin, Blue Hound Visions Website Design, for her work on LawandFiction.com.

Molly Weston, editor of the Sisters in Crime quarterly, *In Sinc*, and Susan Evans, editor of the Guppies' newsletter, *First Draft*, for giving me regular fora to rant and rave, and I hope, inform.

The Guppies and my brother Tom for suggesting books and movies I just had to know about.

All the writers who have asked me questions and allowed me to help them get the facts right.

My mother Alice and my late father Bill, for urging law school and encouraging me to write.

Finally, special thanks to my husband Don Beans, for always understanding what it means when I'm "in writing world."

Index

About the Author

LESLIE BUDEWITZ IS A WRITER AND A PRACTICING lawyer. Her short stories have appeared in *Ellery Queen's Mystery Magazine, Alfred Hitchcock's Mystery Magazine, Thug Lit, The Whitefish Review*, and other journals. Her short nonfiction has been published in the anthologies *Cup of Comfort for Cat Lovers* and *Cup of Comfort for Dog Lovers, Vol. II* and in national and regional magazines.

After graduating from Notre Dame Law School in 1984, Leslie clerked for the Washington State Court of Appeals. She is admitted in state and federal courts in Montana and Washington State and the court of the Confederated Salish and Kootenai Tribes of the Flathead Nation. She has represented plaintiffs and defendants in a wide variety of civil litigation and represented both felony and misdemeanor criminal defendants. She currently represents plaintiffs and defendants in civil litigation.

She writes the *Law & Fiction* column in *InSinC Quarterly*, the Sisters in Crime quarterly, and the *Law & Fiction: Getting the Facts Right* column in *First Draft*, the bimonthly newsletter of the Sisters in Crime Guppies chapter. She enjoys working directly with writers, providing research and answering questions about using the law in fiction. Writers with questions related to law in fiction can reach Leslie through her website, **www.LawandFiction.com**.

Leslie lives in northwest Montana with her husband, a doctor of natural medicine, and their cat. When not writing, she loves to cook, garden, and hike in the mountains outside her door.

Expert marketing advice for writers from Quill Driver Books

$24.95 ($27.95 Canada)

The Social Media Survival Guide

Strategies, Tactics, and Tools for Succeeding in the Social Web

—by Deltina Hay

This is a book for do-it-yourselfers—authors, publishers, and everyone else who wants to promote themselves through social media marketing. *The Social Media Survival Guide* focuses on proven tools that create results. Here are specific strategies, tactics, and tools that will help you reach a global audience and communicate with readers and reviewers personally and effectively. You'll get step-by-step, specific advice on WordPress sites, podcasting, social networking and more.

66 The most authoritative, comprehensive, and technically accurate guide I have ever seen to social networking. 99

—Bob Bly, author of over 70 classic marketing books.

$15.95 ($17.95 Canada)

PR Therapy

Ignite Your Passion for Promoting Your Products, Services, and Even Yourself!

—by Robin Blakely

If doing your own public relations is driving you crazy, maybe it's time for some *PR Therapy*. Let Robin Blakely, the PR "idea girl" for bestselling authors and multimillionaire CEOs, give you her field-tested entrepreneurial know-how on building a PR platform that really works. If you think you can't master publicizing and promoting your work, *PR Therapy* is here to tell you: "Yes, you can! Here's how!"

66 Robin Blakely is the real deal—an energetic, revolutionary PR guru—who finally wrote it all down. *PR Therapy* gives you a step-by-step process and a ton of great tips. 99

—Stacey Wolfe, author of *Psychic Living* and *Never Throw Rice at a Pisces*

Available from bookstores, online bookstores, and QuillDriverBooks.com, or by calling toll-free 1-800-345-4447.

Great books on writing by
BARNABY CONRAD

$14.95 ($16.95 *Canada*)

101 Best Sex Scenes Ever Written
An Erotic Romp Through Literature for Writers and Readers
—by Barnaby Conrad

For writers and readers, no part of a story is more exciting — or more potentially embarrassing — than what William F. Buckley called "the obligatory sex scene." Best-selling author Barnaby Conrad (*Matador* and *The Second Life of John Wilkes Booth*) puts his formidable critical powers to work analyzing what makes a sex scene genuine literature, and he provides a feast of unsurpassed examples from the world's greatest writers. Writers will learn how to write sex scenes with authenticity, credibility, and a genuine feeling for the motives, actions, and emotions of real living human beings.

$14.95 ($19.95 *Canada*)

101 Best Scenes Ever Written
A Romp Through Literature for Writers and Readers
—by Barnaby Conrad

Here in one volume you will find beloved scenes you read in the past, or perhaps great scenes you had forgotten, or totally new scenes to be discovered and savored. Any reader will enjoy browsing Barnaby Conrad's choices of the greatest scenes ever written, but the real beneficiaries of this book will be the countless fledgling writers who will learn by sampling and studying these gems from the masters of the written word.

❝ A superb book! Indispensable! Get it! ❞
—Ray Bradbury, author of *The Martian Chronicles*

$15.95 ($19.95 *Canada*)

101 Best Beginnings Ever Written
A Romp Through Literary Openings for Writers and Readers
——by Barnaby Conrad

For writers and readers, the first part of every story is the most important. Bestselling author Barnaby Conrad identifies the twelve types of beginnings, teaching writers how to start their stories with forceful, compelling prose that hooks their readers from page one.

❝ A book as wise and companionable as its author, and a superb resource for writer, student and literary bystander alike. Bravo! Olé! ❞

—Christopher Buckley, author of *Thank You for Smoking*

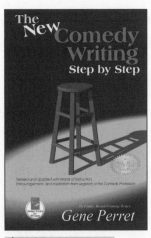

Professional books for working writers from Quill Driver Books

$15.95 ($17.95 Canada)

How to Write & Sell Simple Information for Fun and Profit

Your Guide to Writing and Publishing Books, E-Books, Articles, Special Reports, Audio Programs, DVDs and Other How-To Content

—by Robert W. Bly, author of over 70 classic marketing books

How-to writing is the easiest and most lucrative field an aspiring writer can enter—and copywriting legend Bob Bly is sharing his secrets to how anyone can become a successful how-to writer. *How to Write & Sell Simple Information for Fun and Profit* is a step-by-step guide to building a profitable new career.

❝ Grab this book and devour it. It just might be the catalyst that changes your life. ❞

—Herschell Gordon Lewis, author of *Internet Marketing: Tips, Tricks and Tactics*

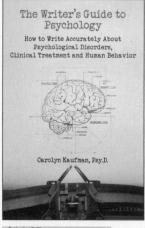

$14.95 ($16.95 Canada)

The Writer's Guide to Psychology

How to Write Accurately About Psychological Disorders, Clinical Treatment and Human Behavior

—by Carolyn Kaufman, Psy.D.

Written by a clinical psychologist who is also a professional writer and writing coach, *The Writer's Guide to Psychology* is an authoritative and easy-to-use reference to psychological disorders, diagnosis, treatments, and what really makes psychopathic villains tick.

The only reference book on psychology designed specifically for writers, *The Writer's Guide to Psychology* presents specific writing dos and don'ts to avoid the misunderstandings frequently seen in popular writing.

❝ This book should be in every writer's professional library and every clinician's, too — whether writers or not! ❞

—*New York Journal of Books*

Available from bookstores, online bookstores, and QuillDriverBooks.com, or by calling toll-free 1-800-345-4447.